BRUCE COST'S ASIAN INGREDIENTS

ALSO BY BRUCE COST

Ginger East to West
(*Aris Books, 1984*)

BRUCE COST'S ASIAN INGREDI-ENTS

BUYING AND COOKING THE STAPLE FOODS OF CHINA, JAPAN AND SOUTHEAST ASIA

FOREWORD BY ALICE WATERS

WILLIAM MORROW
AND COMPANY, INC.
New York

for Shen Yiwen

Library of Congress Cataloging-in-Publication Data
Cost, Bruce, 1945-
    Bruce Cost's Asian ingredients.
    Bibliography: p.
    Includes index.
    1. Cookery, Oriental. 2. Food. I. Title.
TX724.A1C67 1988   641.595   88-8943
ISBN 0-688-05877-9

Printed in the United States of America

  2 3 4 5 6 7 8 9 10

Book Design by Richard Oriolo

FOREWORD

Bruce Cost is one of the greatest cooks I've ever known. My friend Cecilia Chiang, owner of the Mandarin restaurants, once said after eating one of his meals, "You cook food like the *real* Chinese." That Bruce is a wonderful cook is not the only reason why this is a special book. Rather, it is the committed attitude and feel that he has for his ingredients that inspire the book and make it so useful.

At a meal Bruce prepared for us at our house, he brought a durian, a prized Asian fruit, for dessert. This fruit was, to say the least, one of the most extreme things I have ever eaten. Gooey, pungent, sharp, fermented, and sweet, it was so "aromatic" we had to leave it outside until dessert. However, with Bruce's encouragement, we had a great opportunity to experience something we would have been far too timid and ignorant to seek out ourselves.

This book is about a fascination with foodstuffs. It can be your guide through an immense and profound realm of Asian cuisine, into areas that are very foreign and opaque for most cooks. The certainty and definitiveness about the information and techniques he imparts come from great scholarship and study. On the other hand, he truly demystifies many previously forbidding and odd ingredients by giving their intriguing historical context as well as their everyday usage. When reading the book, I find myself wanting to follow him into those Asian markets to avail myself of the treasures inside.

This is a book for both the ambitious and less experienced cook, as well as those who just like the sensuous way he writes. Ultimately, because this book expresses a passion and a respect for ingredients *first* and recipes *second,* it has a very special meaning for me. I've always felt that the taste of a dish is determined by the understanding and careful selection of ingredients. So, as we become more familiar with the specialness and utility of the foods through Bruce's delicious recipes, all Asian cooking seems more accessible.

—ALICE WATERS
CHEZ PANISSE
January 25, 1988

ACKNOWLEDGMENTS

Special thanks to Donald Harper, now of the Department of Far Eastern Languages and Civilization at the University of Chicago, who spent hours poring through Chinese and Japanese reference works to help me place the ingredients in their proper historical context. When he lived in Berkeley, where he taught at the university, Don would drop by with the explanation "I thought you could use this," while plunking down yet another reference work that proved invaluable.

Diane Elwyn not only tested the recipes in this book, she shopped for the ingredients in San Francisco's Chinatown, down two flights of stairs and two steep hills from my apartment, and lugged them back up to me. Besides her familiarity with Asian food from years of living in the Philippines, her kitchen skills, fine palate, and frankly honest opinions helped shape this unusually fine collection of recipes.

There were others whose assistance was invaluable: Wai Ching Lee, my cooking-class assistant, who shared with me foodstuffs her mother sent her from Singapore, such as palm sugars from Malacca or special shrimp pastes; Merle Ellis, the butcher; the Wongs, who own the May Wah Market in San Francisco; Joseph Kwong of the Shew Wo Meat Company; Hoang Huy Bui, a Vietnamese-English translator; Ann Phan, San Francisco Chinatown's premier egg merchant; Allen Clark of the California Department of Agriculture and his counterparts in Washington, D.C.; Keav and Joanna Ty, owners of the Phnom Penh and Angkor Wat restaurants; and Rangsan Fasudhani, the owner of Khan Toke Thai House.

I'm grateful for the friendship, warmth, and sincere interest of my editor, Maria Guarnaschelli, not just in my books, but in all aspects of my life. I also am fortunate to have the continual strong support and encouragement of Susan Lescher, my agent. Final thanks to Lee Fatherree for his ten-month effort that produced the beautiful photographs.

B. C.

CONTENTS

INTRODUCTION

This book is twice as long as the one I proposed in 1984. My idea was to help those who cook Asian food make sense out of the fresh, dried, preserved, and bottled ingredients carried by Oriental markets.

At the time, unless you grew up in a family of Asian cooks, you had to rely on the "special ingredients" sections of your cookbooks for information on how to buy, use, and store what you needed. From experience, I knew that these listings often contained sketchy or even misleading information. Most of the stuff sold in Asian grocery stores was not described in your trusty cookbook. Those odd-looking squashes never seemed to be called for in recipes, and the selection of dried seafood alone was enough to make you want to return your wok and steamer. And what about the variety of meat cuts in a Chinese butcher shop?

When I began doing my research, you had to go to a botany text or East Asia to find the ingredients that later started showing up at markets in the United States, especially the Vietnamese, Thai, and Cambodian foodstuffs. Not surprisingly, their arrival paralleled the influx of people from those regions. It seemed as if every three days some exotic made its debut. It might be *kachai*, a camphorous ginger relative that looks like a cluster of fingers, tiger leaf amaranth, another variety of Chinese spinach, or pea shoots. I realized I had to anticipate ingredients that were bound to appear in this book, such as kaffir limes and lime leaves, because I knew they were being grown behind Thai and Cambodian restaurants on the West Coast.

The influx of new edibles, however, wasn't confined to the West Coast. I found Thai basil in Boston and fresh tamarind and fresh water chestnuts in suburban Virginia. What a short while ago were considered Asian exotics, like fresh ginger, were now for sale in everyday supermarkets, and being called for in newspaper and magazine recipes.

By necessity this book became a source for anyone who cooks, whether it be American or Asian food. There's no reason why Chinese broccoli, or *gai lan*, can't accompany pork chops and a baked potato. Given their increasing availability, many Asian ingredients should soon be found in the larders of American home cooks just as sesame oil, Chinese salted black beans, wonton skins, and lemon grass are now staples for many chefs. Unlike a lot of new foods that come and go (most of which seem to be familiar vegetables with new colors), these Asian staples aren't merely trendy. They've been rigorously tested by hundreds of millions of people over thousands of years, and have proven themselves culinarily.

I got caught up in the rich history of many of these foods and was fortunate to have the help of China scholar Don Harper (see Acknowledgments), who went digging in ancient Chinese and Japanese reference works for tidbits that would shed light on how these foods developed. It's helpful to understand how soybean sauces evolved from ancient methods of fermenting and preserving meat and game, and how this evolution manifested itself in the preserved fish sauces of Southeast Asia, where soybeans can't grow and fish are plentiful. Such information made it possible to arrange these foods in logical categories rather than just listing them alphabetically. For example, in the special ingredients sections of Chinese cookbooks, the paste of fermented soy beans called "bean sauce" is usually found at some alphabetic distance from Hoisin sauce, which is no more than a seasoned and spiced version of it.

Though this book is large, it is by no means an encyclopedia. My goal was to include what was important and to give useful and, where possible, entertaining information about Asian foods. Many of the entries have appeared regularly, in the form of a short article with a recipe, in the *San Francisco Chronicle, Washington Post,* New Orleans *Times-Picayune,* and occasionally in the *Chicago Tribune, Dallas Morning News,* Portland *Oregonian,* and other newspapers.

But I don't want to shortchange the fact that this cookbook also contains some very special recipes that illustrate the use of ingredients. Many of them are my own which I've developed and hoarded over the years, and many are derived from unpublished recipes of the legendary woman with whom I studied cooking over seven years in New York, the late Virginia Lee. Regardless of the extent of your Asian cookbook library, you'll find these recipes unique and delicious.

—Bruce Cost
SAN FRANCISCO
May 16, 1988

...FRESH INGREDI-ENTS

HERBS AND SEASONINGS

THE BASIL FAMILY

ASIAN BASIL
(Osimum spp.)

REGION OF USE: Thailand, Vietnam, Laos, Cambodia, and elsewhere in Southeast Asia

Basil is used more in Thai cooking than in Italian, which is not surprising since sources cite India or Thailand as the plant's probable native home. The herb the Southeast Asians are using and selling here, however, is not the familiar sweet basil of Italian cookery. At least two species and several varieties of basil appear fleetingly on the stands (see Note), but the predominant one is a tropical variety of sweet basil (*O. basilicum*) that the Thais call *bai horapa*. It has small green leaves, purple stems and flowers, and a wonderful basil/anise flavor. Because of the demand, this basil, hardly heard of here a few years ago, is available year-round at markets that carry Thai and Vietnamese produce.

Called also "Thai basil," "Asian basil," *rau húng* (in Vietnamese), or sometimes "licorice basil," the leaves of this herb are tossed into salads, stir-fried dishes, and curries, and are also used to garnish soups. Small baskets of this basil are placed alongside Vietnamese spring rolls, to be wrapped in lettuce, and customers in Vietnamese *phó'* (beef noodle soup) restaurants are served sprigs of it to flavor their hot broth.

At first, all the Thai basil shipped here was grown in Hawaii. Now during the spring and summer months it's grown domestically, in California and elsewhere. It can be stored for a couple of days in the refrigerator with the stems in water and leaves loosely covered with a plastic bag.

BASIL SEEDS. Tiny black basil seeds are sold in Southeast Asian markets; they're used to season cooling drinks and sweets, the simplest being a mixture of soft young coconut flesh, rich coconut cream, and palm sugar. The seeds, which have a mucilaginous coating, are soaked for 10 minutes in cold water, until they are slightly gelatinous, before they are added to other ingredients.

NOTE: Various basil family members, some more closely related to mint, show up sporadically at Southeast Asian produce stands. The most alluring is an herb the Vietnamese call *tia tô*, a kind of lemon balm (*Melissa officinalis*), with leaves of deep purple on one side and a rich dark green on the other. The leaf is hairy, as is a smaller kind with a light green leaf and a distinct lemony flavor. The balms have a stick-in-the-throat quality that renders them best for tossing in a soup just before serving, rather than for use in a salad. Other basil relatives include an aromatic variety with large purple leaves and a type with the shiny green serrated leaves characteristic of basil, but with the flavor of mint. Some are technically varieties of perilla (see page 20).

This delicious green sauce, to be tossed with warm or cold fresh egg noodles, captures the essential flavors of Southeast Asia. Many who have tasted it prefer it to its Italian counterpart. It will keep for a week or so in a jar in the refrigerator if topped with a little oil.

ASIAN "PESTO"
(A Southeast Asian Herb Sauce for Noodles)

Yield: 2½ cups

1½ cups Asian basil leaves (tightly packed)	2 small fresh green chili peppers
¼ cup Asian mint leaves (tightly packed)	1 tablespoon coarsely chopped ginger
¼ cup coriander leaves (tightly packed)	4 large garlic cloves
1 cup peanut oil	1½ teaspoons salt
½ cup raw peanuts	1 teaspoon sugar
	3 tablespoons fresh lemon juice

Combine the herbs in a small bowl and set aside.

Heat the oil in a small skillet until nearly smoking, then remove from the heat and add the peanuts. Allow to sit until lightly browned. Remove the nuts with a slotted spoon and drain, reserving the oil.

Put the peanuts in a food processor or blender and blend to a rough paste. Add the chilis, ginger, and garlic, and continue to blend. Add the herbs and a little of the reserved oil, and continue to blend. Add the salt, sugar and lemon juice, and blend until the herbs are very finely minced.

Transfer the mixture to a serving bowl and stir in the remaining oil. Serve alongside warm or cold noodles, and allow each eater to spoon sauce to taste over a helping of noodles.

NOTE: This quantity of pesto, about 2½ cups, will be more than adequate for a pound of fresh noodles. It's also delicious with the Asian "Ravioli" on page 301.

MINT
(Mentha spp.)

REGION OF USE: Thailand, Vietnam, Laos, Cambodia, and elsewhere in Southeast Asia

Like their close cousin basil, a variety of mints are used in Southeast Asian cooking. A mild fuzzy-leafed variety of tropical spearmint (*M. arvensis*) seems to be the herb of choice among Southeast Asians here. Sold in bunches of foot-long stems with 1½-inch leaves, it's grown year-round in greenhouses in California and is available throughout the country in Southeast Asian produce markets. Darker "curly leaf" mints, one with ½- to ¾-inch leaves, show up regularly, and all may be used interchangeably to season Southeast Asian salads.

WARM GROUND CHICKEN SALAD WITH MINT

Yield: 4 servings

1 *pound boneless, skinless chicken (not just breast)*

1 *egg white, beaten lightly*

1½ *teaspoons cornstarch*

¾ *teaspoon salt*

2 *teaspoons sesame oil*

1 *stalk lemon grass, finely minced*

4 *small fresh red chilis, finely chopped, including seeds*

3 *tablespoons fresh lime juice*

2 *tablespoons fish sauce*

1½ *teaspoons sugar*

1 *teaspoon coarsely ground dried red chili pepper*

1 *cup peanut oil*

15 *mint leaves, cut into shreds*

Lettuce leaves

Chop the chicken by hand until it has the texture of ground meat. Mix it with the egg white, cornstarch, ½ teaspoon of the salt, and the sesame oil. Refrigerate for 30 minutes. Meanwhile, mix the lemon grass, fresh red chilis, lime juice, fish sauce, sugar, remaining ¼ teaspoon salt, and the dried chili powder. Set aside.

Heat about 1 cup peanut oil in a wok until it is hot but not smoking. Add the chicken, stirring rapidly to break up any clumps. Cook, stirring, about 2 minutes, until all the chicken has changed color. Drain, toss with the seasoned sauce and the mint leaves, and serve over lettuce leaves.

PERILLA
(Perilla frutescens)

OTHER NAMES: Shiso (Japanese), Beefsteak plant

REGION OF USE: Japan, Southeast Asia (see Note)

Green perilla leaves, shiso

The Chinese ate this cousin of basil and mint as a vegetable 1,500 years ago, and they valued the oil from its seeds for cooking. Ancient recipes often specified perilla oil if they weren't calling for animal fat. The Chinese gave up on this as a food staple centuries ago, but the Japanese—to whom they introduced the plant—still eat two varieties of it: green (*ao-jiso*) and red (*aka-jiso*).

The large red "beefsteak" leaves are found packed in brine in Japanese groceries, ready for pickling plums, their main culinary responsibility these days. The smaller green perilla leaves are sold fresh in small plastic packages of about a dozen; they're used as a garnish and are sometimes fried whole in tempura batter, but most often they are an aromatic addition to sushi rolls. Interestingly, the Chinese *materia medica* cites perilla as an antidote to fish poisoning.

NOTE: From time to time on Southeast Asian produce stands, varieties of perilla show up among the basil and mint.

CHILI PEPPERS
(Capsicum)

REGION OF USE: Southeast Asia, China, Korea, Japan

Left to right: jalapeño, serrano, and Thai "bird" chili peppers

Chili peppers are a New World fruit, probably originally from Brazil. The Asian cuisines most associated with them—Sichuan, Hunan, Thai, Indonesian, Indian—didn't know of their existence before the seventeenth century, when peppers were introduced to Asia by the Spanish and Portuguese. Those Asian cuisines were already spicy nonetheless, relying on black pepper and ginger, which are native.

Any sort of hot pepper you like can be used in Asian cooking. All peppers, including bell, paprika, and pimiento, are said to be variants of one original New World fruit, and Asians have bred their own kinds. There's a fiery little pepper from Thailand that is now available fresh in this country and is found in stores that carry Southeast Asian goods. Be forewarned, it's hotter than a jalapeño or even the smaller serrano pepper (which the Thais have taken a liking to and now grow in Thailand, where it's called *prik e noo kaset*). The Thai pepper is small, no longer than 1½ to 2 inches, and skinny. It's called a "bird" pepper (because, I've read, birds feed on them—which, if it were true, would mean that Southeast Asia is soon to run out of birds). The peppers are almost always available green, and the red ones show up from time to time in the summer.

The green Thai pepper has an immediate bite to it, whereas the heat of the red comes on more slowly. Both are wonderfully full-flavored, but buy the red if you can and keep them out on a plate. If you don't use them fast enough, they won't spoil, but will dry into the best possible dried peppers. The green ones will rot if you leave them out, but they will keep if stored wrapped in a paper towel in a plastic bag in the refrigerator.

The red ones also come lightly pickled in water, salt, and vinegar in 16-ounce jars under the Thai World Importers and Exporters label. They can be used like the fresh, and as the jar of bright red peppers is beautiful, they're a nice gift for anyone who dotes on hot food.

It should be noted that in Thailand and elsewhere in Southeast Asia, fresh chili peppers are used seeds and all, whereas the cooks of Sichuan and Hunan, China, will often remove the seeds and membranes for aesthetic reasons, for example in a dish of all julienne shreds. This diminishes their heat, but a fiery chili paste may be used in addition.

A succulent dish that is also beautiful, as the whole clams are served in a light coconut sauce with colorful shreds of lime zest, red chili peppers, and ginger.

CLAMS WITH BASIL, MINT, AND CHILIS

Yield: 6 to 8 servings

24 *clams, preferably littlenecks*

3 *small fresh red chili peppers, shredded*

Shredded zest of 1 lime

1 *tablespoon shredded fresh ginger*

3 *garlic cloves, minced*

3 *tablespoons fish sauce*

Grated zest of 1 lime

¼ *cup coconut milk*

1 *teaspoon sugar*

Pinch of salt

½ *cup mixed Asian basil and mint leaves*

2 *teaspoons cornstarch mixed with 2 tablespoons water*

3 *tablespoons peanut oil*

Coriander sprigs, for garnish

Scrub the clams well. Fill a bowl with enough cold water to easily cover the clams, and set aside. Combine the clams with 2 cups water in a wok or large pot, and bring the water to a boil. As the clams open, immediately transfer them with tongs to the bowl of cold water, to stop the cooking. Drain the cooled clams and set aside. Reserve the cooking liquid.

Combine the chili shreds, shredded lime zest, ginger, and garlic in a small bowl.

Mix 1 cup of the clam-cooking liquid with the fish sauce, grated lime zest, coconut milk, sugar, and salt. Set aside the basil and mint, and have the cornstarch mixture handy.

Heat the oil in a skillet or wok. Add the chili pepper combination, and stir-fry until fragrant. Add the seasoned clam stock and bring to a boil. Toss in the basil and mint. Give the cornstarch mixture a stir, and add it. Cook, stirring, until the mixture is smooth and slightly thickened. Add the clams and cook, stirring, until well heated, 1 to 2 minutes. Serve garnished with the coriander.

Kaffir lime with leaves

Citrus trees are thought to have originated in dry subtropical regions of East Asia; the leaves, along with the peels, rinds, and juice of the fruits, are staple seasonings throughout the area.

Historically, one of the most important Chinese flavorings has been orange peel (the orange is a native plant), which is sold dried (see page 246).

In Southeast Asia the lime, *C. aurantifolia,* is an age-old food and medicine. In tropical Asia lime juice is used the way vinegar is to the north in China.

C. hystrix (see page 245), known as the Kaffir lime or as *magrut* in Thailand, is important for its rind and its leaves, both of which are common seasonings in Thailand and environs. Thus far they've only been available dried, but the trees are being grown in California and Florida, and these seasonings are for sale fresh in some markets already.

In the Philippines a lemon called *calamansi* or "sour lime" is squeezed onto food and into dips, and even flavors bottled soy sauce. As with all foreign citrus, these cannot be imported to the mainland United States and Philippine markets here don't carry them. The same is true of the Japanese *yuzu* citron, whose rind seasons dishes in Japan. However the juice and the oil of the rind are sold bottled in Japanese groceries.

FRESH CORIANDER
(Coriandrum sativum)

OTHER NAMES: Cilantro, Chinese parsley, Pak chee (Thai), Yuen sai (Cantonese)

REGION OF USE: China, Southeast Asia

Coriander is the most heavily consumed fresh herb on our planet. It's safe to say if you took an average day's consumption of all other herbs and heaped them in a mound, and put the same day's consumption of fresh coriander next to it, the coriander pile would dwarf the other. The Japanese are the only Asians who don't count it as a staple. The Thais use the roots as well as the leaves in their curry pastes.

Coriander—like dill a member of the carrot/parsley family (Umbelliferae) and a native of the Middle East—appeared in China around 200 B.C. and was eaten like a vegetable. It was regarded as an antidote to stomach upset and was used to treat ptomaine poisoning. It's now the premier herb in China and Southeast Asia as it is in India, the Middle East, Africa, and Latin America. Americans and Europeans are learning to like it all of a sudden, and it's quickly becoming a Western staple.

Availability is rarely a problem. Besides Asian and Latin markets, supermarket chain stores are increasingly stocking fresh coriander.

The near-universal popularity of this herb, aside from its medicinal properties, lies with its ability to heighten other flavors in a dish while at the same time cutting into any unpleasant excess—richness for example. Coriander has a chameleon-like ability to change flavor according to what it's cooked with. People who claim to detest it will relish it in one dish while wanting to pick it out of another. It should top any list of unusual tastes that are worth getting used to.

Bunches of fresh coriander are traditionally sold with the roots. Store it in the refrigerator with the roots in water and a plastic bag loosely covering the leaves. It will keep for a few days or more.

NOTE: Dill (*Anethum graveolens*), used in Thai and Laotian cooking, especially with seafood, is closely linked with its cousin, coriander. In fact the Thais call it *pak chee Lao,* "Laotian coriander." Fennel leaves, which look like dill and are in the same family, are also used, but dill is preferred.

1 *cup peanut oil*	1½ *tablespoons light soy sauce*
½ *cup (heaping) unsalted raw peanuts*	½ *teaspoon salt*
1 *cake bean curd*	1 *teaspoon sugar*
1 *pound coriander leaves*	2 *tablespoons sesame oil*

FRESH CORIANDER AND PEANUT SALAD

Yield: 4 to 6 servings

Heat the peanut oil in a saucepan to nearly smoking. Drop in the peanuts, stir, and turn off the heat. Allow the peanuts to sit until they're golden brown (this should take a few minutes.) Remove the peanuts to drain on a paper towel, leaving the oil in the pan. Cut the bean curd in half diagonally, making two triangles. Reheat the oil, and when it is hot, fry the bean curd until golden brown. Remove and drain the bean curd, saving the oil for another use.

Heat a large quantity of water to boiling and add the coriander leaves. Stir them briefly into the boiling water, then drain immediately and rinse under cold water. Squeeze the coriander with your hands to get rid of most of the liquid (you'll be amazed at how much it will wither down). Chop the coriander and place it in a mixing bowl. Cut the fried bean curd into a fine dice, and add it to the coriander, along with the peanuts. Toss with the remaining ingredients and serve.

TREFOIL
(Cryptotaenia japonica)

OTHER NAMES: Mitsuba
(Japanese), Honewort

REGION OF USE: Japan

Used to a small extent in China, this relative of parsley and coriander is most strongly associated with Japanese cooking, and is found in Japanese produce markets here. Its taste has been described as a combination of sorrel and celery. The Japanese add it to soups, casseroles, steamed custards, and salads, often parboiling it first, and never cooking it for very long lest it lose its fragrance. It's sold in bunches of long light green to whiteish stems with darker trifoliate green leaves. Some trefoil resembles Italian parsley. Trefoil will keep in the refrigerator for a week with its roots in water, lightly covered by a plastic bag.

THE GINGER FAMILY

GINGER
(Zingiber officinale)

OTHER NAMES: Gingerroot, Shōga (Japanese), King or khing (Thai), Geung (Cantonese)

REGION OF USE: China, Japan, Korea, Southeast Asia

It's not an exaggeration to say you can't cook Asian food without ginger. It has extraordinary culinary value. Its clean spiciness makes the freshest seafood taste fresher; it suppresses any hint of rankness in meat; it cuts the richness of fatty dishes; and it works in wonderful harmony with garlic. All Asian countries use ginger, which can't be said of any other seasoning except salt.

Mistakenly called a root, ginger is a tropical rhizome (underground stem) that is thought to be native to Southeast Asia, although it has been cultivated for so long, no one can say for sure where it originated. For millennia it has been valued as a medicinal in every Asian culture. It is thought to aid digestion, alleviate nausea, combat colds, and stimulate the appetite for both food and sex.

In China, which perhaps has more varied uses for ginger than any other culture, the texture of the fresh rhizome counts. It's cut into fine matchsticks, chopped finely, or used in slices that are smashed. In Japan, ginger has its own tool, called an *oroshigane,* on which it's grated, and slices of pink pickled ginger, *gari,* are a familiar accompaniment to sushi. In Southeast Asia, ginger is smashed into a paste with other seasonings at the start of a dish, or it's used cut up as in Chinese cooking.

Fresh ginger is rapidly being adopted by American cooks, and it can be found in most supermarkets. In fact it's now an American product: Some of the world's finest ginger is grown in Hawaii and shipped to the U.S. mainland, like pineapples, by the ton. The late winter and early spring is the peak season for Hawaiian ginger, when the huge, shiny rhizomes are stacked high in Asian markets.

When buying ginger, select the hardest, heaviest rhizomes; those that have been sitting around will be wrinkled and light in weight. Check where the knobs have broken: The longer the rhizome has grown before harvesting, the more fibrous it becomes, and the more fibers you will see at the break. Mature rhizomes are hotter and to some extent more flavorful, but the fibers of an old rhizome may hinder the fine cuts required by Chinese cooking. Where the ginger is to be grated, say for a Japanese dipping sauce, the fiber doesn't matter, and the extra heat and flavor may be preferable.

Since ginger is now available, storing it is no longer the problem it once was. If it's fresh and firm to begin with, it will keep for a week or so sitting on the counter. To keep it longer, it should go into the vegetable crisper in the refrigerator, inside a plastic bag with a paper towel to absorb any moisture, which can cause mold. Freezing ginger turns it to mush, rendering it useless for any cooking where texture is important. Pickling ginger in sherry or vodka shouldn't be necessary unless you live miles from a source. For aesthetic reasons, ginger should be peeled before using.

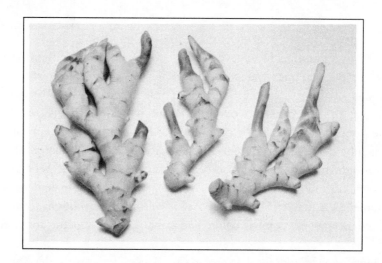

"BABY" OR "YOUNG" GINGER. In the early summer, the immature ginger known as "baby ginger" arrives at Asian markets. From Hawaii, it's beautiful, cream-colored and translucent with bright pink shoots. Baby ginger is expensive—it's more perishable than mature ginger—and has a wonderfully soft texture; but contrary to what's written about it, it is not a superior substitute for mature ginger. The flavor is not as developed and it lacks bite.

Baby ginger is best for pickling—the Japanese *sushōga*, sometimes called *gari*, that is served with sushi is pickled baby ginger. It's baby ginger that comes preserved in syrup in Chinese ginger jars, and it's made into a fine crystallized ginger in Australia. (Asians prefer mature crystallized ginger.) In China it's sliced and cooked like a vegetable—with duck meat, for example, in the Hunan dish Duck with Young Ginger. Baby ginger needn't be peeled.

A slightly more mature ginger, "young ginger," also light in color and lacking mature skin, is available at Asian markets sporadically throughout the summer, and once in a while it shows up during other times of the year. It can be used like mature ginger.

GINGER SHOOTS. These are a Japanese staple, most commonly eaten pickled and dyed red. Known as *hajikama-shoga* or "blushing ginger," these are used a stalk at a time as a garnish for grilled fish. At $10 for a 6-ounce jar, they're not something you snack on.

MIOGA GINGER
(Zingiber mioga)

OTHER NAMES: Mioga
REGION OF USE: Japan

The Japanese alone eat this member of the ginger family, although it was introduced to them by the Chinese, who long ago cultivated it, then let it go wild.

Unlike regular ginger, it's the budlike shoots of this plant that are eaten, rather than the tuber. Mioga ginger is available in the spring in some Japanese markets, especially on the West Coast. Small quantities are grown outside Fresno, California.

GALANGAL
(Alpinia galanga)

OTHER NAMES: Galanga, Galanga root, Laos (Indonesian), Thai ginger, Java root, Ka or kha (Thai), Languas

REGION OF USE: Southeast Asia, especially Thailand, Laos, Cambodia, Java

Among the more unusual fresh seasonings to go on sale in this country recently is galangal, a relative of ginger. Called galingale in England, it was popular throughout Europe in the Middle Ages, when it was dried and ground. It disappeared from Western cooking when the heavy use of spices went out of fashion in the eighteenth century.

The reappearance of this fresh "root"—like ginger, it's actually a rhizome or underground stem—is due to its importance in the cooking of Thailand, where it all but takes the place of ginger.

Thick slices of galangal are starting to turn up in Thai soups in regions of the United States with large Southeast Asian populations. It's not to be eaten in this state, however, as those who have bitten into it can attest. It has a fiery medicinal taste and the texture of a wood chip.

Pounded fresh in a mortar with seasonings such as lemon grass, chili peppers, shallots, and garlic, galangal is an important ingredient in Thai curry pastes. Its ability to curb nausea and settle the stomach is supposedly as great as ginger's, and grated galangal with lime juice is an all-purpose tonic in Southeast Asia.

Galangal resembles ginger, but the rhizomes are larger and pale yellow with zebra-like markings and pink shoots. It's now grown in Fiji and flown here. At six to eight times the price of ginger, it's expensive.

See also "Dried Galangal," page 241.

This is a particularly fragrant, full-flavored example of a genre of Thai soups that use lemon grass. Some of these soups are made sour by tamarind; others, like this one, with fresh lime juice. This is loaded with more galangal than any you're likely to encounter in a restaurant. Any seafood—squid, pieces of fish filet, clams—may be used in place of the lightly poached shrimp; cook it at the last moment in the spicy broth.

HOT AND SOUR SHRIMP SOUP
(Thailand)

Yield: 8 servings

1½ pounds medium-size shrimp

½ teaspoon salt

Few drops sesame oil

4 tablespoons peanut oil

2 quarts chicken stock

6 thin slices fresh or dried galangal

8 garlic cloves, smashed

2 stalks lemon grass (bottom third only), coarsely shredded

1 tablespoon finely shredded lime zest

5 shallots, sliced

4 to 6 small fresh green or red chili peppers, coarsely shredded, including seeds

2 teaspoons salt

2 tablespoons fish sauce

½ teaspoon sugar

¼ cup fresh lime juice

1 teaspoon freshly ground black pepper

⅓ cup mixed coriander and Asian basil leaves, for garnish

Peel the shrimp, reserving the shells. Cut them in half lengthwise, then toss with ½ teaspoon salt and the sesame oil, and refrigerate.

Heat 2 tablespoons of the peanut oil and stir-fry the shrimp shells until pink. Add the chicken stock and bring it to a boil. Skim the stock, then simmer for 10 minutes, and strain.

Add the remaining 2 tablespoons oil to a clean wok. Briefly stir-fry the galangal, garlic, lemon grass, lime zest, shallots, and chilis. Add the stock and bring to a boil. Add the remaining 2 teaspoons salt, fish sauce, and sugar, and simmer 15 to 20 minutes. Stir in the shrimp and immediately turn off the heat. Transfer the soup to a tureen, stir in the lime juice, sprinkle with the pepper and basil-coriander garnish, and serve.

NOTE: If you can get them, 2 or 3 fresh kaffir lime leaves, or about 6 slices of the peel, add flavor to this soup.

FRESH TURMERIC
(Curcuma domestica)

OTHER NAMES: Yellow ginger, Kamin (Thai)

REGION OF USE: Thailand, Vietnam, Burma, Laos, Cambodia, Indonesia

Fresh turmeric, which looks like a small orange-tinted version of its cousin ginger, is now for sale at Southeast Asian markets. It's used fresh in Southeast Asian and South Indian cooking. Sliced or sometimes chopped—it's carrot orange inside—it's added to the stews we call curries. Hoping to get a cooking tip, I asked the owner of the Vietnamese stand where I first found fresh turmeric what she did with it. "It's good for healing scars," she said.

Like ginger, turmeric is a tuber-like stem or rhizome and as such has been dug out of the hilly jungle areas of tropical India and and Southeast Asia for thousands of years, mostly for medicinal purposes. It was so highly valued as medicine—for wounds, internal hemorrhaging, syphilis, insanity, poisoning— that it became the spice of choice in ancient sacrificial rites in China and India. In China during the Zhou period (twelfth to third century B.C.), a turmeric wine was offered to the gods. In India to this day a turmeric-soaked thread is the binding symbol of a Hindu marriage.

When buying turmeric fresh, look for rock-hard rhizomes. It will keep best wrapped in a paper towel inside a plastic bag in the refrigerator. I might add that turmeric seems to be promising as a houseplant. From a rhizome with a bud, I now have a 2-foot plant with long pointed leaves, and am waiting for the yellow flower clusters to appear.

NOTE: Sometimes labeled "turmeric," a variety that's pencil thin and yellow inside, shows up occasionally in Southeast Asian markets. Indians call it "Mango ginger"; Asians sometimes label it "Indian ginger."

OTHER NAMES: Ka chai or krachai (Thai), Kentjur (Indonesian), Camphor root	LESSER GALANGAL
REGION OF USE: Southeast Asia	(Kaempferia galanga)

Once in a great while, in Thai and Vietnamese markets in California at least, these finger-like clusters of roots—related to ginger, they're actually rhizomes —show up fresh. The Chinese use them medicinally, but throughout Southeast Asia they're tossed in stews and curries, either peeled whole or shredded. They're used more as a vegetable than as a seasoning. Mildly medicinal and refreshing, their flavor is less biting than the large species of galangal.

If you absolutely need krachai and can't get it fresh, it's available shredded and pickled in brine in Southeast Asian food markets. The label reads "Preserved Rhizome (Ka Chai)." These aren't a bad substitute for the fresh.

THAI CURRY PASTES

Anyone who has eaten in a Thai restaurant has noticed curry dishes such as Chicken in Green Curry Sauce or Beef in Red Curry Sauce. These dishes are flavored with fragrant pastes which if homemade will keep their fresh, spicy bite for up to a month. They needn't be used only for Thai curries, either. The pastes are excellent seasonings for fried rice, pasta, soup, home-fried potatoes, scrambled eggs, and sautéed meat and seafood dishes.

The flavor of these pastes varies from restaurant to restaurant, but the colors are standard. Green and red are the most popular, green being the most incendiary. Red curry paste has dried red chilis as the base (the recipe is on page 236). Fresh green chilies are the base for green curry paste, and a yellow paste includes turmeric, fresh or dried.

GREEN CURRY PASTE

Yield: about 2 cups

1 tablespoon coriander seeds

2 teaspoons cumin seeds

2 teaspoons fennel seeds

2 teaspoons black peppercorns

8 cloves

1 nutmeg

20 fresh serrano chilis or 12 fresh jalapeños

4 large shallots

8 garlic cloves

1 bunch coriander, including roots

2 small stalks lemon grass (bottom third only)

3 ¼-inch slices galangal or ginger

Zest of 1 lime

1 tablespoon shrimp sauce

½ cup peanut oil

1½ teaspoons salt

Place the coriander seeds, cumin seeds, fennel seeds, peppercorns, and cloves in a small skillet, and toast over medium heat, shaking, until fragrant. Then grind the spices in a mortar or spice grinder.

Grate the whole nutmeg, add it to the spices, and set aside.

Combine the chilis, shallots, and garlic in a food processor or large mortar. Cut the fresh coriander and lemon grass into 1-inch lengths and add these with the galangal and lime zest, to sauce along with the shrimp paste, ¼ cup of the oil, and the salt. Blend to a coarse paste. Add the spices and continue to blend until the ingredients are very finely minced. Remove to a bowl; stir in the remaining oil, transfer to a jar and store in the refrigerator. It will keep for a month.

(See Green Curry Noodles with Beef and Chinese Chives, page 46, and Squid Stuffed with Green Curry Shrimp, page 36.)

Turmeric, preferably fresh, gives this paste its name. If necessary, 2 teaspoons of ground turmeric may be substituted, and ginger may be substituted for the galangal.

YELLOW CURRY PASTE

Yield: about 2 cups

24 to 30 dried red chilis (30 if small "bird" peppers are used)

3 tablespoons coriander seeds

1 tablespoon cumin seeds

1½ teaspoons black peppercorns

2 tablespoons chopped fresh turmeric

2 tablespoons chopped fresh galangal

1 bunch coriander (roots and 1 inch of stems only)

12 garlic cloves

½ cup chopped shallots

1 large stalk lemon grass (bulb only), chopped

½ cup peanut oil

2 teaspoons salt

2 tablespoons ground fish sauce (anchovy cream) or shrimp sauce

2 tablespoons fresh lime juice

In a dry skillet over medium heat, toast the peppers, coriander seeds, cumin seeds, and peppercorns until fragrant. Then grind the spices in a mortar or spice grinder to form a coarse powder.

Put the turmeric, galangal, coriander roots, garlic, shallots, lemon grass, and 2 tablespoons of the oil into a food processor, and grind to a coarse paste. Add the spices, salt, ground fish sauce, and lime juice, and continue to blend. Transfer to a bowl and stir in the rest of the oil. It will keep in a jar in the refrigerator.

(See Yellow Curry Fried Rice with Mussels, page 277.)

Best served as an appetizer cut into rounds—each with a toothpick,
if you like—these squid are stuffed with a spicy shrimp mixture, dipped in a
light batter, and fried until golden.

SQUID STUFFED WITH GREEN CURRY SHRIMP

Yield: 10 to 12
appetizer servings

2 ounces pork fat

1 pound squid (about 8
small ones)

½ pound shrimp, chopped
coarsely

1 egg white

5 fresh water chestnuts,
chopped

½ cup chopped coriander
(leaves and stems)

BATTER

1 egg yolk

½ cup cold water

½ cup flour

1 tablespoon Green Curry
Paste (see page 34)

½ teaspoon salt

Peanut oil for deep
frying

Bring water to boil in a small saucepan and add the pork fat. Simmer for 2
minutes, drain, and let cool. Meanwhile clean the squid, leaving the body whole.
Set the bodies aside along with the tentacles. Score each squid body by pressing it flat on a cutting board and, with a knife held almost horizontally, make
diagonal cuts about ¼ inch apart. (Be careful not to cut all the way through.)
Turn the squid body over and repeat.

Make the stuffing by mixing together the shrimp, egg white, water chestnuts,
coriander, curry paste, salt, and 2 heaping tablespoons of the pork fat, chopped
finely. Stuff each squid loosely with the mixture, leaving a little room near the
end. Skewer the ends with toothpicks.

Heat oil for deep frying while you make the batter. Blend the egg yolk with
the cold water and pour in the flour. Mix by stirring just a few times. The
mixture should be lumpy and not well mixed.

When the oil is hot, about 350°F, dip each squid into the batter and fry 3
to 4 minutes until golden. Fry the tentacles also. Drain on paper towels. Cut
each body into ¾-inch-wide sections and rearrange in their original shapes on
a serving platter. Salt the tentacles lightly and put them in the middle.

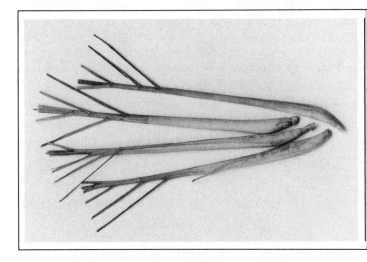

LEMON GRASS
(Cymbopogon citratus)

OTHER NAMES: Sereh (Indonesian), Takrai (Thai)

REGION OF USE: Southeast Asia

Lemon grass is the reason a Thai or Vietnamese dish often will have a compelling balmlike flavor that you can't quite put your finger on. It's not exactly lemon, but more of a subtle lemon perfume. In Indonesia young girls are sent to cut lemon grass, because of an old belief that it's at its most fragrant when picked by someone with a virgin's pure thoughts. Unlike most other herbs used in the Asian tropics, lemon grass will grow in moderate climates. It's grown in abundance in California these days. In fact it's difficult to stop once it takes hold.

Fresh lemon grass is sold by the stalk, which is gray-green, 2 feet in length, and looks something like a scallion though it is fibrous to the point of being woody. For this reason, unlike seasonings such as garlic and ginger, it is valued for the flavor it imparts rather than for any substance it adds. Only the bulblike 6- to 8-inch base of the stalk is used, after the top is trimmed and a layer of tough outer leaves is peeled off. For soups this is cut into coarse shreds around 2 inches in length or sliced into little rounds. For curry-style dishes, lemon grass is chopped coarsely, then pounded to a paste with other seasonings in a mortar. It's part of a standard paste with chili peppers and shallots that seasons the various pork, seafood, or chicken stuffings that are wrapped in banana leaves and steamed and grilled in Southeast Asia. A wonderful Laotian dish calls for a whole crab to be steamed on a bed of freshly shredded lemon grass.

Some sources confuse lemon grass with citronella (*C. nardus*). They are close relatives and the oil of each is used commercially in food products and cos-

metics. Oil of citronella is the more valued for perfume, and is a highly regarded mosquito repellent.

Lemon grass is easy to grow if you can find a stalk with vestiges of roots.
It can be kept in water until the roots develop, then transferred to a planter
that gives it plenty of room to spread. The more closely the environment
approximates its warm, moist, tropical home the better, but lemon grass will
thrive anywhere it doesn't frost.

DRIED LEMON GRASS. You may also buy lemon grass shredded and dried, in
which case it must be soaked in hot water for 30 minutes before using. It's
also sold dried and ground, but this isn't recommended. Since tracking down
dried lemon grass will take you to the same stores that carry it fresh, it makes
little sense to use these substitutes. It should be noted that dried lemon grass
is a common ingredient in herbal teas.

A Southeast Asian country-style soup that is simple and tasty.

½ chicken, skinned, boned, and cut into strips	3 cups coconut milk	**CHICKEN, GALANGAL, AND COCONUT SOUP**
½ egg white	4 tablespoons fish sauce	
2 teaspoons cornstarch	½ teaspoon sugar	Yield: 6 to 8 servings
4 cups fresh chicken stock	½ teaspoon salt	
8 slices galangal	1 cup peanut oil	
3 stalks lemon grass, bottom 6 inches to 8 inches only sliced on the diagonal	Juice of 1 lemon	
8 small fresh chili peppers, red or green, coarsely chopped	1 teaspoon ground black pepper	
	Coriander leaves	

Toss the chicken with the egg white and cornstarch, and refigerate for 30 minutes.

Heat the chicken stock and add the galangal, lemon grass, and chilis. Cover, and simmer for 10 minutes. Uncover, add the coconut milk, fish sauce, sugar, and salt, and simmer for 15 minutes.

Meanwhile, heat about 1 cup oil in a skillet or wok. When it is hot, add the chicken pieces. Stir to separate and cook just until the pieces change color, then drain. Transfer the soup to a terrine, and add the chicken. Sprinkle with the lemon juice, pepper, and coriander leaves, and serve.

NOTE: Rice noodles, cooked in the usual manner, may be added to this soup. They should be put in the terrine just before the soup is poured in.

OTHER NAMES: Prickly ash, Sansho	**KINOME**
REGION OF USE: Japan	(Zenothoxylum piperitum)

Spring sprigs of a kind of prickly ash, *kinome* has a refreshing, slightly minty fragrance and is the most widely used garnish in Japan when chefs can get their hands on it. It's the same little tree whose berries are dried and sold as *sansho,* also called "Japanese pepper," and is a first cousin of the Chinese Sichuan peppercorn, *Z. simulans.*

Kinome sprigs can be found, at least if you're friendly with Japanese produce dealers or restaurateurs, but as of this writing it's not available commercially in the United States.

MATRIMONY VINE
(Lycium chinense)

REGION OF USE: China, Southeast Asia

OTHER NAMES: Chinese box thorn, Gow gei (Cantonese)

Shoots of this spiny shrub are increasingly available at Chinese and Southeast Asian produce stands. Stripped from the thorny stalk (which is discarded), the leaves, which have a distinct peppermint taste, are stirred into rich soups just before they're served, or they're cooked with pork—a traditional combination.

An ancient Chinese medicinal, matrimony vine is one of those ingredients that while it adds a particular flavor, eating it once in a while, no matter how, is a must if you care about a long and healthful life. Traditionally one eats the leaves in the spring, the flowers in the summer, the berries (called wolfberries —see below) in the fall, and the root in the winter. There are abundant matrimony vine extracts, tinctures, and pills, not to mention the dried parts of the plant itself, for sale in Chinese herbal shops.

The leaves are also commonly used to make tea in China and Japan. In fact, when the plant was introduced to England it was thought to be the tea plant. (The name has no significance in China; the plant is a relative of a species native to the West that is so named.)

WOLFBERRIES. Available dried at herb shops and some food stores, these berries of the matrimony vine look like small pointed reddish-orange raisins. Eaten plain, they're sweet with a slight licorice flavor. Children are often given a handful at the medicine counter as a quick, tonic snack, but usually they're added to braised dishes featuring chicken, pork, or turtle. Wolfberries have a reputation for improving eyesight and kidney function, and are believed to cure diabetes.

THE ONION FAMILY

The onion family, with the exception, ironically, of the common bulb onion, has been vital to East Asian cooking since antiquity. The origins of much of the onion family are obscure. Few of the cultivated species—leeks, shallots, chives, garlic, and scallions—have wild ancestors. Some scholars feel that most of these are native to Central Asia; others refuse to be more specific than citing the Northern Hemisphere. The Chinese use the widest variety, the Japanese —who use mostly two kinds of scallion—the narrowest.

SCALLIONS
(Allium fistulosum, A. cepa)

OTHER NAMES: Green onion, Spring onion, Bunching onion, Chinese onion

REGION OF USE: East Asia

The scallion is among the earliest recorded and most consistently employed ingredients in Chinese cooking, and the kind of scallion or "Chinese onion" referred to in early texts may be native. Its close relatives are staples throughout East Asia.

The term "scallion" includes several kinds of onions. They may be common white bulb onions (*A. cepa*) that are grown to inhibit bulbing and harvested when young (in the spring), or they may be a species of onion (*A. fistulosum*) that includes the Chinese onion, which never bulb. Welsh onions (no connection to Wales) are of this type.

On the market here, depending on the time of year and the region of the country, "scallions" take in a lot of varieties. In Louisiana, for example, rather than allowing shallots to bulb and the tops to die as is their normal course, they're harvested young as scallions.

NOTE: The only onions traditionally eaten in Japan are varieties of green onions: *naganegi,* popular in Tokyo (it looks like a small leek) and *aonegi,* popular in Osaka. Both are difficult to obtain here, though the *naganegi* occasionally shows up in Japanese markets.

In Southeast Asia squid are barely poached and then tossed, while still warm, with cool greens and herbs. Too much iceberg lettuce accompanies the versions in Thai restaurants in the United States. The salad below is filled with fresh, clean tastes and is a pleasure to look at.

THAI SQUID SALAD

Yield: 4 to 6 servings

1 *pound fresh squid*

1 *celery stalk, thinly sliced on the diagonal*

1½ *tablespoons fish sauce*

1½ *tablespoons fresh lime juice*

1 *teaspoon sugar*

Pinch of salt

1 *teaspoon chili oil*

2 *teaspoons peanut oil*

2 *garlic cloves, finely minced*

2 *scallions, white part, only finely minced*

10 *mint leaves, cut into strips*

2 *tablespoons chopped coriander leaves*

1 *small red chili pepper, finely chopped*

1 *cucumber, peeled, seeded, and sliced*

Clean the squid. Cut off the tentacles just below the eyes. Squeeze out the beak and discard it, and put the tentacles in a bowl. Split the white body of the squid with a knife, and lay it inside up on a cutting board. Holding the knife almost parallel to the squid, score the body with straight cuts about ¼ inch apart. Turn the squid 90 degrees and repeat, so you have a diamond pattern. (Be careful not to cut through.) Cut the body into six more or less equal pieces and add to the bowl with the tentacles. Repeat with the remaining squid.

Bring a large pot of water to a boil. Add the squid and the celery. Stir just to separate the pieces, and cook for just 20 seconds. Drain immediately, and rinse under cold water to stop the cooking. Set on paper towels to dry.

Mix the fish sauce, lime juice, sugar, and salt in a small bowl. Add the oils and the garlic and set aside. Combine the scallions, mint, coriander leaves, and chili pepper in another small bowl.

Arrange the cucumber slices on a small platter. Make sure the squid and celery are thoroughly dry, and toss them with the sauce. Add the scallion mixture and toss well. Arrange over the cucumbers, and serve.

SHALLOTS
(Allium ascalonicum)

REGION OF USE: Southeast Asia, China

While we may associate shallots with French cooking, they're more vital to the cuisines of Thailand, Laos, Vietnam, Kampuchea, Malaysia, and Indonesia. In Southeast Asia, it's exceptional when they're left out of a dish. Typically, the first step is to pound shallots into a fragrant paste with lemon grass, chili peppers, sometimes galangal, and other seasonings. They're occasionally blackened over a flame before they're used, or they may be sliced and fried to a golden crispness and used for a garnish. Southeast Asian markets in fact are the place to buy the best shallots at the most reasonable prices, no matter what kind of cooking you do.

NOTE: There is a small onion (*A. bakeri* or *A. chinense*) that is cultivated in China—it also grows wild in the mountains of Kiangsi—that has been routinely written of as a shallot and confused with the shallot described here. This Chinese "shallot" is grown mostly to be pickled and shows up here in jars or cans labeled "pickled shallots" or "pickled scallions."

<table>
<tr><td>

CHINESE LEEKS
(Allium ramosum)

</td><td>

OTHER NAMES: Jiu (Mandarin)

REGION OF USE: China

</td></tr>
</table>

These are not the leeks of Western cookery (*Allium porrum*), and they aren't to my knowledge available on these shores. Referred to in ancient and modern writings, these members of the onion family were given the English name "leek" somewhere along the line, and it stuck. They are worth mentioning since food writers credit the Chinese with having had the leek since antiquity.

The Western leek does show up on Asian vegetable stands from time to time, however, and, in the spring, often beautiful, young thin ones at reasonable prices. They shouldn't be passed up.

<table>
<tr><td>

CHINESE CHIVES
(Allium turberosum)

</td><td>

OTHER NAMES: Gow choy (Cantonese)

REGION OF USE: China, Southeast Asia

</td></tr>
</table>

Not to be confused with the European chive (*A. schoenoprasum*), this species of chive takes three forms as it appears on produce stands:

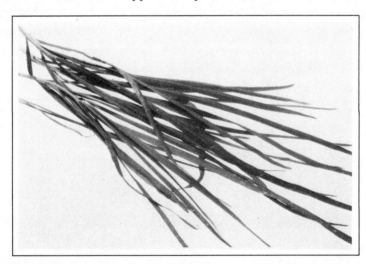

CHINESE CHIVES. This foot-long chive with its grassy, dark green leaves is sold in bunches about 3 inches in diameter at Chinese and Southeast Asian produce stands. They're a common spring roll ingredient and are also cooked with noodles or, cut into 2-inch lengths, may be stir-fried with slices of lamb or pork. Delicately flavored, though stronger than Western chives, they may be used as you would Western chives, scrambled in eggs for example. Chinese chives must be used quickly as they don't keep longer than a few days in the refrigerator.

Yellow chives and flowering chives

YELLOW CHIVES (ALSO CHIVE SHOOTS). These chives, traditionally available in small, expensive bunches from August through November, are highly prized for their sweet, mellow onion flavor. They combine well with shreds of pork or poultry and are stirred into noodle dishes at the last minute, as they require only the briefest cooking. They're simply green Chinese chives grown under an inverted flower pot or straw mat to block the light and thus blanch them.

FLOWERING CHIVES. The stiff flowering stem plucked from Chinese chives, these are also expensive and sold by the small bunch. They are stronger in flavor than the Chinese chive leaf, but may be used in much the same way. After cutting off the bottom inch or so, use the flower and all. They mince easily. (Flowering chives should not be confused with flowering garlic stalks, sometimes called "garlic chives" (see page 47).

This simple but elegant pasta dish is kind of a spicy
Thai lo mein. Fried chopped peanuts are
tossed in at the end.

GREEN CURRY NOODLES WITH BEEF AND CHINESE CHIVES

Yield: 4 to 6 servings

1 cup peanut oil

¾ cup raw peanuts

¾ pound (12 ounces) flank steak

1 tablespoon dark soy sauce

2 teaspoons cornstarch

1 tablespoon sesame oil

½ pound fresh Chinese egg noodles

1 bunch Chinese chives

4 tablespoons Green Curry Paste (see page 34)

½ cup chicken stock

1½ teaspoons salt

Heat the oil to nearly smoking in a wok; add the peanuts and turn off the heat. Allow them to sit until the oil cools. Using a slotted spoon, transfer the peanuts to paper towels; leave the oil in the wok. Chop the peanuts coarsely and set aside.

Slice the flank steak as thinly as possible across the grain. Cut the slices in half and mix them with the soy sauce, cornstarch, and sesame oil, and set aside.

Bring a large quantity of water to boil. Add the egg noodles and cook 3½ minutes. Drain, and rinse under cold water to stop the cooking. Toss with a little peanut oil and set aside.

Cut the ends off of the chives, rinse and dry them, and cut into 1-inch lengths. Set aside.

Reheat the cup of oil in the wok. When it is hot but not smoking, add the beef. Turn down the heat, and stir quickly to separate the pieces. When the beef starts to change color—some of it should still be slightly pink—remove it to a colander to drain. Remove all but 3 tablespoons oil from the wok. (Or you may want to just transfer 3 tablespoons oil to a clean wok.) Heat the oil and add the curry paste. Stir briefly, and add the chives. Stir for 20 seconds, and then add the noodles, chicken stock, and salt. Stir for 30 seconds. Add the beef, and stir until well combined and piping hot. Turn off the heat, toss in the chopped peanuts, transfer to a platter, and serve.

GARLIC
(Allium sativum)

Probably native to Central Asia, garlic has been integral to the food and medicine of East Asia for millennia. East Asians in fact consume the most garlic per capita on earth, measurably more than the people of the Mediterranean. Korea is first in the world, although the Chinese in the far north consume about as much as the Koreans; Thailand is second; and the countries that surround Thailand—Laos, Cambodia, Vietnam—would put the Italians and Greeks to shame. (Two of the most garlic-laden dishes I've ever eaten were Asian. One was Sichuan pig's-ear salad that boasted ⅔ cup of raw chopped garlic. The other was a Korean squid dish that looked at first as if it were covered with chopped peanuts. The restaurant menu didn't even bother to mention it had garlic in it!)

Pickled garlic is common in Asia; for the Koreans, pickling young garlic in vinegar, soy sauce and sugar is a spring ritual.

The Japanese alone among East Asians eschew the use of garlic in their cooking, although it's used medicinally. The Japanese have historically referred to Koreans as "garlic eaters."

GARLIC CHIVES. The flowering stalks of the garlic plant, sold in bunches, are offered for sale occasionally. At around ¼ inch thick at the base and over 12 inches in length, they look like an adult version of the flowering chive.

PANDANUS LEAF
(Pandanus odorus)

OTHER NAMES: Screw pine leaf, Fragrant screw pine leaf, Daun pandan (Malay), Bai toey (Thai)

REGION OF USE: Southeast Asia

How European sailors traveling in the South Pacific could have named the graceful tropical pandanus a "screw pine" is a mystery. More akin to palms, and familiar to anyone who spends time Hawaii, none of the several varieties have much in common with pine trees.

The young, thin, pointed leaves picked from the bush-sized *P. odorus* are used as a seasoning in Thailand, Malaysia, Indonesia, and elsewhere in Southeast Asia. Typically, one or two leaves are cooked in a sugar syrup that is then strained—they also color the syrup green—as a first step in turning out various puddings, cakes, and custards made with rice, tapioca, and even mung bean flours. Pandanus leaves are sometimes cooked in plain rice. The name "screw pine" further throws you off when it comes to the flavor, which is best described as new-mown hay with a floral dimension.

Fresh pandanus leaves from Hawaii, up to 20 inches in length, are increasingly available in small bunches at Southeast Asian produce stands. Look for leaves that are shiny green on one side; they lose luster as they dry and age. Store them in plastic wrap in the refrigerator.

One-ounce packages of cut dried leaves, labeled "Dried Bay-Touy Leaves," are imported from Thailand, but first inquire about the fresh, which are much preferred.

This Malaysian recipe comes from Wai Ching Lee, who has assisted me with cooking classes and who only recently left her home in Singapore. She scattered dried blue pea flowers—tough to get unless someone mails them to you—into the rice, which when cooked was splashed with patches of violet. The "jam," which is actually a thick custard, must be cooked slowly over low heat and stirred regularly for hours. The pandanus leaves flavor the jam and color it a yellowish green.

COCONUT EGG JAM (*KAYA*) WITH STICKY RICE

Yield: 10 to 12 servings

2 cups glutinous rice

12 eggs

2⅓ cups sugar

1½ cups thick coconut milk

2 or 3 pandanus leaves, tied in a knot and lightly bruised

Pinch of salt

1 cup thin coconut milk, or more as needed

1 teaspoon salt

Soak the glutinous rice in water to cover for 8 hours or overnight.

Meanwhile, break the eggs into a bowl and stir in the sugar (don't beat—there should be no foam). Pour the mixture through a fine-mesh strainer into another bowl. Add the coconut milk, pandanus, and a pinch of salt. Pour the mixture into the top of an enamel, stainless steel, or glass double boiler, and cook over low heat, stirring often until thick (almost pasty), about 4 hours. (This may be done a day ahead; the jam keeps for weeks.)

Two hours before serving, put the glutinous rice into a pan or bowl, add the salt and light coconut milk just to cover, and steam for 1 hour on a plate or spread over cheesecloth in the top of a steamer. When the rice is cooked, press it into a round serving dish—a 12-inch glass pie pan will do—spread the jam over the top, and serve cut into small wedges.

TAMARIND
(Tamarindus indica)

OTHER NAMES: Asam
(Indonesian), Mak kam
(Thai), Tamarindo (Spanish)

REGION OF USE: Southeast
Asia (also India, the Middle
East, Africa and Latin
America)

After vinegar and lemon or lime juice, many North American cooks would be hard put to name the next most popular sour flavoring. Yet tamarind, from the pods of a large tropical tree, is hardly a secret. It adds a tasty prunelike sourness to curry-style dishes and chutneys in India, pickles in Iran, sour and hot soups in Thailand, refreshing beverages in Latin America—and to Worcestershire Sauce. The edible pulp of the pod is savored like a fruit in West Africa, even though the sugar it contains does little to mitigate its mouth-puckering sourness.

As a tonic, vitamin-rich tamarind is reportedly good for the liver and kidneys. In tropical Asia it's used to bring down a fever. It's also respected as a thirst quencher. The name comes from the Arabic *tamr hindi,* meaning "date of India." It is not a relative of the date, however, and while it has grown in India for centuries, the tree is thought to be native to tropical Africa.

Like lemon and vinegar, tamarind is usually added in liquid form to whatever calls for its flavor, and this is obtained by soaking and straining the pulp of the pod. The pods, 3 to 4 inches in length with a resemblance to fava bean pods, are now widely available in Latin markets, where they're called *tamarindo,* in Asian stores specializing in Thai and Vietnamese staples, and in Indian food stores.

When ripe—the way they are almost always sold—the brownish gray shells of the pods are often cracked, revealing a reddish brown pulp. Occasionally the immature pods, with a greenish cast, are sold in Southeast Asian markets to be cooked whole in soups and stews. You may also buy just the pulp in 8-ounce or 1-pound plastic-wrapped blocks, and these are acceptable for cooking. Less acceptable and lacking the full flavor of the freshly soaked pulp are the liquid concentrates carried in Indian food stores.

Recipes refer to ball-shaped sizes (e.g., "the size of a walnut") when calling for the amount of tamarind to be soaked. To soak, simply shell the pod or pinch off what you need from the brick and soak it in hot water for 15 minutes.

A ball 1 inch in diameter needs about ¼ cup water. After soaking, the fibrous material should be worked with the fingers while still in the liquid to remove every smidgen of pulp. This should be poured through a fine-mesh strainer, and worked again with the fingers into the mesh to remove all that is flavorful. The resulting liquid is added when called for. The pulp of the fresh pods will dissolve faster and be less fibrous than that from the brick.

Tamarind pods should be used here if you can get them.
Their prunelike tang makes an unusual and tasty
base for this shrimp dish.

SHRIMP IN TAMARIND SAUCE

Yield: 4 servings

1 pound fresh shrimp

2 teaspoons cornstarch

1 teaspoon sesame oil

¼ cup tamarind liquid (from fresh pods; see Note)

Pinch of salt

2 tablespoons fish sauce

1 tablespoon sugar

1 tablespoon fresh lemon juice

2 tablespoons minced fresh ginger

6 tiny fresh "bird" or 2 serrano chili peppers, finely chopped

2 large shallots, chopped

1½ cups peanut oil

Coriander leaves for garnish

Shell the shrimp. Cut them in half lengthwise, toss them with the cornstarch and sesame oil, and refrigerate for at least 30 minutes.

Combine the tamarind liquid, salt, fish sauce, sugar, and lemon juice, and set aside. Combine the ginger, chili peppers, and shallots, and set aside.

Heat the oil in a skillet or wok until hot but not smoking. Add the shrimp and stir quickly to separate. Remove the shrimp when just pink, and drain in a colander.

Remove all but 2 tablespoons of the oil from the skillet. Heat the remaining oil over high heat, and add the ginger/chili pepper combination. Stir until fragrant, and then add the tamarind sauce. When boiling hot, add the shrimp and stir over high heat for a minute or so, until the sauce is reduced. Serve garnished with coriander leaves.

NOTE: To obtain tamarind liquid, pour ½ cup hot water over 5 or 6 fresh peeled tamarind pods, and let sit for 15 minutes or so.

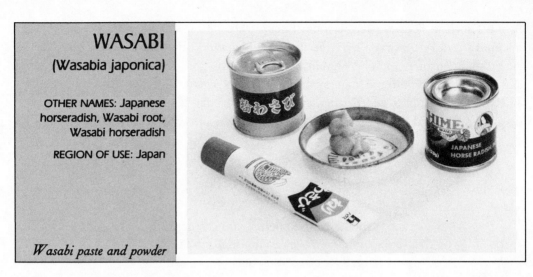

WASABI
(Wasabia japonica)

OTHER NAMES: Japanese horseradish, Wasabi root, Wasabi horseradish

REGION OF USE: Japan

Wasabi paste and powder

Unrelated to horseradish, *wasabi* is most familiar as the tearfully pungent green paste that accompanies sushi. Some Japanese cookbooks give the impression that the 4- to 5-inch wasabi root (indigenous to swampy earth next to cold mountain streams in Japan) is sometimes available fresh in this country. Maybe so, but Japanese produce dealers in California claim they don't carry it, and according to the USDA, with the exception of Hawaii, wasabi is not allowed in the United States. It's also not a crop grown with any success outside Japan. It's a shame, since the freshly grated root has a compelling herbal fragrance that is missing in the dried and powdered product that is popularly used. Even in Japan the powdered product is more readily purchased than the fresh, which is available but expensive.

The fresh root, if it can be gotten (in Japan it's sold in water-filled tubs) should be pared and then rubbed on a fine grater just before using.

POWDERED WASABI. Powdered wasabi comes in tins of 1 ounce, 2 ounces, 4 ounces, and up. Like ground mustard, this light green powder should be mixed half and half with tepid water and then allowed to sit at least 10 minutes to develop its flavor. A little lump of this paste traditionally accompanies sushi, and should be mixed with a little soy sauce to make a dip. Unless you go through a lot of it, buy wasabi in small quantities. Like any spice, once the package is opened it deteriorates over time. Some American chefs have begun to experiment with wasabi, mostly using it as a base for a dip sauce for grilled meat and fish.

WASABI PASTE. Available in 1.2-ounce tubes, convenience is about all the paste has going for it. It lacks the bite of the freshly mixed powder, especially when it sits in the refrigerator after it's opened.

MISCELLANEOUS SOUTHEAST ASIAN HERBS AND EDIBLE LEAVES

"Rice-paddy herb" and "saw leaf herb"

Unlike Chinese, Japanese, or Korean cooks, Southeast Asians use a variety of herbs, both cultivated and wild. In Thailand or Vietnam, cooks may gather leaves from various trees, shrubs, and vines before preparing a salad, or for use as a last-second ingredient in a soup. Not just for flavor, each is thought to offer some medicinal effect. The selection of herbs at Southeast Asian produce stands here, while still limited, is growing, with the basil/mint family predominating (see page 17).

On weekends in San Francisco's Chinatown, sidewalk vendors—literally selling from small cloths on the pavement—offer an array of home-grown and -gathered leaves. Three herbs, besides those which are treated individually in this book, are beginning to show up regularly at Southeast Asian markets, and more can be expected. Two of these are "souring herbs" for use in Southeast Asian hot and sour seafood soups. One, *Eryngium foetidum,* a coriander relative, sold leaves only in small bunches and called the "saw leaf herb" by Cambodians (*ngò gai* to the Vietnamese), is a 3- to 4-inch serrated green leaf with fine thorns at the tips of the serrations. The other, *ngò ôm* to the Vietnamese and sold in tiny bunches of sprigs, has rounded ½-inch leaves that sprout at intervals along the length of its soft stems. It's sometimes called the "rice-paddy herb."

The most important and versatile of these herbs is polygonum *(P. pulchrum),* *rau răm* to the Vietnamese, which comes in generous bunches. The stems are pinkish, with pointed 1½-inch-long green leaves, some of which have purplish markings. Never cooked, the highly aromatic (some might say soapy-tasting) leaves are used fresh in Thai, Vietnamese, Cambodian, and Laotian salads. They're also used as a garnish, like fresh coriander. The leaves would be an authentic and fragrant addition to the Thai Squid Salad (see page 42).

BAMBOO SHOOTS

(Bambusa and others)

OTHER NAME: Takenoko
(Japanese)

REGION OF USE: China,
Japan, Korea, Southeast
Asia

Like canned water chestnuts and bean sprouts, canned sliced bamboo shoots have been available for a couple of decades, even in supermarkets. Today sweet fresh water chestnuts are a fixture at Asian markets and fresh bean sprouts can be found almost anywhere, but bamboo shoots—with rare exceptions—still come in cans. However, this isn't necessarily bad.

In Asia fresh bamboo shoots are available in the spring, when the bamboo plant sends them forth, and there are also some highly prized winter varieties. If husked and cooked immediately after they're cut, fresh bamboo shoots have a savory sweetness to go with their refreshing crunchiness. But because they rapidly develop an acrid and bitter flavor after being cut, depending on the species they usually must be boiled from ten minutes to an hour and a half— traditionally in rice-rinsing liquid—before they can be used for cooking. By this time they aren't dramatically better than the canned variety.

With few exceptions, the fresh bamboo shoots that have shown up in Chinese markets on the East and West coasts have been as terrible as they are expensive; they don't travel well. (To my knowledge, edible varieties of bamboo, many of them tropical or subtropical, have not been raised successfully on these shores.) The bamboo shoots for sale in large plastic tubs in Asian markets aren't fresh, as some think; they're processed like canned bamboo shoots, only they're sold in bulk.

Among the fine canned bamboo shoots available, perhaps the best is Ma Ling, packaged in China in 16-ounce cans. For winter bamboo shoots (twice the price) Companion brand is very good, and so are Companion's Giant Bamboo Shoots. An unusual variety are the "Slender" bamboo shoots packaged in a beautifully labeled 28-ounce can from Kiangsi, China. They're shaped like asparagus, and the two go well together in a simple stir-fried dish with any kind of light seasoning or sauce.

Before they are used, canned bamboo shoots should be boiled for a minute to rid them of any tinned taste, then run under cold water. Extra shoots may be stored for up to two weeks in the refrigerator in a water-filled container if the water is changed every two days.

RECOMMENDED: Ma Ling, from China, available in 16-ounce cans. Companion brand Winter Bamboo Shoots, and Giant Bamboo Shoots.

THE CABBAGE FAMILY

Cabbages, referred to sometimes as "Brassicas," their family name, take up the lion's share of space on most Asian produce stands. They include various bok choys, celery cabbages, mustard cabbages, and Chinese broccoli, and the similarity in appearance of many of them—various bunches of stems and leaves with white or yellow flowers—is confusing to non-Asians. Over a dozen varieties are grown (mainly in California) and sold in the U.S.

This, however, is a paltry selection compared to the variations available in Asia. The famed Cornell University botanist L. H. Bailey, who authored two volumes on the cultivated Brassicas, encountered hundreds of varieties of these plants and wrote: "The Brassica group is indeed perplexing, . . . the most bewildering I have attempted."

This family of plants, particularly the bok choys, are by far the most popular leafy vegetables in China and Southeast Asia. It's probable that they were first cultivated for the edible oil in their seeds—the mustards being the earliest—and once cultivated, they were cooked and enjoyed, or at the least, their rich nutritional value was immediately appreciated.

BOK CHOY
(Brassica chinensis)

OTHER NAMES: Chinese white cabbage

REGION OF USE: China, Southeast Asia

Bok choy, short variety

Hong Kong farmers alone grow over twenty kinds of bok choy—"horse's tail" bok choy, "horse's ear" bok choy, "soup spoon" bok choy, and so on—of which four or five kinds are regularly available here and are described below. The vegetable we call simply *bok choy,* with its snow-white stalks, slightly bulbous base, and dark green leaves, is, along with *bok choy sum* (see next page) and the celery cabbages, one of the most popular and well-known Chinese leafy vegetables.

Available all year, bok choy is a versatile vegetable that may be simply cut up and cooked, leaves and all; or it's a good foil for stir-fried meats and seafood, and is popular when combined this way in noodle dishes. Its stalk has a mild, refreshing flavor, and the leaves are pleasantly tangy and bitter.

BOK CHOY SUM OR "CHOY SUM"

OTHER NAMES: Flowering bok choy, Flowering white cabbage, Flowering cabbage, Bok choy

REGION OF USE: China, Southeast Asia

Almost identical to bok choy in appearance, *bok choy sum* can be distinguished by its yellow flowers. (The Cantonese *sum* means "younger and flowering" when applied to vegetables; literally it means "heart.") It's also slightly smaller, with narrower stalks and green leaves a shade lighter. Cooked exactly like bok choy, flowers and all, it's at least as popular and commands a slightly higher price. Ask for "choy sum," although some Hong Kong dealers might give you *yow choy* (see below).

"BABY" BOK CHOY SUM OR "SHORT LEGS" CHOY SUM. Increasingly available, this is simply a miniature bok choy sum. The advantage of it is that its stalks, with their leaves and flowers, can be cooked whole, which makes for an attractive presentation.

SHANGHAI BOK CHOY

OTHER NAMES: Green stem bok choy, Blue River (Yangtse) bok choy

REGION OF USE: China

The leaves of this vegetable are spoon-shaped and the stems are flatter than regular bok choy; leaves and stem are the same light green. Although it grows to a foot or more in height, it's often harvested as a baby plant of 6 inches or less and sold four or five plants to the bunch. This plant is delicious when cooked like bok choy, but it's at its best when just the hearts of the baby vegetables, after a layer or so of outer leaves are stripped away, are stir-fried or steamed briefly. Cooked whole or cut in half lengthwise, the brilliant green of the cooked hearts makes an attractive adornment to a red cooked meat dish, such as Yangchow Pork with Pine Nuts (page 262), or they may be cooked and served by themselves. Shanghai bok choy is available, with occasional lapses, year-round.

This dish has special aesthetic appeal as well as flavor. If you
save the extra bok choy leaves for another use, it
won't seem so extravagant!

HEARTS OF BOK CHOY, CABBAGE FLOWERS, AND MUSHROOMS

Yield: 6 to 8 servings

6 dried black mushrooms

12 to 14 heads baby Shanghai bok choy, with flowers if possible

8 to 10 bunches bok choy sum or yow choy sum or enough to get two cups of 4-inch stalks with flowers

3 eggs

2½ teaspoons sesame oil

2½ cups fresh chicken stock

2 teaspoons salt

½ teaspoon sugar

4 tablespoons fresh chicken fat or peanut oil

1½ tablespoons cornstarch

1 tablespoon Shaoxing wine

1 teaspoon finely ground white pepper

Place the mushrooms in a small bowl, and pour boiling water over them to cover. Allow to soak for 30 minutes.

Meanwhile, remove the outer leaves of the Shanghai bok choy until you have a heart about 4 inches long and 1 inch wide at the base. Trim the base. Pluck the choy sum flowers, leaving each with a 3- to 4-inch stem, and set aside.

Make egg crepes: Beat the eggs with ½ teaspoon of the sesame oil. Lightly oil a well-seasoned 8- to 10-inch crepe pan and place over medium-high heat. When it is hot, pour in enough of the beaten eggs to coat the bottom when you swirl the pan around. Pour any excess back into the uncooked egg. When the egg has set and the edges begin to curl, remove the crepe from the pan. Repeat until all the egg has been used, stacking the crepes as you go. Roll up the stack of crepes, and cut it into ¼-inch slices. Leave the slices rolled, and arrange them, overlapping, in the middle of a large platter, with space in the center for the mushroom slices.

In a small saucepan, blend the chicken stock with the salt and sugar. Place the pan over medium heat. Drain the mushrooms, reserving the liquid. Slice the mushrooms into ¼-inch strips, and rub them with 1 tablespoon of the chicken fat. Blend the cornstarch with 3 tablespoons of the reserved mushroom liquid, and set aside.

In a wok or skillet, heat the remaining 3 tablespoons fat and add the bok choy hearts. Stir briefly, and add the choy sum flowers. Stir for 30 seconds, and then add the hot chicken stock. Bring to a boil, cover, and steam for about 1 minute (do not overcook). Remove the vegetables with a slotted spoon, reserving the stock, and arrange them around the eggs. Drop the mushrooms into the hot stock and cook for 30 seconds, then transfer them to the platter. Give the cornstarch mixture a quick stir and add it to the stock. Add the wine and white pepper and cook, stirring, until the mixture has thickened. Pour the sauce gently over the vegetables, dribble with the remaining 2 teaspoons sesame oil, and serve.

| TAIWAN BOK CHOY | OTHER NAMES: Fengshan bok choy |
| | REGION OF USE: China, Taiwan |

This yellowish green bok choy, which shows up from time to time on produce stands, has broad delicate leaves that are almost lettuce-like in texture. Like a lettuce, it wilts easily. It has a sweet, delicate flavor and may be cooked like celery cabbage or other bok choys.

YOW CHOY SUM OR "YOW CHOY"

OTHER NAMES: Oil vegetable, "Choy Sum"

REGION OF USE: China, Southeast Asia

Yow choy means "oil vegetable"; its seeds produce an oil not unlike rapeseed oil, which was used for lamps and sometimes for cooking. It's the ubiquitous green of Hong Kong, where it's called simply *choy sum*, or "flowering green" (the same term that's used for bok choy sum around Guangzhou and in Guangdong Province, and also by most Chinese vegetable dealers in this country).

A personal favorite, yow choy has narrow stems and oval leaves, all of the same plain green color, and it's full of yellow flowers that are smaller than those of bok choy sum. It's bitter, with a mustard-like tang, and is the most fibrous of the bok choys; yet it's delicious—you can taste that it's healthful—stir-fried plain or with a little black vinegar. As with any bok choy, yow choy will keep loosely wrapped in plastic in the vegetable bin in your refrigerator.

CHINESE BROCCOLI
(Brassica alboglabra)

OTHER NAMES: Chinese kale, Gai lan (Cantonese)

REGION OF USE: China, Southeast Asia

This is a dull-green plant with smooth, round stems and a resemblance to Western broccoli, although with larger leaves (meant to be eaten) and small clusters of white flowers. It has a slightly earthier flavor than broccoli; and it's a little more bitter, but quite delicious.

Available all year, Chinese broccoli is harvested just as the first flower buds begin to open. This is one of the world's most nutritious vegetables, with one of the highest calcium contents of any food. It's also rich in iron, vitamin A, and vitamin C. In Chinese restaurants, the vegetable is typically cooked with oyster sauce, Canton-style, and it has an affinity for that sauce. It's sometimes blanched before it's stir-fried, and can be cooked as you would broccoli.

NOTE: Chinese broccoli is often confused with the Italian vegetable broccoli de rabe (literally "turnip broccoli"), which it closely resembles. Although they're in the same family, broccoli de rabe is not in the broccoli subgroup but is rather a turnip top, as its name implies.

CELERY CABBAGE
(Brassica pekinensis)

OTHER NAMES: Napa cabbage, Chinese cabbage, Tientsin cabbage, Shantung cabbage, Michihli cabbage, Hakusai (Japanese), Wong nga bok choy or "wong bok" (Cantonese)

REGION OF USE: China, Japan, Korea

Of strictly Chinese origin, celery cabbages are the most important leafy vegetables in northern China, like bok choys in the south. (Some argue they're the same species, bred for different climates.) In spite of its Chinese identity, celery cabbage is a longtime staple of Japanese cooking, and in Korea it's the common ingredient in *kimchi,* the national pickle that's eaten every day by everyone.

First grown here around 1890, celery cabbage has been cultivated in the United States, both in the Northeast and in California, for years. The long, slender variety known as Michihli or Chihli (presumably after the Gulf of Chihli on the North China coast) until recently was a fixture of Asian vegetable stands and American supermarkets, and is still sold from time to time. It has been replaced in popularity by the squat, nearly white napa cabbage (no relation to Napa, California, although Northern California raises most of the country's crop). Napa is the most delicately flavored and textured celery cabbage of three kinds sold here, which include a napa type with green leaves.

Celery cabbage may be steamed, stir-fried, braised with chestnuts, cooked in casseroles as a foil for rich meats, used in soups—or it may be salted and pickled. It keeps for a week or more, minus some vitamin C, loosely wrapped in plastic in the vegetable crisper of the refrigerator.

More than just a peppery condiment to perk up one's appetite, *kimchi* is sustenance in Korea and the surrounding area of northern China, and it has been for centuries. It's served every day the year round.

The popular version here consists of napa cabbage preserved in salt, garlic, and ground chili pepper. In Korea, kimchi usually contains seafood—a protein source—such as shrimp, squid, or cuttlefish. Elaborate versions may also include oysters, octopus, abalone, chestnuts, dates, or pine nuts; daikon juice and chicken stock may be used in the pickling process.

KIMCHI
(The fiery Korean Pickle)

Yield: 1 quart

5 to 6 pounds celery (napa) cabbage

½ cup uniodized salt, preferably kosher or coarse sea salt

4 scallions, cut into ½-inch lengths

3 tablespoons finely minced fresh ginger

3 tablespoons finely minced garlic

2 tablespoons coarsely ground dried red chili peppers

4 teaspoons sugar

Quarter the cabbage lengthwise, then cut across the leaves at 1½-inch intervals. In a stainless steel, glass, or enamel bowl, toss the leaves with the salt, and pour in water just to cover. Allow the cabbage to sit at room temperature overnight.

The next day, drain the cabbage in a colander but don't rinse it. In another mixing bowl, toss the cabbage with the remaining ingredients. Put into a sterilized canning jar.

Let the pickle stand at room temperature for 2 to 4 days, opening the jar once or twice a day to release the gas that builds up, and to taste the kimchi (it will mellow). (Poking a chopstick or skewer down along the sides of the bottle will help the bubbles escape.) Once the flavor is right, store in the refrigerator. It will keep for several weeks.

CHINESE MUSTARD CABBAGE OR GAI CHOY
(Brassica juncea)

OTHER NAMES: Chinese mustard greens, Leaf mustard, Indian mustard

REGION OF USE: China, Southeast Asia

Because of their antiquity, mustards hold a special place in Chinese (and Indian) culinary history. Among the earliest cultivated greens, they were first raised, it is thought, for the oil in their seeds. Because the leafy plants themselves are exceptionally nutritious, their cultivation has been continually refined over the centuries. Most of these mustard cabbages—and this makes them unique among leafy vegetables—are, like olives, raised to be preserved.

Among the innumerable varieties, each seems to have its own specialty. Some are raised just to make particular kinds of pickles, such as Sichuan Province's famous Preserved Vegetable (see page 178) or the chopped and salted leaves known as Red-in-Snow (see page 180). The stems of some mustards are delicious when pickled in vinegar and sugar.

Of the mustards eaten fresh, a large, bulky plant known as Swatow mustard is grown for its heart, which is expensive. With some mustards, the fresh stems are prized for banquet-style vegetable dishes—they are usually parboiled first in water to which a little bicarbonate of soda is added to turn them a brilliant green; yet the leaves of the same plant may be considered useful only in a mundane soup.

It should be noted that most mustard green leaves, cut into strips and deep-fried briefly until they're translucent and crisp, make an excellent bed for fried seafood as they look like seaweed.

The fresh mustards available on produce stands here are as follows:

BROAD-LEAF MUSTARD CABBAGE (DAI GAI CHOY)—Curved stem or semi-closed head variety. Often just the bottoms of these are sold, cut off where the leaves start, since the stems are valued for salting and drying. That's why they're often a little more ragged looking than other produce. Sometimes the stems are cooked fresh. If the whole large plant is sold, it all may be salted and dried, or the leaves can be shredded and tossed in a soup.

BROAD-LEAF MUSTARD CABBAGE (DAI GAI CHOY)—Straight stem. After the leaves are carefully cut away, the inch-wide stems of this mustard are delicious parboiled in water with a little baking soda, then stir-fried and served in a light sauce; or they make one of the world's great sweet pickles. The leaves are best shredded for soups or for salting.

GAI CHOY SUM—This skinny-stemmed mustard looks like yow choy. However, its leaves are slightly serrated, its stems have subtle ridges characteristic of mustard, and its flowers are not readily apparent. This mustard can be stir-fried, leaves and all.

A specialty of Tung Fong, a small jewel of a *dim sum* parlor
in San Francisco, these pickles are sweet with a mustardy
bite—addictive is the word.

3 *bunches mustard greens, preferably with long, straight stems*	2 *cups mild white rice vinegar*	**PICKLED MUSTARD GREEN STEMS**
1⅓ *tablespoons salt*	1½ *cups sugar*	
	6 *dried red chili peppers*	Yield: 1 quart

Carefully trim the leaves from the stems (save the leaves for Salted Mustard Green Leaves, page 66, or another recipe). Cut the stems into 3-inch lengths and sprinkle with 1 tablespoon of the salt. Let stand for 1 hour.

Transfer the stems to a clean quart jar, leaving behind any accumulated liquid. Bring the vinegar, sugar, chilis, and remaining 1 teaspoon salt to a boil, and pour over the stems. Allow to cool, cover the jar, and refrigerate. They'll be delicious after a day or two.

A Japanese specialty, to be stirred into warm
rice. Use the leaves from another recipe, or start
from scratch.

SALTED MUSTARD GREEN LEAVES	*Mustard green leaves, stems removed* *Salt*

Rinse and dry the leaves. Roll them up a few at a time, and cut them into fine julienne strips. Measure what you have (tightly packed), and put them in a mixing bowl. For every cup of mustard greens, add 1 teaspoon salt. Let stand for an hour.

Squeeze most of the moisture out of the leaves with your hands. Chop them coarsely and transfer to a clean jar, where they will keep, refrigerated, for a week or so.

When you cook rice, stir these greens in as a seasoning, using ½ cup greens to about 4 cups cooked rice. Or you can make a simple fried rice by stir-frying 4 cups cooked rice in 3 tablespoons oil in a wok or skillet, and stirring ½ cup of these greens in just before you turn off the heat.

NOTE: Daikon greens may be substituted for the mustard greens in this recipe.

ASIAN RADISH
(Raphanus sativus)

OTHER NAMES: Daikon, Japanese radish, Chinese turnip, Lo bok (Cantonese), Korean turnip

REGION OF USE: Japan, China, Korea

Left to right: green radish, Chinese lo bok, *and Japanese* daikon

To tenderize octopus, the Greeks bash the poor creature ninety-nine times against a rock. The Japanese simply clean the animal and knead it for 5 minutes or so in a large bowl of grated *daikon,* the long white radish (or turnip if you will) that is a fixture of Asian produce stands. This not only softens the octopus, it further cleans it. The gratings, which turn gray during the process, are discarded and the sweet-smelling and relatively tender octopus is ready to cook.

Although in Asia there are several radish varieties, including a kind in Japan the size and shape of a soccer ball, just three types are available here, two of them white. The true daikon, or Japanese radish, sold at Japanese, Chinese, and Korean markets is cylindrical, 12 to 20 inches long, and about 2 inches in diameter. There's a shorter, fatter, white variety (lo bok, or Chinese radish) and also a stubby green turnip about 12 inches in length sometimes called a "Korean turnip."

Though a staple of Chinese cooking, the daikon can lay claim as Japan's most fundamental vegetable. It's cooked, it's pickled, and it's eaten raw, usually in grated form. For this it has its own tool, a *daikon-oroshi,* which is standard equipment in a Japanese kitchen. Daikon is certain to accompany Japanese fried food, as it's thought to aid in digesting anything oily. Tempura dipping sauce, for example, always contains grated daikon.

The daikon is a star in the Japanese art of cutting vegetables into decorative shapes. A rudimentary exercize for a Japanese chef is to cut a cylindrical section into one long rectangular sheet that's almost transparently thin.

These radishes are as integral to Korean cooking as to Japanese, but the Chinese don't have quite the same reverence for them. In Chinese cooking they're most often cut up and simmered with meat in stew-type dishes. When cooked this way, the radishes become tender and absorb the richness of the main ingredient. Unlike most root vegetables, however, they taste light and refreshing rather than heavy or starchy.

Daikon sprouts

Daikon leaves are a popular green in Japan, and they're usually available in Japanese markets. They're sometimes salted and stirred into warm rice. (See Salted Mustard Green Leaves, page 66.)

Daikon sprouts, *kaiware*, are a popular garnish and salad ingredient in Japan. If you can get daikon seeds, the sprouts will prove easy to grow by the window in any sort of shallow tray. After a couple of weeks of watering, just snip them off.

A simply made, country-style dish using the
familiar long white radish and a flavoring of dried
orange peel.

		DAIKON IN ORANGE PEEL SAUCE
1 or 2 pieces dried orange peel	1½ tablespoons dark soy sauce	
¼ cup Shaoxing wine	1½ tablespoons sugar	
2 pounds Asian radish (daikon or lo bok)	½ teaspoon salt	
	¼ cup water	
2 garlic cloves, chopped	3 tablespoons peanut oil	Yield: 6 servings
1 tablespoon chopped fresh ginger	3 scallions, cut into 1½-inch lengths	

Soak the orange peel in the wine for 30 minutes, then chop it and return it to the wine until ready to use.

Cut the daikon into 1¼-inch cubes and set aside. Combine the garlic and ginger, and set aside. Combine the soy sauce, sugar, salt, and water, and set aside.

Over high heat, heat a wok or skillet and add the oil. Add the daikon and cook briefly, stirring. Add the garlic and ginger and cook, stirring, 15 seconds. Add the orange peel and wine, and cook until the liquid has evaporated. Then stir in the soy sauce mixture. Turn the heat to medium, cover, and cook for 20 minutes, checking from time to time. Add a little water if necessary.

At the end of the cooking time, reduce the sauce by stirring the daikon over high heat until most of the liquid has been absorbed. Stir in the scallions and serve.

WATERCRESS (Nasturtium officinale)	OTHER NAMES: Sai yeung choy (Cantonese) REGION OF USE: China, Japan, Korea

The difference between the Western and Eastern use of this refreshing, peppery green is that Westerners are most apt to eat it raw, whereas Asians cook it, albeit briefly. For example, used as a "salad" vegetable around Shanghai, watercress is blanched, the moisture is wrung out, and then it's chopped and tossed with a light sesame oil dressing. However, the Chinese most often stir-fry it with a little salt, sugar, and wine, or use it in soups.

Watercress spread from Western Asia and Europe to the rest of the world —the Chinese name means "overseas vegetable"—and all ancient cultures have been eating it for centuries, either harvesting it wild like the Romans or cultivating it like the Chinese. A shallow freshwater plant, in some places it's considered a pest.

Store watercress in the refrigerator, with its stems in water and the leaves covered loosely by a plastic bag.

CELTUCE (Lactuca sativa var. asparagina)	OTHER NAMES: Asparagus lettuce, Stem lettuce REGION OF USE: North, East, and West China

After experimenting with seeds sent to them from China in 1938, the Burpee company offered seeds in their 1942 catalogue for a kind of lettuce they called *celtuce*. This lettuce, which originated in China, is grown for its thickened tender stem, which reaches 3 feet, rather than its leaves. The stem, similar to a romaine lettuce stem when it goes to seed, is peeled, sliced, and cooked much like any vegetable.

Although celtuce can be obtained in other markets, it occasionally shows up on Chinese produce stands, particularly those with owners or clientele from northern China or Shanghai.

CHINESE CELERY
(Apium graveolens)

OTHER NAMES: Smallage, Hon kun or Heung kun (Cantonese), Tang O (Thai)

REGION OF USE: China, Southeast Asia

This celery should be easy to spot on Chinese and Southeast Asian produce stands; it looks like celery with skinny, stemlike stalks. Shorter bunches could be mistaken for Italian parsley because of the family resemblance, particularly in the leaves. Chinese celery, like all celery, is a marsh plant that grows widely in temperate climates and in tropical mountain regions. It's probably closer to wild ancestral varieties in appearance and flavor—it's tastier—than the cultivated broad-stemmed celery of the United States and Europe.

There is debate among experts as to the vegetable's origins. Some feel that, like most of the Umbelliferae family, it originally grew in the Middle East; others think this celery may have been wild in East Asia to begin with. Celery has an established medicinal history in both East and West. The Chinese consider it a cooling, calming, digestive. Chinese celery is tossed, leaves and all, into soups and stews throughout Southeast Asia and in China. The Chinese also enjoy it lightly cooked, even parboiled just until it turns bright green to be tossed in "salads." It is rarely eaten raw.

CHRYSAN- THEMUM LEAVES

OTHER NAMES: Shungiku (Japanese), Garland chrysanthemum, Chop suey greens, Tong ho (Cantonese)

REGION OF USE: Japan, China

Edible chrysanthemum leaves, written of as a Japanese green, are very much a Chinese vegetable as well. Although they're recognizable to anyone who has been in a flower garden, these greens are not among the flower-garden varieties of chrysanthemum; they've long been specially bred for consumption.

With a soft, spinach-like texture, a subtle musty-floral fragrance, and a slight astringency, these are a popular salad green, though not in the Western sense. Young and freshly picked, they're occasionally eaten raw in Japan, but usually the Japanese and Chinese parboil them briefly—which changes their color from a pale to a deep green—and toss them with a light dressing containing sesame seeds or oil (see recipe, page 000). In Japan this vegetable is also added, literally at the last minute, to soups and stews. In China it's also stir-fried with salt, sugar, and wine.

Edible chrysanthemum leaves are available in Japanese, some Chinese, and once in a while in Vietnamese markets in the fall, and sporadically throughout the winter and spring. Don't be alarmed if they look slightly wilted; they begin to droop as soon as they're picked. If you get them fresh enough, the leaves can be plucked from the stem and tossed with other greens in a Western salad.

Before using, any buds should be plucked and discarded, and the leaves should be rinsed thoroughly, as this may be the world's sandiest vegetable.

A refreshing forest-green dish. This is ideal as
part of an assortment of bright, tasty
items to start off a meal.

2 bunches edible
  chrysanthemum leaves
10 fresh water chestnuts,
  peeled and chopped
1½ teaspoons light soy
  sauce

½ teaspoon salt
1½ teaspoons sugar
1½ tablespoons sesame oil

CHRYSANTHE-MUM LEAF AND WATER CHESTNUT SALAD

Yield: 4 to 6 servings

Cut off the tough end of the stems of the chrysanthemum leaves, and rinse the leaves thoroughly to get rid of any sand.

Bring a large quantity of water to a boil, add the leaves, and turn off the heat. Stir until thoroughly wilted, about 20 seconds, then drain and immediately run under cold water to stop the cooking. Squeeze the leaves with your hands, to rid them of as much water as possible. Chop the leaves and place them in a bowl with the water chestnuts.

Combine the seasonings, add them to the bowl, and toss the salad thoroughly. Serve at room temperature.

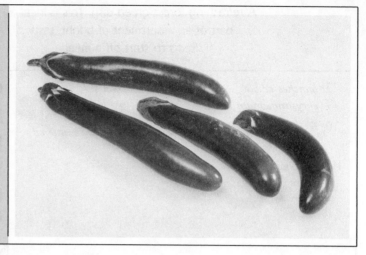

ASIAN EGGPLANT
(Solanum species)

OTHER NAMES: Chinese eggplant, Japanese eggplant, Pea eggplant

REGION OF USE: China, Japan, Korea, Southeast Asia

Chinese eggplants

People who love eggplant and who cook with the familiar deep purple variety sold in American grocery stores are depriving themselves of a much finer eggplant-eating experience. Western eggplant also requires some preparation that isn't necessary with this vegetable. The standard first step in most recipes is to cut and salt the eggplant and let it stand for 30 minutes, after which its bitter juices can be rinsed away; it's then deemed ready to cook.

With the long thin lavender variety sometimes called Chinese eggplant or the smaller nearly black Japanese eggplant, this salting and rinsing isn't necessary. Compared to their larger cousins, they're sweet, tender, and relatively seedless, and processing them before they're cooked is a waste of time. Just cut them up and cook them.

We associate eggplant with the Mediterranean, but it was unknown there in ancient times; the Italians first saw eggplant around the fifteenth century. Eggplant is native to Southeast Asia—where varieties still grow wild—which may explain why Southeast Asian markets offer the largest variety. From India east through China and Japan, they've been eaten for thousands of years.

Asian eggplants, unlike the standard purple eggplant, wrinkle and soften quickly, and should be used within a few days of purchase.

PEA EGGPLANTS (SOLANUM TORVUM). Southeast Asians cultivate marble-sized eggplants, green and white, known as "pea eggplants," for pickling, adding raw to chili sauces such as Thailand's *nam prik,* or cooking in curry dishes. Bitter for the most part, three or four varieties are now available at Thai and Vietnamese produce stands.

A flavorful, peppery Southeast Asian "salad." The
eggplant is steamed, then pulled apart by hand to produce
an unusual texture.

1½ pounds Western-style eggplant, whole and unpeeled (see Note)	1 tablespoon minced fresh ginger	**HAND-SHREDDED EGGPLANT WITH DRIED SHRIMP**
2 tablespoons fish sauce	1 tablespoon minced fresh red chili peppers, preferably Thai "bird" peppers	
1½ tablespoons fresh lemon juice		
1½ tablespoons sugar	1 tablespoon ground dried shrimp	Yield: 6 servings
6 tablespoons peanut oil	½ cup chopped coriander leaves and stems	
1 tablespoon minced garlic		

Place the eggplants in a covered steamer and steam for 20 to 25 minutes. Uncover, and allow to cool.

Meanwhile mix the fish sauce, lemon juice, and sugar together, and set aside.

Heat a small skillet and add the oil. When it is hot, add the garlic, ginger, and chilis, and stir just until fragrant. Add the lemon juice mixture, and when the sauce comes to a boil, turn off the heat and pour the sauce into a bowl to cool.

When the eggplant is cool, cut it into 2-inch sections, discard the skin and most of the seeds, and pull it apart by hand into shreds no more than ¼ inch thick.

Just before serving, pour out and discard any liquid that has accumulated around the eggplant. Toss the eggplant with the sauce, the shrimp powder, and the chopped coriander. Serve.

NOTE: This is an instance where the tougher Western eggplant works better; if you are trying the dish with Asian eggplants, reduce the steaming time.

ANGLED LUFFA
(Luffa acutangula)

OTHER NAMES: Vegetable sponge, Chinese okra, Sze gwa ("Silk Gourd," Cantonese), also Loofa or Loofah

REGION OF USE: Southern China, Southeast Asia, occasionally Japan

Distinguished by its ten sharp ridges and dull green skin, this long, narrow squash is tapered in girth, growing wider away from the stem. Wild varieties, whose vines can grow well out of reach, may be found in India, where it's presumed to be native. The fruit on the market, which occasionally may be 3 feet long, is actually immature; it reaches 9 feet, at least in the tropics. The older "ripe" fruits are bitter, producing a juice valued medicinally as a purgative.

Whatever its medicinal uses, when cooked this squash has a pleasant earthy flavor and a texture reminiscent of zucchini. Sliced or cut like thick French fries, the vegetable may be stir-fried alone with salt and pepper or perhaps a little oyster sauce, or it may be cooked in combination with chicken or seafood; it goes nicely with squid. Before cooking, pare off the ridges and scrape the skin lightly. Cook as you would any squash.

Angled luffa is eaten throughout the tropical world; it's a favorite in Jamaica, for example.

This sweet, bland, earthy-tasting squash soaks
up a good sauce like a sponge. It's excellent with
oyster sauce.

LUFFA WITH OYSTER SAUCE

Yield: 4 to 6 servings

1 pound angled luffa (1 or 2 squash)

3 tablespoons oyster sauce

2 tablespoons water

½ teaspoon sugar

½ teaspoon salt

3 tablespoons freshly rendered chicken fat (see page 320) or peanut oil

1 tablespoon chopped garlic

½ teaspoon white pepper

Cut the ridges off the luffa, leaving some of the peel. Cut the luffa into 2-inch slices; cut those pieces into quarters lengthwise. Set aside. Mix the oyster sauce, water, sugar, and salt, and set aside.

Heat a skillet or wok to hot and add the fat or oil. Add the garlic, and stir-fry briefly. Add the luffa and cook, stirring, about 1 minute. Add the oyster sauce mixture and cook, stirring another 1 to 2 minutes or until most of the liquid has been absorbed. Sprinkle with the white pepper, and serve.

BITTER MELON
(Momordica charantia)

OTHER NAMES: Balsam pear, Bitter cucumber, Bitter gourd, Fu gwa (Cantonese)

REGION OF USE: South China, Southeast Asia

Abundant to overflowing in Chinese markets in the summer, bitter melon is not your average Chinese vegetable; it's not beloved by all Chinese. The enjoyment of this melon—which looks a cucumber covered with warts—is confined mostly to tropical South China, Southeast Asia, and especially India, where it's pickled.

Foods are said to be made up of five sensations: sweet, sour, salty, bitter, and pungent or "hot" as in chili peppers or mustard. It's rare that the bitter predominates, so the bitter melon, which lives up to its name, takes some getting used to. Like most ancient Asian foods, it was originally a medicine, believed to purify the blood; the leaves were used to treat sore-eyed elephants. It's one of the few fresh "fruits" stocked in Chinese herb stores in Asia.

Although bitter melon is a Cantonese staple, it's tough to get it in Chinese restaurants in the United States, with the exception of some *dim sum* parlors that serve rounds of it stuffed with shrimp or pork and covered in a black bean sauce. Salted and fermented black beans almost always accompany this strange cucumber relative.

To prepare bitter melon, scrape away its seeds and the surrounding inner membrane. It may be parboiled for 5 minutes, then cut into strips and stir-fried with other ingredients—usually meat and black beans. Or it may be cut into rounds, which are then stuffed; this mitigates its bitterness.

FUZZY MELON
(Benincasa hispida)

OTHER NAMES: Hairy melon, Fuzzy or hairy gourd, Mo gwa (Cantonese), Chinese vegetable marrow

REGION OF USE: China, Southeast Asia

Close relatives of the large winter melon—all are varieties of a species called "wax gourds" thought to be native to Java, where they still can be found growing wild—fuzzy melons come in two shapes. One, squashlike, is narrow and cylindrical, sometimes crooked; the other looks like a stubby pill capsule. They're most enjoyed in southern China, where they've been cultivated seemingly forever. Harvested young, at about 12 ounces to 1 pound, they're easy to spot because they're truly hairy, a condition they'd outgrow if allowed to mature.

Fuzzy melons are eaten in a variety of ways: cut into wedges and steamed; stuffed and steamed; shredded, blanched in oil, then stir-fried with dried shrimp; cubed and cooked in soup. Their texture can best be described as refreshing. They should be peeled before using.

JAPANESE SQUASH
(Curcurbita moschata)

OTHER NAMES: Japanese pumpkin, Kabocha (Japanese), Nam gwa (Cantonese)

REGION OF USE: Japan, China, Southeast Asia

A staple of Japanese cooking, these pumpkin-shaped squashes, about 8 inches in diameter with skins in varying shades of dull green, are not natives of Asia. Like most others of their genus—summer squashes, winter squashes including the acorn and butternut—they originated in the New World. Seeds of this species found in New Mexico have been carbon-dated to 3400 B.C.

As with many vegetables, the Japanese learned of this squash from the Chinese. The Chinese and Japanese characters mean "southern gourd." Presumably the squashes were brought to tropical Asia by the Spanish and Portuguese, and the Chinese got them from regions south. Species of it are grown in Malaysia.

The flesh of these squashes—there are a couple varieties, one of them called "hatchet pumpkin" because of its tough skin—is a rich, deep yellow to orange color, and it makes a flavorful, sometimes superior, substitute for American pumpkins and winter squash. A friend who cooks Italian food prefers kabocha for preparing pumpkin risotto.

In Japan the vegetable is versatile. It's deep-fried in tempura batter, simmered in the stew known as *oden,* or simmered alone in *dashi;* it's braised or steamed, and used in salads. A large crop of it is grown on the West Coast. Like winter squashes, it keeps well unrefrigerated before using.

A spicy, unusual soup that's designed
to be served slightly chilled, but is
just as good hot.

FUZZY MELON AND COCONUT SOUP

Yield: 6 to 8 servings

2 teaspoons coriander seeds

1 teaspoon fennel seeds

1 teaspoon cumin seeds

2 tablespoons peanut oil

1 cup sliced shallots

2 teaspoons finely minced fresh turmeric, or ½ teaspoon powdered

2 tablespoons minced fresh green chilis, including seeds

2 fuzzy melons, about 12 ounces each, peeled and cut into ¾-inch cubes

3 cups fresh chicken stock

2 tablespoons fish sauce

1½ teaspoons salt, or to taste

½ teaspoon black pepper

1 cup rich coconut milk

Chopped fresh coriander and mint for garnish

Lime wedges for garnish

In a small, dry skillet, over medium heat, toast the seeds and grind them finely.

Heat the oil to hot in a large saucepan and add the shallots, turmeric, and chilis. Cook, stirring, until fragrant, about 1 minute. Add the ground spices and stir briefly. Then add the melon cubes and stir to coat.

Add the chicken stock and bring to a boil. Lower the heat, add the fish sauce, cover, and simmer for 25 minutes or until the melon is very tender. Blend in a food processor or blender to a fine purée. Stir in the salt and pepper, and the coconut milk. Chill slightly. Sprinkle with the chopped herbs and serve lime wedges on the side.

WINTER MELON
(Benincasa hispida)

OTHER NAMES: Winter gourd, Ash pumpkin, Chinese preserving melon, Kundur (Malay), Dung gwa (Cantonese)

REGION OF USE: China, Southeast Asia

Winter melon, ironically, grows in the tropics and is harvested in the summer. Its name comes from the waxy white blotching on the mature melon, which looks like a light dusting of snow, and from the fact that it keeps well in cold storage into the winter months. Watermelon green is the normal color. Winter melons grow to 100 pounds, although those harvested around Sacramento, California, are much smaller.

Despite their resemblance, winter melons are not closely related to watermelons or other true melons, but rather are squashes—or more properly, wax gourds, like the small fuzzy melons.

The most spectacular use of winter melon is as the serving vessel, sometimes intricately carved, for a soup poetically named "Winter Melon Pond." Versions are numerous, but it's basically a combination of ingredients—including chicken, ham, mushrooms, abalone, and bamboo shoots—that is steamed in a broth inside the melon, and then the whole thing is brought to the table. A helping of the soft white flesh is served along with the rest of the soup. Winter melon is in fact commonly used in soups and often with ham—a combination reminiscent of melon and prosciutto.

Though seemingly an odd choice, since the fruit is not sweet, winter melon is a popular candy preserve. It's also the filling for "melon cakes," a flaky pastry sold in Chinese bakeries. Winter melon may be purchased by the pound or by the whole melon, which is less expensive—but not practical unless you're serving the whole thing.

A slice of winter melon, wrapped in foil, will keep in the refrigerator for five or six days.

FRESH FUNGI

REGION OF USE: All of East Asia

*Left to right:
enoki, oyster, and
shiitake mushrooms*

Unlike plants that germinate from seeds, many species of mushroom can be found in areas around the world, where conditions are right, because the spores are light enough to be swept up into the atmosphere and deposited far away. Thus morels grow in China and the tree fungus called "cloud ears" grows in Europe and the United States, and neither was transplanted by man.

Among Asian food shops in this country, only Japanese markets have a selection of fresh mushrooms; in Chinese and Southeast Asian stores most of the fungi are dried. This doesn't mean fresh mushrooms aren't enjoyed in these regions. Some, such as the shiitake, are simply preferred dried by the Chinese; in fact the very best of these are always sold that way. In China the same is true for the popular black and white tree fungus (see pages 151 and 155).

Many of the fresh fungi that are enjoyed in Asia aren't available here. However, with the growing passion for edible fungi, this situation is changing rapidly. Recently, for example, a Taiwanese group in San Jose, California, has begun cultivating one of China's prized fungi, the "monkey's head" fungus. It's available on a limited basis commercially. In fact, many of the new mushrooms for sale in markets here are Asian mushrooms that have been cultivated for centuries.

CLOUD EARS (AURICULARIA). Almost always sold dried (see page 153), large fresh specimens of this tree fungus show up once in a great while in Chinese markets. I've seen a reddish-tinged variety in one market in San Francisco's Chinatown. According to a San Francisco Mycological Society expert, these can be gathered in Northern California, but they're not abundant. (For more information, see "Tree Ears," page 153.)

ENOKI MUSHROOMS, OR ENOKITAKE (FLAMMULINA VELUTIPES). Used in Japan and familiar by now to anyone in this country who shops in a supermarket, these tiny whitish mushrooms with skinny stems are sold in clumps in plastic bags. Their spongy, sometimes moldy roots, shaped like the bottles in which they're cultivated, should be cut off before they're used. They grow naturally on the stumps of the Chinese hackberry, which the Japanese call the *enoki* tree. Although advertised here as a great salad ingredient, the Japanese never eat them raw. They're usually cooked for a minute or two in soups, or with other ingredients in a broth; or they may garnish fish or chicken to be grilled. Enokis should be rinsed before using. They'll keep for about three days in the package they came in.

MATSUTAKE, OR "PINE MUSHROOMS" (AMARILLARIA EDODES). Probably the best-loved mushroom in Japan and Korea (where they're called *songi*), these are harvested wild in pine forests in the fall, and have a slight pine fragrance. Autumn matsutake hunts in Japan culminate in an outdoor feast. Domestic matsutake are now available here in Japanese markets and gourmet food stores, mostly in the fall. They're expensive, and Japanese Americans claim that those from their own red pine forests are a little tastier.

In Japan, matsutake are cooked briefly—sometimes lightly seasoned and grilled in foil pouches. The caps should be wiped before they're used, and for sauté-ing, the slices should be cut at least ¼ inch thick. Matsutake have never been successfully cultivated; they're rarely sold dried, and the canned are a poor substitute for the fresh.

"MONKEY'S HEAD" FUNGUS, OR "BEAR'S HEAD" MUSHROOM (HERICIUM). These delicious, juicy mushrooms, highly prized in China, are now available in limited quantities from Chinese who have begun to cultivate them here. They indeed resemble the top of a primate's head covered with snow-white fur. Highly perishable, they begin to lose flavor and turn yellow within twenty-four hours of harvesting. If you can find them, slice them in ¼-inch slices and sauté them briefly. The creamy white, fringed slices are quite beautiful.

OYSTER MUSHROOM, ABALONE MUSHROOM, OR TREE OYSTER MUSHROOM (PLEU-ROTUS OSTREATUS). Like its kin the shiitake, this fungus grows on dead trees and has been cultivated in Asia for ages. Popular throughout East Asia, it's widely available here in gourmet produce departments and Japanese super-markets. In Chinese stores, it's only available canned. With a subtle taste of the sea that gives it its name, it's a versatile mushroom that can be stir-fried, grilled, or even deep-fried in a tempura batter.

SHIITAKE, OR BLACK MUSHROOM, OR BLACK FOREST MUSHROOM (LENTINUS EDODES). Fresh shiitakes are rapidly becoming one of the most widely culti-vated mushrooms here, and are now something of a staple of American cook-ing. Nevertheless the Chinese prefer them dried; in fact in Asia the best—with thick caps that have white fissures—are grown only to be dried. Fresh shi-itakes may be stir-fried, grilled, steamed, or added to soups—in other words, used like any mushroom. (See "Black Mushrooms," page 151).

STRAW MUSHROOMS, OR PADDY STRAW MUSROOMS (VOLVARIA ESCULENTA).
Cultivated on rice straw in southern China, Hong Kong, Taiwan, and Malaysia, and on manila hemp waste in Java and the Philippines, these perfect little bite-size mushrooms, which could have come from a Walt Disney cartoon, unfortunately are available only canned or dried at present. Requiring constant warmth for growing, they are enjoyed fresh only in southern Asia, where they're the most important fresh mushroom. Growing and canning straw mushrooms is a huge business in Taiwan. Unfortunately the canned taste canned, and unlike some mushrooms, the dried in this case is merely a substitute. Straw mushrooms come peeled—with their edible shroud removed—or unpeeled.

A colorful dish—the mustard stems are a brilliant green—that is
both rich and refreshing. It's important to use fresh
chicken fat and a good stock.

MUSTARD GREEN STEMS AND BLACK MUSHROOMS		
Yield: 6 to 8 servings	10 *large dried black mushrooms* 3 + *tablespoons freshly rendered chicken fat (see page 320)* 2 *tablespoons cornstarch* 2 *pounds mustard greens*	2 *quarts water* 1 *teaspoon baking soda* 3 *tablespoons peanut oil* 2 *cups chicken stock* 2 *teaspoons salt* 1 *teaspoon sugar*

Place the mushrooms in a bowl, and add boiling water to cover. Soak for 30 minutes. Then drain the mushrooms, reserving the liquid, and squeeze them out over the soaking liquid. Cut the mushrooms in half diagonally, slicing with the knife almost parallel to the cap. Rub with a little chicken fat and set aside. Blend the cornstarch with ¼ cup of the reserved mushroom liquid, and set aside.

Remove the leaves from the mustard stems (use the leaves in Salted Mustard Green Leaves, page 66, if you like), and cut the stems into 2-inch lengths.

Bring the water to a boil and stir in the baking soda. Add the mustard stems and cook for 2 minutes. Drain, and immediately rinse the stems under cold water.

Heat a wok over high heat and add the oil. Add the mushrooms and stir-fry 30 seconds. Add the mustard greens and stir-fry for another minute. Add the stock, salt and sugar, and bring to a boil. Re-stir the cornstarch mixture, and add it. Cook until the mixture is thickened and clear. Dribble with 3 tablespoons melted chicken fat, and serve.

LEGUMES

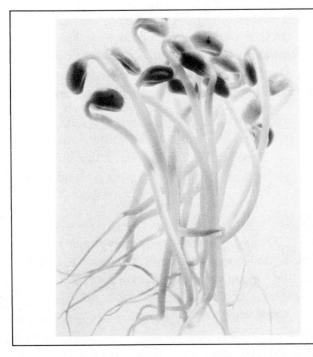

BEAN SPROUTS

REGION OF USE: China, Vietnam

Soybean sprouts

While they are healthful, sprouts—from beans or otherwise—aren't quite the miracle food they were touted to be a decade or so ago. According to Harold McGee in *On Food and Cooking,* their nutritional value lies between the raw bean (or seed) they started as and the mature green vegetable they would have become. One can surmise that the Chinese grew them ages ago as a sort of instant vegetable, one that doesn't require a patch of land and proper weather. Few other vegetables can be harvested in the dead of a bitter winter, and they are a fine source of vitamin C.

Two varieties of bean sprouts are available at Chinese markets. Most common is the sprout of the green mung bean; not so common is the larger, woodsy-flavored soybean sprout. The Chinese also sprout and eat the broad (fava) bean (see page 147).

MUNG BEAN SPROUTS (PHASEOLUS AUREUS). Sold in large sacks or tubs, these are offered fresh every day at Chinese and other Asian markets. They should be crisp and bright white, without a trace of the brown that begins to color the root and "neck" of the sprout as it ages. In all but the homiest of home dishes, the Chinese pluck off the head (bean) and tail (root) of the bean sprout. The task takes time but makes a big difference in texture and appearance. In Hong Kong, pearly white mounds of fresh-plucked bean sprouts are offered for sale daily.

Blanching bean sprouts is sometimes recommended before using them, but it isn't necessary. They should, however, be thoroughly rinsed. If it's impossible to buy them the day you use them, store them in a plastic bag in the vegetable crisper, where they'll keep for a couple of days.

SOYBEAN SPROUTS (GLYCINE MAX). A tradition at Chinese New Year's, these sprouts are longer and thicker than mung bean sprouts, and they're topped with a full-size yellow bean. They're often blanched and tossed with a sesame oil dressing or stir-fried in simple combinations, such as with mushrooms and bamboo shoots.

NOTE: For anyone who wonders why home-grown bean sprouts are never as long and straight as those at Chinese markets, the secret is that commercial growers put a light weight over the beans for the sprouts to push up against.

A recipe from Sue Yung Li, a highly regarded documentary film maker and talented cook who lives in San Francisco but travels frequently to China. Sue Yung points out that Ningbo, an ancient trading port 100 miles south of Shanghai, is known for fresh seafood and salted vegetables.

SOYBEAN SPROUTS, NINGBO STYLE

Yields: 6 to 8 servings

1½ *pounds fresh soybean sprouts*
1 *scallion*
3 *tablespoons peanut oil*
½ *teaspoon salt*
¼ *cup chicken stock*

½ *cup chopped Salted Mustard Green Leaves (see page 66)*
1 *teaspoon sesame oil*
1 *teaspoon sugar*

Trim the stringy roots from the sprouts. Wash the sprouts and drain well.

Wash and trim the scallion. Tie the whole stem into a loose knot. ("Knot" is a homophone of "good luck" in the Ningbo dialect.)

Heat the peanut oil in a wok or pan, sprinkle in the salt, add the scallion, and saute until it is soft but not brown. Stir in the sprouts and cook over high heat until all the stems are coated with oil, about 1 minute. Add the chicken stock and cook for another minute or so. Stir in the mustard greens and simmer for 2 minutes.

Using a slotted spoon, transfer the sprouts to a bowl to cool. Add the sesame oil and sugar to the liquid in the pan, and bring just to a boil. Pour into a dish and allow to cool. When the sauce is cool, pour it over the sprouts and refrigerate overnight in a covered container. Serve cold or at room temperature.

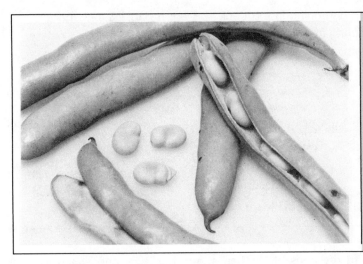

BROAD BEANS
(Vicia faba)

OTHER NAMES: Fava bean, Horse bean

REGION OF USE: China (mostly Shanghai and north), Japan

Just as Chinese and Italian markets are the place to go for noodles, Chinese and Italian produce stands are the place to go in the spring when broad beans first appear. It's a surprise to Westerners that these "Italian beans" are a Chinese staple. Legumes, plainly cooked, are unusual in the cuisine to begin with.

Popular throughout Europe and elsewhere, the broad bean is a native of the Mediterranean, where it has been cultivated since the Stone Age. They're not exactly new to China: Some sources say they were introduced in the third millennium B.C. In China they're prepared mostly around Shanghai, Beijing, and the northern regions; they don't grow well in the tropical south, and are not a staple of Cantonese cooking.

The Shanghainese use both the fresh and the dried bean; they're also eaten sprouted. Salted fried broad beans are a popular snack and are readily available in Chinese groceries here. You set them out as you would peanuts.

To prepare fresh broad beans for stir-frying, remove the beans from the pod, and then, using your thumbnail or a knife, split the outer skin of each bean and discard it. It's time-consuming but worth it. They're traditionally cooked with minced ham and simple seasonings. Dried beans are soaked, cooked with soy sauce and sugar, and served at room temperature (see page 147).

What's an Italian dish doing in this book? It's not Italian; it's authentically Chinese. In the spring fresh broad beans are heaped just as high in Chinese markets as anywhere. The ham accompaniment here is traditional.

BRAISED BROAD BEANS WITH HAM

Yield: 6 servings

4 *pounds fresh broad bean pods*

¼ *cup freshly rendered chicken fat (see page 320) or peanut oil*

½ *cup sliced scallions*

1 *cup chicken stock*

2 *teaspoons sugar*

1 *teaspoon salt*

1 *tablespoon Shaoxing wine*

½ *cup finely minced ham, preferably Smithfield*

Remove and discard the pods of the beans, and the large outer shell as well (this can be facilitated by parboiling the beans briefly). Heat a pan or wok and add the fat. When it is hot, add the scallions. Cook, stirring, for 10 seconds; then add the beans. Sauté briefly, and add the stock, sugar, salt, and wine. Cook over high heat until most of the liquid has been absorbed and the beans are tender, 5 to 6 minutes. Toss with the ham and serve.

LONG BEANS

(Vigna sinensis var. sesquipedalis)

OTHER NAMES: Asparagus bean, Yard-long bean, Dow gok ("Horn bean," Cantonese)

REGION OF USE: China, Southeast Asia

Truly long beans, these legumes, sold by the bunch at Chinese and Southeast Asian produce stands, are around 18 inches in length, and varieties with names like Fowl's Gut Bean and Yak's Tail can grow to twice that. An ancient vegetable, the wild plants still grow in tropical Africa—probably where the long bean originated, although some scholars feel they were taken there from Southeast Asia.

Since cookbooks often instruct you to treat these as you would regular green beans, it's a common misconception that they're related. Green beans—including pole beans, bush beans, and snap beans or French beans—are an entirely different genus of plants, native to the Central American highlands. Long beans are close kin to the black-eyed pea (some argue they are simply a variety), which was brought to the United States by African slaves. In fact black-eyed peas, much to the wonderment of southern tourists to big-city Chinatowns, are a fixture of markets that stock Southeast Asian goods. Black-eyed peas and rice have been enjoyed for far longer in Malaysia than in Alabama.

Several varieties of long bean are eaten in Asia, as are the leaves of the plant and the beans themselves when they're allowed to mature. Two varieties are available at Asian produce stands here: a light green type that is at its best from mid-May to mid-June, and a darker green one that peaks between mid-June and mid-August. I've heard discussions as to which is better, but although both are sold regardless of season, their quality really depends on the time of year.

Those expecting the sweet crispness of green beans will be disappointed. Briefly steamed or stir-fried, unless the flavors around them are assertive, long beans don't have a lot to offer. Their value is as a long-cooked bean; they hold up well when added to a stew. Or in dishes such as the popular Sichuan Dry-Fried Beans (see page 90), they may be deep-fried in very hot fat, then cooked with chopped meat and other seasonings. (True dry-frying originally meant baking them under glass in the sun until they wrinkled, rather than immersing them in oil.)

Even when hanging on the vine, long beans are never stiff and crisp like green beans. However, they shouldn't be terribly limp when you buy them. They'll keep for a week in the vegetable crisper.

The best I've ever tasted were grown on the Chino Ranch in Rancho Santa Fe, California; they were purple, were harvested when about 10 inches long, and turned a brilliant green when cooked.

SICHUAN DRY-FRIED LONG BEANS Yield: 4 to 6 servings	1½ pounds long beans (about 1 bunch) 2⅛ cups peanut oil ½ pound ground pork 2 tablespoons chopped fresh red chili peppers, including seeds 1 tablespoon chopped fresh ginger	1 tablespoon dark soy sauce 1 teaspoon sugar 1 teaspoon salt 1 tablespoon Shaoxing wine

Cut the beans into 3-inch lengths, and set aside.

Heat 2 cups of the oil in a wok or heavy skillet until nearly smoking. While it's heating, chop the pork to a finer consistency. Combine the chilis and ginger and set aside.

When the oil is hot, add the beans (making sure they are thoroughly dry), and cook for 2 to 3 minutes or until they wrinkle. Remove and drain.

Drain off the oil (it may be strained and used again) and reheat the wok. Add the remaining 2 tablespoons oil and the pork. Cook, stirring, over high heat just until the granules are broken up and the meat changes color. Add the soy sauce and stir for 20 seconds, then add the chilis and ginger and cook for another 30 seconds. Add the beans, sugar, salt, and wine, and cook, stirring, until piping hot. Serve.

PEA SHOOTS (Pisum sativum)	REGION OF USE: China, especially around Shanghai

The late master cooking teacher Virginia Lee would talk longingly of edible pea plants, which were a staple of her native Shanghai. Very recently they've shown up for brief periods in the spring at Chinese markets here—curiously, only at those owned by Chinese who've come from Vietnam.

These shoots are harvested when the pea plants are only about 12–18 inches out of the ground. While they are growing, any flowers that develop are plucked off, so the sweet pea flavor goes into the leaves and tender stems. They're delicate and tasty when gently stir-fried Shanghai-style with a little salt, sugar, and Shaoxing wine.

SNOW PEAS

(Pisum sativum var. saccharatum)

OTHER NAMES: Sugar pea, Pea pod

REGION OF USE: All of Asia

An East Asian–bred variation of the garden and field pea—whose origins are in West Asia—the snow pea was one of the first Chinese vegetables to appear in this country, and it has been pretty much adopted. Not of particularly ancient origin, these peas, flat edible pea pods actually, were developed because they're easier to grow in warm climates such as southern China. Having grown these and cooked them a few minutes after picking, I find that those that appear on the stands are for the most part a poor substitute, as peas rapidly deteriorate.

String snow peas before cooking by pinching off a smidgen of the tip and pulling down one side. Repeat with the other tip and side.

Sugar snap peas, the edible pods plump with peas, were bred relatively recently in this country and now appear regularly on Asian produce stands. This is perhaps the best (and easiest) way to cook them. Snow peas may be substituted.

1 *pound sugar snap peas or snow peas*	1 *teaspoon salt*	**SNAP PEAS WITH FRESH SHIITAKES**
¼ *pound fresh black (shiitake) mushrooms*	1 *teaspoon sugar*	
2 *tablespoons chicken stock*	5 *tablespoons freshly rendered chicken fat (see page 320) or peanut oil*	Yield: 6 servings
1 *tablespoon Shaoxing wine*		

String the peas but don't open them, and set aside. Slice the mushrooms thinly and set aside. Mix the stock, wine, salt, and sugar together and set aside.

Heat a wok or skillet over high heat and add the fat or oil. When it is hot, add the mushrooms and stir until they begin to wilt and give up their moisture.

Then add the pea pods and stir-fry over high heat for 1½ to 2 minutes. Add the seasoned chicken stock and continue to stir until the liquid has almost disappeared and the peas are crisp yet tender. Serve.

LOTUS
(Nelumbo nucifera)

OTHER NAMES: Water lily

REGION OF USE: China, Japan

Related to the water lilies found throughout the world, this plant is indigenous to a wide swath of Asia, from Iran through China to Japan and northeastern Australia. It was brought to Egypt around 708 B.C. and grown for its beauty, as it is throughout Asia. Japan has cultivated beautiful variations. Lakes in the Kashmir region of India are filled with lotus, and its rhizomes, buried in the mud, are harvested and cooked or pickled as they are in China and Japan.

The lotus plant, which has religious significance throughout Asia (Buddha is often depicted sitting on or holding a lotus flower), is planted near temples and palaces and has been represented for centuries in Asian art.

THE RHIZOME. Referred to as "lotus root," the rhizome is shaped something like a large sausage link; when sliced, it is beautifully porous. It should be peeled and sliced quickly, and immediately dropped into acidulated water, as it discolors faster than apples. The flesh, fibrous and chewy, has a slight astringency and a flavor that reminds some people of artichokes. In Japan lotus root is used for tempura and in simmered dishes. The Chinese, who make the most use of lotus root, eat it steamed, stir-fried, braised, and in soups; slices are also blanched and doused with a light dressing and served cold.

Look for rhizomes that are free of bruises. If the sections remain uncut, the root will keep in the vegetable crisper for two or three weeks.

The Chinese make a lotus starch from the rhizomes, which they use like cornstarch. Lotus seeds, which are eaten fresh in Asia, are sold dried, and lotus leaves are sold dried as food wrappers.

FOUR ROOTS

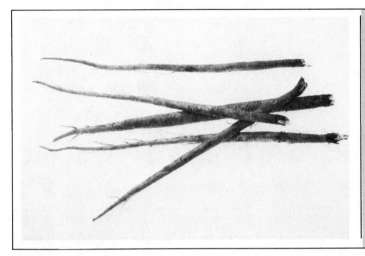

BURDOCK
(Arctium lappa)

OTHER NAMES: Gobo
(Japanese)

REGION OF USE: Japan

We could include China as a region of use for burdock, but only as a medicine. This slender, hairy taproot, which reaches 4 feet in length, is thought to have been introduced to the Japanese as a medicine by the Chinese around a thousand years ago, and it has been a staple of the Japanese diet ever since. Harvested in the fall, burdock is not hard to grow, and in fact is something of a weed in temperate climates.

Available in Japanese groceries, burdock roots should be firm. The smaller and thinner the better—around a foot in length is ideal—and dirt should still be clinging to them. To prepare it, scrub the root with a stiff brush, leaving the skin, which has most of the flavor, intact. Once cut, burdock should be put immediately into lightly acidulated cold water, as it discolors rapidly.

In Japanese cooking, burdock, which is neutral in flavor, is added to slow-simmered dishes or is sautéed in oil and seasonings and served warm or at room temperature. Upon occasion the Japanese will sprinkle it with ground hot pepper.

Burdock will keep for a couple of weeks in a paper bag in the refrigerator.

JICAMA
(Pachyrrhizus erosus)

OTHER NAMES: Yam bean, Sha got (Cantonese)

REGION OF USE: Southeast Asia, China

Considering its lack of natural charms, jicama, the starchy turnip-shaped tuber native to the American tropics, has had some great press. It's suddenly available in American supermarkets, having been caught up in the same trend that popularized yellow bell peppers.

You will find jicama on Southeast Asian vegetable stands, as the Vietnamese and others sometimes use it in spring rolls or stew it like other starchy tubers. Thanks to the Spanish, the Philippines was the first place it was introduced in Asia. Chinese farmers began to raise it there and brought it to Malaysia. It's grown in China, but you'll rarely see it at Chinese produce stands here. The Chinese find it useful almost exclusively for its starch, which is used like cornstarch.

It's doubtful anyone in Asia has reached for jicama when they wanted a fresh water chestnut. Given that jicama can be relatively tough and insipid, it's not much of a substitute, in spite of what's written.

TARO
(Colocasia antiquorum)

OTHER NAMES: Sato imo (Japanese); Puak (Thai); Wu tow (Cantonese)

REGION OF USE: China, Southeast Asia, Japan

This starchy tuber of tropical Asian origin is one of those ancient foods cultivated for so long that no wild ancestor exists. From all indications, it was a staple of prehistoric man and provided starch in the diet of Chinese and Southeast Asians before rice was used. There's only one species of taro, which spread around the world long ago, and there are now enough varieties—over forty-five in Hawaii, two hundred in the West Indies—to cause a lot of confusion.

Taro reached Egypt from Asia about the time of Christ and has been cultivated in the Nile River delta for the past twenty centuries. The Spanish introduced it to the New World tropics, where it has become a staple (West Indians call it *dasheen,* a corruption of the French *de la Chine,* meaning "from China").

The plant, though it needs lots of water and a generally warm climate, is robust. A sixth-century Chinese agricultural work, the *Qi Min Yao Shu,* describes methods for cultivating taro in the frigid far north of China. Wherever conditions are right—throughout the South Pacific, for example, where centuries ago people quickly became dependent on taro—the plant has escaped cultivation and spread.

Available at Asian and Latin markets, taro "roots," large or small, are barrel-shaped with hairy brown skin and noticeable rings. The flesh is cream colored to white and is often speckled with purple.

As with many of the earliest-cultivated plants, taro ceased producing seeds long ago and is propagated by vegetative means. The top of the tuber is simply cut off and planted, which is why the top slice is missing from the larger variety sold at local markets. The other smaller, more expensive Hawaiian tubers, 2 to 3 inches in length, are mostly harvested whole since the plant produces more than one tuber.

Taro is versatile, although to suggest (as some guides do) that it be prepared "like a potato" isn't helpful or particularly accurate. The tuber is usually steamed until just tender as a first step. It is then most commonly added to a stew with a rich meat. The Chinese use it as a foil for pork belly or in duck casseroles. Taro may be steamed, sliced, and pan-browned; or it may be fried like French fried potatoes. Chinese restaurants present seafood combinations in fried baskets made of taro. It's also turned into a pudding.

The popular golden fried "taro puff" (wu gok) offered in *dim sum* restaurants is made by steaming and mashing taro with fresh lard and wrapping it around a pork and mushroom filling (see page 97). Poi, the creamy purple concoction invented by Polynesians, is a fermented paste of taro, whose bland sourness goes unappreciated by tourists and others who encounter it in Hawaii.

Unlike potatoes, taro does not keep for more than a week or so. Its speckled flesh contains crystals of calcium oxalate, which is a serious skin irritant, and which only cooking will destroy. It should be noted that taro turns a rather unappetizing purplish gray when cooked and mashed.

A most popular *dim sum* item, these golden fried savories (called *wu gok*) aren't at all difficult to make. And once the dough and filling are prepared, they may be kept in the refrigerator for a couple of days and assembled quickly whenever you're hungry.

TARO PUFFS

Yield: about 20

DOUGH

1½ *pounds taro root*	1 *tablespoon sugar*
⅔ *cup wheat starch*	½ *cup lard, preferably fresh*
⅔ *cup boiling water*	
1½ *teaspoon salt*	

FILLING

4 *dried mushrooms, soaked (liquid reserved)*	3 *tablespoons oyster sauce*
½ *cup finely diced bamboo shoots*	1 *tablespoon Shaoxing wine*
12 *ounces ground pork*	½ *teaspoon white pepper*
1 *tablespoon dark soy sauce*	1 *tablespoon cornstarch*
1 *teaspoon minced fresh ginger*	3 *tablespoons peanut oil*
1 *teaspoon salt*	2 *teaspoons sesame oil*
2 *teaspoons sugar*	*Peanut oil for deep-frying*

Peel and cut the taro into thick slices, and steam in a covered pan or steamer over boiling water until soft, 30 to 45 minutes.

Meanwhile, cut off and discard the mushroom stems; cut the caps into small dice, and set aside with the bamboo shoots. Chop the pork briefly, and combine with the dark soy sauce and ginger. Blend ¼ cup of the mushroom soaking liquid with the salt, sugar, oyster sauce, wine, white pepper, and cornstarch, and set aside.

Heat a wok or skillet over high heat and add the peanut oil. Add the pork and cook, stirring, until the grains separate and change color. Add the mushrooms and bamboo shoots, and cook and stir another 30 seconds. Stir the cornstarch mixture and add it. Cook until the dish thickens and has a sheen. Turn off the heat and stir in the sesame oil. Allow to cool slightly, transfer to a bowl, cover, and refrigerate for at least 4 hours.

Finish making the dough: Put the wheat starch into a mixing bowl and slowly add the boiling water, stirring with chopsticks. When it becomes a paste, stop. (You may not need all the water.)

Mash the steamed taro with your fingers to form a fine paste, and add it to the wheat starch with the salt and sugar. Mix well with your fingers. Add the lard and continue to mix and knead the mixture as you would dough. When it is well blended, refrigerate for at least 4 hours.

When you are ready to cook the puffs, heat a quantity of oil for deep-frying to about 350°F. Meanwhile, spread a ¼-inch layer of dough over the palm of your hand (about 3 × 3 inches). Put a couple of teaspoons of filling in the center, and fold the dough up and over it. Shape the dough like a football. Repeat with the remaining dough and filling.

When the oil is hot, fry two or three puffs at a time for 3 minutes or longer, until golden brown and cooked through. Drain on paper towels and serve cut into thirds.

CHINESE SPINACH
(Amaranthus gangeticus)

OTHER NAMES: Amaranth, Jacob's coat, Yin choy (Cantonese)

REGION OF USE: China, Southeast Asia

Chinese spinach is not spinach at all, but a member of the large amaranth family, some species of which are cultivated for their flowers and others for their seeds, which are a popular grain in India and elsewhere. High in nutritional value—even more so than spinach—several species of these greens are eaten in southern Asia, and have been since ancient times.

The variety available here from spring to fall is an herblike plant usually no more than 14 inches in height; it is sold with the roots, which are pinkish red. The leaves are dark green, have a fuzzy texture, and are tinged with red. Like spinach, the whole plant can be eaten, but the leaves and tender stems are preferred. Amaranth is delicious when substituted in any spinach recipe and requires even less cooking time. Southeast Asians cook it with a little mint.

More delicate than spinach, these greens need only the briefest cooking.
You can look at this dish as a kind of pasta with greens or as
an unusual version of ham and eggs.

CHINESE SPINACH WITH EGG CREPE NOODLES

Yield: 4 to 6 servings

4 eggs

1 teaspoon sesame oil

2 tablespooons peanut oil

2 bunches amaranth (leaves and tender stems only)

1 cup chicken stock

1½ teaspoons salt

½ teaspoon sugar

2 teaspoons cornstarch mixed with 2 tablespoons water

2 tablespoons melted chicken fat (see page 320)

1 tablespoon minced Smithfield ham

Make egg crepes as you would flour crepes: Combine the eggs and sesame oil, and beat lightly. Heat and lightly oil a well-seasoned 8- or 10-inch skillet. When it is hot, pour in enough of the beaten egg to coat the bottom of the pan when you swirl it around. Pour any excess back into the uncooked egg. When the egg has set and the edges start to curl, remove from the pan. Cook, oiling the pan a little each time, until all of the egg is used. Stack the crepes and roll them up. Cut the rolls into ¼-inch slices.

Heat a wok or skillet over high heat and add the peanut oil. Add the amaranth and stir-fry briefly, until barely wilted. Add the chicken stock, salt, and sugar, and bring to a boil. Stir in the cornstarch mixture. When the mixture has thickened, turn off the heat. Dribble in the chicken fat, stir in the egg noodles, and serve sprinkled with the ham.

SWEET POTATO
(Ipomoea batatas)

OTHER NAMES: Fan shue
("foreign tuber,"
Cantonese), Satsuma-imo
(Japanese)

REGION OF USE: China,
Southeast Asia, Japan

The sweet potato is the one New World food that may have reached the Far East before Columbus's voyage. Thor Heyerdahl argues persuasively that the Polynesians got it centuries ago, by way of natives of pre-Inca Peru, who brought it to Easter Island in a balsa raft. There are indications that it was growing in Hawaii by 1250, and that the Maoris were growing it in New Zealand in 1350.

The introduction of the sweet potato to New Guinea in the sixteenth century touched off a dramatic population increase in the highlands. The Chinese found the sweet potato in the Philippines in 1594, when a famine in Fujian province prompted the governor to send an expedition there in search of food plants. Today the sweet potato is the most important root crop in the Yangtze valley, and it's the number one starch in some parts of China. In the early seventeenth century, the Japanese took sweet potatoes from China to the Ryukyu Islands, and from there about a century later they took the tuber to Satsuma, where it was cultivated extensively; thus its name in Japan is *Satsuma-imo* ("Satsuma yam").

The appeal of the sweet potato in Asia wasn't so much its flavor as it was the vegetable's high yield and short growing time. Baked sweet potatoes are a street food in China and Japan, particularly welcome during the winter. Not a glamorous food, they are usually eaten baked or boiled, or cooked in broth. Both the Chinese and the Japanese make confections of them. Starch made from sweet potatoes is often cooked in gelatinous slices or made into noodles. The varieties sold on Asian produce stands are akin to the kinds grown in Asia for centuries. Sweet potatoes are far more perishable than potatoes and should be used within a week or two after purchase.

WATER SPINACH
(Ipomoea aquatica)

OTHER NAMES: Swamp spinach, Long green, Ung choy (Cantonese), Kang kong (Malay)

REGION OF USE: Southern China, Southeast Asia (also southern India, Africa, Australia)

This is not a relative of the spinach we know (which also is enjoyed in Asia), but it's cooked and eaten like spinach. The vegetable, 18 inches or so in length with long stalks and narrow pointed leaves, is sold in hefty bunches in Chinese and Southeast Asian markets from early winter to fall. Considering that half or more of the stems is too tough to eat, it's a pricey vegetable, but it's worth it for both its flavor and its nutritional value. It's rich in iron and minerals.

A native of tropical India, water spinach thrives in swamps, although it's also cultivated on dry land. In Asia it's stir-fried, most popularly with fermented white bean curd, shrimp sauce, or just garlic. Use all the leaves and the top third to half of the stems, with the leaves attached, cut into 2- to 3-inch lengths.

WATER CALTROPS
(Trapa bicornis)

OTHER NAMES: Ling gok (Cantonese), Water chestnut

REGION OF USE: Southern China

Periodically on display at Chinese produce stands, these shiny black, somewhat nefarious-looking, horned nuts usually elicit a "What's that?" from non-Asians who pass by. When an English-speaking worker at the stand replies, "Water chestnuts," he or she is telling the truth while at the same time misleading the questioner.

These are indeed called water chestnuts, but they are not related to the far-better-known water chestnut of Chinese cookery, *Elocharis dulcis,* a chestnut-shaped corm, and the two should not be confused.

Resembling little water buffalo horns, these nuts grow on a floating water plant that is closely related to a plant common in streams in the eastern United States, *Trapa natans.* Sometimes called a "Jesuit's nut" as well as a water chestnut, it produces a similar edible nut with four horns rather than two. To add confusion, these too are harvested and sold in Asia.

Trapa bicornis must be boiled for an hour before it is used, to destroy possible parasites harmful to the digestive system. The Chinese eat these shelled and cooked in combination with other ingredients, preserve them as sweetmeats, or make a starch from them that resembles water chestnut starch.

WATER CHESTNUTS
(Elocharis dulcis)

OTHER NAMES: Ma tai (Cantonese)

REGION OF USE: China, Southeast Asia

Water chestnuts, once available only canned in this country, are now for sale fresh. For anyone who has only tried the canned or has never had them at all, the fresh are a wonderful surprise. They have a sweet crispness reminiscent of coconut meat and are as refreshing as spring water.

Water chestnuts, which do resemble chestnuts with the addition of a small tufted point, are corms (underwater stem tips) from which a kind of water grass sprouts. Cultivated throughout China, they're a favorite of the ducks that paddle around the streams and ponds where they grow.

Originally valued as a medicine, water chestnuts are considered *yin,* or cooling, and are thought to sweeten the breath. A paste made from dried and ground water chestnuts is fed to children who accidentally swallow coins. The powder—available in Chinese grocery stores—is an excellent substitute for cornstarch (see page 313).

To peel water chestnuts, first rinse off any mud. Cut off the flat top and bottom, then pare the circular edge with a small knife. You may keep them briefly in cold water until ready to use. An occasional water chestnut turns up fermented, with a taste like sweet wine—it's not unpleasant or harmful, but you may not want to use it. Discard any with discolored flesh.

Pick over water chestnuts individually, choosing only those that are rock-hard. The very best have a slight sheen. If you can't find them, the canned variety will do, but only for a cooked dish where they are a minor feature.

NOTE: Another starchy water tuber (like the water chestnut, it too is a corm) grows off of a swamp plant called an arrowhead (*Sagittaria sinensis*). Round and pale yellow in color with husklike leaves, the vegetable shows up on Chinese produce stands only during the winter. The Shanghainese sometimes fry slices of it like potato chips; the southern Chinese eat it chopped up and cooked thoroughly, usually as a foil to pork. It's never eaten raw. Its Cantonese name is *sha gu*.

MEAT

CHINESE

For meat, the Chinese markets are the best of the Asian markets and the most prevalent—on some streets in Chinese communities there are two or three to a block. If it's odd, as in "odd part," and they don't have it, no one does.

To the Chinese, meat primarily means pork. They domesticated the familiar pink pig, *Sus domestica,* thousands of years ago, and in their markets every part of the animal, from the ears to the tail, is for sale. High-quality beef, often including sirloin steak, is available too; but the pork as a rule is superb and as fresh as can be. Unlike many Western meat markets, Chinese butchers buy little precut meat. As anyone who has walked around a Chinatown knows, truckloads of whole pigs are delivered daily.

After you have made a few visits and established yourself as a customer, most butchers will be happy to cut to order whatever you don't see. Because of the high volume in Chinese meat markets in large cities, and the competition, there are bargains to be had.

PORK

PORK CHOPS. Fine, rather thin, center-cut pork chops are for sale; if you want them thicker, just ask. Regular customers will be presented with a whole loin to select from.

PORK LOIN. Not always on display, whole pork loins or any portion, with or without bones, are available. Some shops offer just the boneless tenderloin, from which you can buy any size piece.

SPARERIBS. Because of their universal popularity spareribs are expensive, though less so in these markets. The Chinese rarely buy a rack whole, but rather have the butcher cut it across the bones (using a hand saw), forming two to four strips. You end up with more manageably sized ribs. If the rack is cut into four strips, the individual pieces will be practically bite-size once they're cut apart.

GROUND PORK. In Chinese butcher shops in Asia, you can actually buy wonderful hand-chopped pork. Here pork is ground by machine; it's best to improve its texture by chopping it briefly with a cleaver before you use it. What's sold here is quite fatty—not to cheat you, but because it's used in stuffings and sauces, and fat means juiciness and flavor. Chances are you won't get your pork ground to order, but what you do get won't have been sitting around. Ground pork costs substantially less at Chinese markets than elsewhere.

PORK SHOULDER. Another bargain, this delicious cut of meat, sold with rind and bone, is often around $1 a pound. On display you'll usually see split sections of 2 to 3 pounds each, but whole shoulders, up to 9 pounds, are kept in the back. Shoulder is enjoyed braised for several hours with dark soy sauce, Shaoxing wine, rock sugar, and sometimes star anise and cassia (see page 111). When it is cooked, the Chinese would just as soon eat the sticky rind and meltingly soft fat as the meat. Shoulder steaks with skin and rind, as well as butt steaks, are sold also.

PIGS' FEET. Beloved by people who enjoy gelatinous skin, chewy bits of gristle, and soft flavorful marrow, these are a favorite of the Chinese. Buy the forefeet, which are meatier than the hind feet. They're about 20 cents more per pound, but still under $1. You'll want the butcher to split and cut these into about eight pieces each, Chinese style. Pigs' feet are simmered for hours with soy sauce and rock sugar. The Cantonese make a postpartum stew from them, with sweetened black vinegar and lots of fresh ginger. The hocks, the meaty portion of the forefeet, are sold as well.

PORK BELLY. Sold on the commodities market, like gold, this is available only as bacon in Western markets. The Chinese love pork belly cooked fresh. It's simmered and/or steamed for hours. Sometimes it's steamed and smoked, and then sliced and stir-fried with leeks or peppers. For the slow simmering with wine, soy sauce, and rock sugar known as "red cooking," it's best to use belly with the ribs still attached; but you'll have to get to the butcher early in the morning to get this cut.

PIGS' EARS. Cooked for 1 to 2 hours or until the cartilage is soft and crunchy, a fine pigs' ear salad is made in Sichuan province by shredding and mixing them with bean sprouts, lots of fresh garlic, and a dressing of soy sauce, vinegar, and chili oil.

PIGS' TAILS. Not terribly expensive, these are either cut into pieces and slow-simmered like feet, or simmered and then marinated—in soy sauce, five spices, and hoisin sauce—and grilled (see page 115).

SNOUTS. Easier to recognize than other cuts, snouts are not to everyone's taste. They have a particular gelatinous, chewy quality when slowly simmered in a soy-seasoned liquid, the way they're usually cooked.

PORK TONGUE. Delicious marinated and roasted like the barbecued pork strips (cha siu) one sees hanging in Chinese delicatessens, tongue is also simmered slowly or sometimes simmered, sliced, and stir-fried. It is, I think, a juicier and more flavorful alternative to beef tongue.

CAUL FAT. A transparent membrane laced with fat that encloses the organs in the abdominal cavity, caul fat is highly useful. As a wrapping, it seals the juices in meats to be roasted or broiled, or it holds together stuffed foods to be fried. The caul fat itself melts away during cooking. The French use it to wrap pâtés.

Occasionally found fresh, caul fat usually is sold frozen, in plastic bags of a pound or so, which is way more than you're likely to need. Thaw it until you can peel off as much as your recipe calls for, and refreeze the rest. Rinse it in lukewarm water before using.

PORK KIDNEYS. The world's most wonderful entrail and under $1 a pound! A friendly butcher will clean these for you—a tedious task—by splitting them and cutting out the dark core of blood vessels. They should be sliced and leached in several changes of cold water for at least 12 hours before they are used. After parboiling for 30 seconds, which gives them a silken texture, the kidney slices can be tossed in a salad (see page 112) or stir-fried. They combine well with seafood. Many restaurants don't bother to leach kidneys, so expect a slight urine flavor if you order them when dining out.

PORK LIVER. A fine liver indeed, full-flavored with the tenderness of the best calves' liver. Pork liver lends itself to grilling, broiling, or stir-frying. The

Chinese like it barely cooked. It's often served thinly sliced in broth or congee, Chinese "rice porridge."

PORK HEART. Like squid, pork heart must be cooked either briefly or over a long period—anything in between makes it tough. In the case of pork heart, a long time means an hour.

PORK STOMACH. Pork stomach is versatile and very tasty but needs simmering of 1½ hours to be tender. If simmered with soy sauce and star anise, it can just be sliced and eaten. If simmered in water or a light stock with wine and ginger, it can then be sliced and stir-fried, or it can be slivered and tossed in a Beijing-style salad with a mustard-sesame sauce (see page 114).

Before simmering, pork stomach should be scoured on the inside with coarse salt, rinsed, and parboiled for 5 minutes.

PORK BLOOD. Sitting in a cylindrical coagulated mass in its pan, this looks like crimson cranberry sauce. Slices of pork blood are simmered briefly, then drained before they're added to soups. Hot and Sour Soup, for example, traditionally has blood as one of its ingredients. The flavor is like a delicately textured liver.

PORK BRAINS. These aren't always a cinch to get, even at a Chinese butcher shop; and with the highest cholesterol count known to man, maybe it's a good thing. They beat calves' brains on all counts. For one thing, they needn't be as tediously picked over to remove the membrane. These are wonderful as part of a Chinese custard that is steamed and cooled, then lightly fried in cubes.

PORK INTESTINES. Available large and small, these are simmered along with other innards, such as stomach, in anise-flavored broth and are often served atop noodles. Large intestines are sometimes simmered, then deep-fried and served thinly sliced.

PORK SPLEEN (MELT). An English reference book says this is "sold in Western society for pet food." In China and elsewhere in Asia, they've found that this long liver-like organ enhances stock, and it's sold for that; it's also included in steamed or simmered "offal" dishes.

SUCKLING PIGS. With a day or two notice, you can have a tender 30-pound pig for around $2 a pound at most Chinese butcher shops.

FAT. If you're a regular customer, the butcher will give you a bag of scrap fat, which is fine for rendering for lard. Leaf lard, sometimes called "flair fat," is the easiest to render—but some bakery or restaurant will probably have bought it already. Pure white back fat is always for sale.

BEEF

Far less popular than pork, there is nevertheless a variety of beef cuts at Chinese butcher shops, including high-quality, beautifully cut steaks for those with Western tastes. Ground beef is usually for sale. Rib roasts are hard to find, since a haunch of rare beef has little appeal to the Chinese. Beef filet is considered insipid. But there is a discriminating selection of what Westerners consider scrap meats, many of which must be cooked for hours. The texture of these is appreciated especially; the taste, almost always mitigated with star anise, a little less so. A full range of beef innards, though less popular than those of pork, can be found as well.

FLANK STEAK. In spite of stir-fry recipes that call for sirloin steak, flank steak is the most popular and best cut for this. The texture is what appeals. It has to be sliced thinly and marinated before it's cooked.

BEEF SHIN, TENDONS. Shin is extremely popular because of its texture after it's cooked, typically for hours with star anise, dark soy sauce, and a little sugar. It's often served cold and thinly sliced, decorated with its own aspic. Shin tendons are enjoyed cooked in a soy and anise–seasoned liquid until they become gelatinous and translucent—often offered as a *dim sum* item.

OXTAIL. Any cut of meat, poultry, or fish where tender morsels are to be found along the bone is prized by the Chinese. Oxtails are thus in ample supply, ready to be chopped into 2-inch pieces by the butcher. They require stewing for at least 4 hours.

PLATE (ROUGH FLANK OR "BEEF NAM"). Akin to pork belly, this rich layered cut of beef with its tough membranes and fat is a favorite. Cut into rectangles and cooked for hours, it makes a rich broth, and the meat itself is very flavorful. It's sometimes cooked with curry paste.

CHINESE "STEW" CUTS. These include *flap*, a roughly textured cut from the bottom sirloin that can also be marinated and stir-fried; *rib beef*, from the spareribs of beef; *short ribs*; and various cuts of *round*, which may also be marinated and stir-fried. Lean thin slices of tough cuts such as round are sometimes marinated in bicarbonate of soda overnight in the refrigerator, then rinsed, seasoned, and added to soups. The soda tenderizes them, but leaves them relatively flavorless.

HONEYCOMB TRIPE. The white lining from the second stomach of a cow vies for the favorite part of the animal among the Chinese. It needs simmering for 1 to 1½ hours. After it's tender it may be eaten as is, or it can be sliced and stir-fried with chilis, fresh coriander, and shreds of ginger.

OTHER INNARDS AND PARTS. These include tongue, liver, kidneys, brains, and sometimes hooves for making gelatin.

OTHER ITEMS

While lamb or veal is rarely available at Chinese meat markets,* many carry fresh goat, presumably for their Moslem customers. Also, curiously, most butchers carry fish paste for making fish balls, which are sometimes offered ready-to-cook as are finely textured beef balls.

VIETNAMESE

A good Vietnamese meat counter will offer almost the same array as a Chinese one, with perhaps a little less pork and a little more beef. Whole beef tenderloins (fat removed) are sometimes displayed. Piles of beef bones are offered for making phó', the beloved beef noodle soup (see page 117). Every imaginable cut of round is there, to be sliced paper-thin and added raw to this soup. Like the Chinese meat markets, they offer a variety of pork and beef innards.

JAPANESE

By any standards, the Japanese meat counter is pristine. You'd never know the offerings had anything to do with living animals. The meat is precut and often packaged specifically for the few meat dishes in the cuisine. You'll find trimmed and sliced sukiyaki beef—usually either New York strip or rib eye. There's ground chuck and ground pork, and trimmed and thinly sliced pork cutlets or butt. The latter are for pan-frying or deep-frying. That's about it.

*Historically lamb and mutton were the meats of China's northern invaders, and while they're eaten by some northern and western Chinese, most find the flavors too strong, probably out of ages-old cultural prejudice. Veal holds little interest, particularly because of the cost.

These easily prepared lettuce packages—everything can be made ahead—are garnished and seasoned by each eater. Whatever the lettuce employed (and it's not a bad use for iceberg), the leaves should be able to maintain some crispness in spite of the heat of the filling.

THAI LETTUCE PACKAGES

Yield: 6 to 8 servings

SAUCE

¼ cup minced garlic	1 tablespoon sugar
½ cup fish sauce	1 teaspoon chili oil
⅓ cup fresh lime juice	

GARNISHES

Chopped fried peanuts	Thinly sliced fresh red chili peppers
Sliced peeled, seeded cucumbers	2 to 3 heads lettuce (romaine, iceberg, red leaf, or other leaf lettuce)
Shredded basil or mint leaves	
Coriander leaves	
Chopped red onion	

FILLING

3 tablespoons peanut oil	1 cup finely diced bamboo shoots
1 pound ground pork	1 cup chopped fresh red and green chili peppers, including seeds
1½ tablespoons dark soy sauce	
½ teaspoon salt	
1½ teaspoons sugar	

Mix the sauce ingredients together and set aside. Prepare the garnishes, but wait to arrange them on serving dishes just before serving. Separate the leaves of the lettuce—large ones may be cut in half or trimmed—and rinse and dry them. Set them aside.

Prepare the filling (this may be done hours earlier and reheated): Heat a wok or skillet over high heat and add the oil. When it is hot, add the pork. Stir just to separate the grains, then add the soy sauce and cook 3 minutes. Add the salt and sugar and stir-fry briefly. Add the bamboo shoots and chilis, and cook over medium heat for 3 to 4 minutes. Turn off the heat and set aside.

Just before serving, arrange the garnishes on plates or in bowls. Put the sauce out in individual bowls. Reheat the filling and set it out with the garnishes and lettuce leaves on the side.

Each eater takes a lettuce leaf, puts in a heaping spoonful of filling, garnishes it, seasons it with sauce to taste, then rolls up the leaf and eats.

More succulent than fresh ham, the pork shoulder is a cut prized by the Chinese. Surrounded by stir-fried hearts of Shanghai bok choy or spinach, and coated with the rich brown glaze of the reduced sauce, this dish is a glorious focus of a meal.

RED BRAISED WHOLE PORK SHOULDER

Yield: 10 to 14 servings

1 *pork shoulder (5 to 7 pounds) with bone and rind*

3 to 4 quarts water

¾ *cup Shaoxing wine*

6 *star anise*

1 *3-inch cinnamon stick*

8 *garlic cloves, smashed*

10 *thin slices fresh ginger*

2 or 3 pieces dried tangerine peel

2 *dried chili peppers*

1 *whole scallion*

⅓ *cup dark soy sauce*

6 *approximately 1-inch-square crystals Chinese rock sugar*

1 *tablespoon coarse salt, or to taste*

Bring the water to a boil in a large pot, and add the pork. When it comes to a boil again, skim, and reduce the heat to medium. Add the wine and cook, partially covered, for 20 minutes.

Add the star anise, cinnamon stick, garlic, ginger, dried tangerine peel, dried chilis, and scallion, and cook for another 20 minutes. Add the remaining seasonings and continue to cook for another 2 to 3 hours, turning the meat occasionally. The rind and fat should be very soft when it's done. Remove the pork from the liquid and keep the meat warm. Strain the sauce into a large skillet and reduce to a syrup over high heat. (This may take 15 minutes or longer.)

When the sauce is reduced—it should be the consistency of thin syrup—put the pork in the center of a large platter, arrange vegetables, if any, around the pork, and pour the sauce over the meat.

Few first-course dishes are as delicious and elegant as these pork kidneys. The dish will be particularly memorable to anyone who has never tried these inexpensive delicacies. Served room temperature, this "salad" may be prepared ahead and then tossed whenever you're ready to serve it.

PORK KIDNEY SALAD WITH MUSTARD DRESSING

Yield: 6 to 8 servings

6 *pork kidneys*

2 *small celery stalks, sliced thinly on the diagonal*

1 *teaspoon finely chopped garlic*

1 *teaspoon finely chopped fresh ginger*

1½ *tablespoons light soy sauce*

1 *teaspoon Shaoxing wine*

1½ *tablespoons red wine vinegar*

¼ *teaspoon salt*

½ *teaspoon sugar*

½ *teaspoon white pepper*

1½ *teaspoons prepared Dijon mustard*

2 *tablespoons sesame oil*

2 *teaspoons finely chopped fresh red chili pepper (seeded)*

1 *tablespoon finely chopped coriander leaves and stems*

Split the kidneys in half and place them, inside up, on a cutting surface. Cut out and discard every bit of the core of dark red veins. Turn the kidneys over, and holding your knife parallel to the cutting surface, cut the kidneys as thinly as possible into slices of about 1 × 2 inches. (Don't worry about odd shapes.) Put the slices in a pot of cold water and allow them to soak, changing the water occasionally, for 12 hours or overnight. Then drain and rinse.

Heat a large pot of water to boiling and add the celery slices. After 10 seconds add the kidney slices, and cook for another 20 to 30 seconds. Drain immediately, and run under cold water to stop the cooking. Drain thoroughly and set aside.

Combine the garlic, ginger, soy sauce, wine, vinegar, salt, sugar, white pepper, and mustard. Add the sesame oil, and set this dressing aside until ready to serve. About 10 minutes before serving, toss the kidneys and celery with the dressing, chili peppers, and coriander, and allow to sit. Toss once more just before serving.

The kinship between Italian and Chinese cooking—the use of pasta, for example—is my excuse for adapting a simple recipe of Marcella Hazan's. Both cultures love pork liver and make good use of caul fat. Here the liver is topped with fresh Asian seasonings, wrapped in the lacy fat membrane, and simply grilled or broiled.

GRILLED PORK LIVER WRAPPED IN CAUL FAT

Yield: 4 to 6 servings

1 pound caul fat (you won't use all of it, but it's tough to buy less)

1½ pounds pork liver

½ cup finely chopped fresh ginger

½ cup finely chopped scallions

½ cup finely chopped coriander leaves and stems

2 teaspoons coarsely ground white pepper

2 tablespoons light soy sauce

1 teaspoon salt

¼ teaspoon sugar

¼ cup sesame oil

Unravel about half the caul fat and rinse it in warm water. (Freeze the rest.) Cut the pork liver into strips about 1 inch thick and 4 to 5 inches long. Combine the remaining ingredients, and smear 1 tablespoon or so of the mixture over the top of each liver strip. Wrap each strip in a piece of caul fat large enough to comfortably cover it. Grill or broil the strips 3 to 5 minutes on a side; they should still be pink in the middle when done. Slice, and serve.

I found this dish by pointing at random to an item in the Chinese part of a dual-language menu at a small restaurant in San Francisco's Chinatown. With its mustard and sesame paste combination, this is a Beijing specialty, rare among the predominantly Cantonese dishes enjoyed in that community. If you've never tried pork stomach, this is a tasty introduction.

PORK STOMACH SALAD WITH CUCUMBERS AND MUSTARD SAUCE

Yield: 8 servings

2 pig's stomachs (about 1½ pounds total)

Salt

¼ cup Shaoxing wine

5 thick slices fresh ginger

2 teaspoons powdered mustard

2 tablespoons sesame seed paste

3 tablespoons brewed tea

2 tablespoons light soy sauce

½ teaspoon salt

2 teaspoons sugar

2 tablespoons white vinegar

1 teaspoon minced garlic

1 tablespoon sesame oil

2 teaspoons chili oil

½ cucumber, peeled, seeded, and sliced

½ cup coriander leaves

Remove any excess membrane or fat from the stomach lining, rub with coarse salt, and rinse. Simmer in lightly salted water for 5 minutes. Drain then simmer in new water with the wine and ginger slices for 1½ hours, or until tender.

Meanwhile prepare the sauce: Mix the mustard powder with 2 teaspoons water and let stand for 15 minutes. Stir the tea into the sesame paste until well blended, then stir in the soy sauce, salt, sugar, vinegar, garlic, and oils. After the mustard is set, stir it in.

When the stomachs are done, drain them. When cool enough to handle, slice them thinly. Toss with the mustard-sesame sauce, the cucumber, and the coriander, and serve.

These are quite tasty and easy to do. If left whole—which is easier for grilling—it's the presentation that's problematical. The 5-inch tail itself can be thought of as a handle to hold on to while you gnaw at the morsels along the section of spinal column it's attached to. For oven roasting, have the butcher cut up the tails.

8 *pigs' tails (cut up for roasting, left whole for grilling)*	4 *teaspoons red bean curd "cheese" (see page 210)*	**BARBECUED PIGS' TAILS**
3 *tablespoons white rice vinegar (5 tablespoons for grilling)*	1 *teaspoon five spices (see page 237)*	Yield: 4 to 6 servings
¼ *cup light soy sauce*	2⅔ *tablespoons sugar*	
¼ *cup hoisin sauce*	4 *teaspoons bean sauce*	

TO ROAST: Preheat the oven to 350°F. Score the skin twice lengthwise along each tail part. Put all the meat in a pot with water to cover. Bring to a boil, reduce the heat to medium, and simmer for 5 minutes. Then drain and dry the pieces.

Mix 3 tablespoons vinegar with the light soy sauce, hoisin sauce, red bean curd, five spices, sugar, and bean sauce. Smear the mixture all over the pieces of meat, and spread them out on a foil-lined baking sheet. Bake for 40 minutes. Turn the pieces, brush them with more sauce, and cook for another 20 minutes. Allow the meat to sit for 6 to 7 minutes before eating.

TO GRILL: Score the skin twice along each tail part. Put the tails in a pot with water to cover and bring to a boil. Reduce the heat to medium, add 2 tablespoons vinegar, and simmer uncovered for 45 minutes.

Meanwhile, mix 3 tablespoons vinegar with the light soy sauce, hoisin sauce, red bean curd, five spices, sugar, and bean sauce. Start your charcoal fire.

When the meat is done, drain the pieces, dry them, and smear them with the sauce. Grill over a medium fire, turning the pieces, for 10 to 15 minutes. Baste once. Allow to sit 6 to 7 minutes before eating.

NOTE: For a simpler method, after simmering, dry the pieces and toss them in some dark soy sauce, salt, and pepper before roasting or grilling.

An elegant and flavorful stew
that could, on first glance, be mistaken
for a French country dish.

OXTAIL AND WHITE RADISH WITH STAR ANISE

Yield: 6 servings

1 *oxtail (about 2 pounds), cut up*

1 to 1½ *pounds white Chinese radish (lo bok) or Japanese radish (daikon)*

8 *cups water*

5 *star anise*

¼ *cup Shaoxing wine*

4 *garlic cloves, smashed*

6 *thin slices fresh ginger*

1 *tablespoon dark soy sauce*

2 *tablespoons light soy sauce*

2 *pieces, about 1 inch square, rock sugar*

1½ *teaspoons salt*

1 *cup coriander leaves*

Parboil the oxtail for 2 minutes and rinse. Cut the radish into odd-shaped chunks about 1 inch in diameter, and set aside. Bring the water to a boil in a pot and add the oxtail, anise, wine, garlic, and ginger. Bring to a boil again, then reduce the heat to medium, partially cover, and cook for 1 hour.

Add the soy sauces, rock sugar, and salt, and continue to cook for another 2½ hours (you may have to add more water). Add the radish pieces and cook for another 30 minutes. By now the meat should be tender. Uncover the pot, and stirring from time to time, cook until the sauce is greatly reduced and is slightly syrupy. Stir in the coriander leaves and serve.

This tasty cut of beef with its gristly layers
must be cooked for hours, but the soup it yields—here a Vietnamese
phó' (beef noodle soup)—is worth it.

VIETNAMESE BEEF SOUP WITH RED CURRY AND RICE STICKS

Yield: 6 to 8 servings

2 pounds beef plate or "rough flank," cut into 1½-inch squares

4 quarts water

4 star anise

1 1-inch cinnamon stick

4 ounces ¼-inch-wide rice sticks (dried noodles)

1 tablespoon peanut oil

2 tablespoons red curry paste, or more to taste

2 teaspoons salt

1 teaspoon sugar

GARNISHES

¼ cup thinly sliced scallions

Fish sauce

Coriander leaves

Bean sprouts

Sliced fresh red chili peppers

Lime wedges

Sprigs of Asian basil

Put the beef in a pot with water to cover. Bring to a boil, then drain and rinse. Put the beef back in the pot with 4 quarts water, the star anise, and the cinnamon stick, and bring to a boil again. Turn the heat to low and simmer 3 to 4 hours, until the beef is tender. Keep an eye on it; the liquid should reduce by almost half.

Meanwhile put the noodles in a bowl, cover with hot water, and set aside.

When the soup has cooked 3 to 4 hours, heat the oil in a small pan and add the curry paste. Cook, stirring, until just fragrant, and add to the soup. Add the salt and sugar, and cook another 20 minutes. Drain the noodles and add them. Cook until the noodles are tender, another 8 minutes or so, and serve garnished with the scallions. Serve the rest of the garnishes on the side.

POULTRY AND EGGS
POULTRY

CHICKENS. The chicken was once a tropical Asian jungle bird, and there are still wild chickens in Southeast Asia. Needless to say it's beloved in that part of the world, and so are its eggs—which may have been the reason the chicken was domesticated in the first place.

If you're fortunate enough to have a Chinese or Southeast Asian poultry market near you (they often share space with seafood), it's where you should buy your birds no matter what kind of cooking you do. They are fresh-killed —they come with heads and feet just like in real life—and are one of the last holdouts against the little yellow factory-raised birds from Maryland and their counterparts in the West. These plump chickens are at least 20 cents more per pound than supermarket birds, but Asians even on meager incomes will gladly pay it for the flavor.

You'll more than likely have to buy these chickens whole. With the exception of some large poultry markets, those that offer parts, offer parts from the other kind of chickens. Some large Asian communities have live poultry markets; if you know what to look for you can choose your own, and it will be butchered on the spot.

When you buy one of these chickens, make sure you get it with the fat in the cavity—it's excellent for rendering (see page 320)—and with the giblets if you like them.

It should be noted that when cooking chicken in master sauce (see page 205), sometimes called soy-braising, the skin of a mass-produced chicken will reject the sauce and it will turn out splotchy, whereas the fresh-killed chicken will turn a golden brown.

DUCKS. Like the pig, the familiar white duck is a Chinese food product, domesticated centuries ago. Depending on where you hear the story, a clipper ship sailed into either New York or San Francisco from Beijing in the 1870s with around a dozen ducks, heralding the beginning of America's duck industry. It's the descendants of those white Pekins that are raised by the millions from Long Island to California. Since that time, because duck is such a staple of Chinese cooking, Chinese markets have always had the freshest and the best. If you can get to a Chinese market, it makes no sense to buy frozen supermarket ducks. While Vietnamese markets carry fresh ducks, no other Asian markets compare to the Chinese in volume.

Outside San Francisco, the Reichardt duck farm in Petaluma raises 1.1 million ducks annually, and well over 1 million of these go to Chinese markets. Even though they're the same breed, I've found that Long Island ducks—the kind sold fresh in Chinese markets in the Northeast and shipped frozen elsewhere—average a pound heavier (5 pounds or more), are fattier, which means they take longer and are more difficult to cook, but ultimately are tastier than ducks raised elsewhere. Those raised at the world's largest duck farms in the Midwest under the Maple Leaf or C & D labels (same ownership), which are available frozen throughout the United States, should be a last resort. The flesh is a little mushy and the skin, highly prized by the Chinese, is sometimes damaged.

There are myriad Chinese duck dishes, and many use more than one cooking technique. A duck may be seasoned and steamed, to melt the fat and perfume the flesh with the seasonings, then deep-fried the next day to crisp the skin. Or, after steaming, the duck may be smoked with tea, rice, and sugar (see page 128).

At Chinese poultry markets, be sure to take advantage of the wonderful bargain in fresh duck livers—they're under $1 a pound.

SQUABS. Plump, tasty squabs—pigeons under a month old, and not the kind that peck around city streets—are available at Chinese poultry markets, and you'll pay for them, around $5 a bird. Non-Asian restaurants and markets look to the Chinese for these birds. They're sometimes available alive, but plucking them is a hassle—unlike a chicken you can't scald them to loosen their feathers.

Squabs can be simply seasoned and roasted or grilled, or seasoned and fried, Chinese-style; or like duck they can be seasoned, steamed, and fried. At around 1 pound apiece, they're an ideal size and have many times the flavor of a Cornish game hen.

QUAIL. You need patience to pick at one of these little birds, but they're tasty. They're sometimes available fresh or even alive, and almost always available frozen, six or eight to a pack, in Chinese poultry markets.

OTHER POULTRY. Pheasant, partridge, wild duck, and other game birds are available at some Chinese and Southeast Asian markets.

EGGS

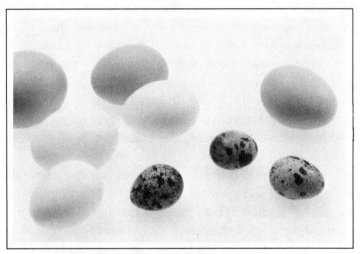

Double yolk, hen, pullet, and quail eggs

Today the word "egg" on a menu or in a recipe assumes the product of the domestic fowl, the chicken. But in Asia, where chickens were first domesticated, other eggs are enjoyed as well. The egg stand, with its eggs in a multitude of sizes, shapes, and colors, is a fixture of Chinese and Southeast Asian street markets. San Francisco's large Chinatown has the equivalent in its weekend egg truck, and Asian poultry stores offer a variety throughout the country.

HENS' EGGS. Chinese and Southeast Asian markets offer your best bet for farm-fresh eggs in various sizes and colors, from jumbos with double and triple yolks to pullet eggs—including the prized "first born" (the eggs of the hen the first time she lays).

QUAIL EGGS. These are enthusiastically consumed throughout Asia and are available here in Chinese, Southeast Asian, Japanese, and Korean markets. The Japanese skewer them and fry them, and break them into soups or into nests of grated daikon. The most familiar Chinese use of them is the *dim sum* called quail egg *siu mai*. Quail eggs are a staple in Vietnam and Thailand.

Quail eggs are cuter but not distinguished in taste from hens' eggs. They're easily found now, as gourmet stores have begun to carry them. They'll keep for two weeks if refrigerated.

DUCK EGGS. Ducks may have been the first birds domesticated for egg production. If so, credit the Chinese, who are the most avid consumers of duck eggs. The Chinese salt and preserve them, as well as eating them fresh. Ducks bred for laying will rival hens in production. The eggs have a stronger and some swear a more delicious taste than hens' eggs and are slightly oilier. For certain pastries French chefs tout them over hens' eggs.

Fresh duck eggs are available at Chinese poultry stores, and in some Chinese and Vietnamese grocery stores.

PIGEON EGGS. Loved by the Chinese, small white pigeon eggs are delicious, seasonal, and expensive—the birds lay only two eggs, and if you take both of them they'll stop laying. You can get them by special request through some Chinese poultry merchants who carry squabs.

The drumstick sections of chicken wings
are readily available at Asian poultry markets, and this is one
of the best possible uses for them.

2 pounds drumstick sections of chicken wings 1 tablespoon dark soy sauce Scant 2 teaspoons salt, preferably kosher or coarse 2 teaspoons black peppercorns	1 small dried red chili pepper 1 tablespoon cornstarch 1 tablespoon flour 2 tablespoons Shaoxing wine ¼ cup finely chopped fresh coriander Peanut oil for deep-frying	**FRIED CHICKEN "DRUMETTES" WITH CORIANDER** Yield: 6 servings

Toss the chicken pieces with the soy sauce and salt. Grind the peppercorns and chili pepper together, and add to the chicken along with the cornstarch, flour, wine, and coriander. Mix thoroughly.

Heat oil for deep-frying (2 cups or more) in a wok or heavy skillet, and fry the chicken, six or seven pieces at a time, 5 to 7 minutes, until golden brown. Drain and serve.

TWO CHICKEN SALADS:
THAI AND SICHUAN

"Oriental" chicken salads have become a standard
on American menus. Here are two using the popular texture-enhancing
method known as "hand cutting."

THAI CHICKEN SALAD

Yield: 6 to 8 servings

1 whole chicken, about 4 pounds, cut into large pieces

½ cucumber

3 fresh red or green chilis, seeded and cut into matchstick shreds

¼ red onion, thinly sliced

1 heaping tablespoon matchstick shreds of fresh ginger

2 cloves garlic, minced

¼ cup fresh lime juice

3 tablespoons fish sauce

5 teaspoons sugar

½ teaspoon salt

2 tablespoons peanut oil

1 teaspoon chili oil

½ cup fresh coriander

¼ cup chopped roasted or fried peanuts

Bring a large quantity of water to a boil in a large pot. Add the chicken pieces, bring to a boil again, and skim the surface. Reduce the heat to medium, and simmer for 5 minutes. Cover, remove from the heat, and let the chicken sit for 20 minutes in the hot water. Remove and allow to cool. (At this point the chicken may be refrigerated overnight; the stock can be reserved for another purpose).

When the chicken is cool enough to handle, remove and discard the skin. With your hands, pull the meat apart into shreds about ¼ inch wide and 1½ inches long, and put them into a bowl.

Peel and seed the cucumber, cut it into matchstick shreds, and add it to the chicken. In another bowl, mix the chilis, onion, ginger, and garlic; toss with the lime juice, fish sauce, sugar, salt, and the oils. Allow this dressing to sit for 10 minutes. Then add it to the chicken and cucumber, and mix thoroughly. Stir in the coriander, transfer to a serving dish, sprinkle with the peanuts, and serve.

2 whole chicken breasts	2 tablespoons Chinese white rice vinegar	## SICHUAN CHICKEN SALAD
2 celery stalks	1 teaspoon sugar	
2 small fresh red or green chili peppers, minced, including seeds	¼ teaspoon salt	Yield: 6 to 8 servings
1 tablespoon finely minced ginger	1 teaspoon freshly ground white pepper	
3 garlic cloves, finely minced	2 tablespoons sesame oil	
2 scallions, white part only, minced	2 tablespoons chopped fresh coriander (leaves and stems)	
2 tablespoons light soy sauce		

Poach the chicken breasts as described for Thai Chicken Salad. Drain, allow to cool, and shred by hand.

Cut the celery thinly on the diagonal; stack and cut into matchstick shreds. Parboil for 10 seconds, drain, and run under cold water to stop the cooking. Drain again, and set aside.

Mix the chilis, ginger, garlic, and scallions with the soy sauce, vinegar, sugar, salt, and white pepper, and allow to sit for 5 to 10 minutes. Toss with the chicken, sesame oil, celery, and coriander. Allow to sit 5 minutes, toss again, and serve.

CHICKEN STOCK, CHINESE STYLE

The art of making Chinese-style chicken stock is worth knowing, whatever kind of cooking you do. There are two methods, both different from Western techniques. One produces the nutritious liquid essential to everyday Chinese cooking. The other, little known, makes a "banquet stock." Crystal clear yet rich with flavor, this was the base of the two most memorable soups I've ever tasted. In one, twelve "goldfish" sculpted from fish purée with scales of steamed egg yolk—each with a fluttery cabbage-leaf tail—were served in broth in a round moatlike dish. When the dish was set down, the liquid jiggled, causing the fish to swim in a circle. The other soup had two layers. On the bottom was a gossamer cake of duck liver mousse, over which the clear broth had been ladled. A handful of fresh coriander leaves and a healthy dash of white pepper were added.

Unlike a Western stock clarified by egg shells and slow simmering, Chinese clear "banquet" stock is made by steaming. A whole plump chicken is parboiled briefly, then put in a bowl of water, and the whole bowl steams in a large steamer for 4 hours or so. The liquid around the chicken, skimmed of fat, becomes your deliciously rich "banquet" stock (see page 125).

Everyday chicken stock is also made differently from that in the West. Vegetables other than a slice of ginger are rarely added. The Chinese believe vegetable aromatics such as carrots and celery absorb more flavor than they add, and then this is lost when they're discarded.

To make Chinese chicken stock, put equal amounts of chicken bones (the fresher the better) and water in a pot with a slice or two of ginger, and bring it to a boil. When it boils, skim the brown foam from the surface, reduce the heat to a simmer, cover, and cook for 3 to 4 hours. You may strain it after it cools slightly and refrigerate it at this point; but I usually make stock at night and let it sit covered until the morning, then strain it. Stock will keep in the refrigerator if you bring it to a boil every four to five days. You needn't cook with the layer of fat that congeals on top, but it protects the stock from spoiling. To make an extra-rich stock, use a fresh whole chicken, cut in pieces, employing the same method.

Sichuan banquet cuisine has its own repertoire of dishes
that bear only a passing resemblance to the fiery food we associate
with that province. Centuries ago, it seems, a separate court cuisine was
created by political exiles from the north. Representative
is this extraordinary soup, which takes time but
is not difficult to make.

CLEAR STOCK
1 *fresh chicken (4 to 4¹/2 pounds)*
8 *cups water*

SOUP
3 *large scallions*
6 *slices fresh ginger*
¹/2 *cup boiling water*
1¹/2 *pounds fresh duck liver*
2 *ducks' eggs or 3 hens' eggs, lightly beaten*

2¹/2 *teaspoons salt*
¹/2 *teaspoon sugar*
1 *tablespoon Shaoxing wine*
1 *teaspoon freshly ground white pepper*
¹/2 *cup fresh coriander, or more to taste*

DUCK LIVER MOUSSE WITH CLEAR STOCK
(A Sichuan Banquet Soup)

Yield: 8 servings

The day before, or at least the morning before, you prepare the soup, make the clear stock: Bring a large quantity of water to a boil in a pot large enough to hold the chicken, and drop in the chicken. When the water comes to a boil again, drain and rinse the chicken. Get a large steamer going. Put the chicken, along with 8 cups of water, into a heatproof bowl; then place the bowl in the steamer, and steam for 4 hours or longer. You'll have to add water to the bottom of the steamer from time to time. When it is done, the water around the chicken will be a rich, clear stock, and the chicken, devoid of flavor, won't be of much use.

To make the soup, first, smash the scallions and ginger slices together in a small bowl; cover them with boiling water (about ½ cup). Allow to sit until cool.

Meanwhile, pick over and cut away all veins from the livers. Cut the livers into small pieces and process them in a blender at high speed for about 2 minutes. Scrape the purée into the center of a clean dampened cotton cloth (thin sheet material or layers of cheese cloth), and gather up the edges. Holding the cloth bag over a bowl, by a process of squeezing and milking, force as much of the liver as you can through the cloth into the bowl. It will take time, but you should end up with only ¼ cup or so of tough tissue in the cloth when you're done. This should be discarded.

To the liver, add ¼ cup of the scallion/ginger juice, the eggs, 1½ teaspoons of the salt, the sugar, the wine, and ¾ cup of the chicken stock. Mix until well blended.

Scrape the liver mixture into the bottom of a heatproof, preferably clear, bowl. Put the bowl into a hot steamer, and steam for 15 minutes. Meanwhile heat 4 to 5 cups of the chicken stock over medium heat, and season it with the remaining teaspoon of salt.

When the liver is done, carefully ladle the stock over the liver. Sprinkle with the pepper and coriander leaves, and serve. Each eater should be served a helping of liver along with some stock.

This duck may be simmered, refrigerated overnight, brought to room temperature the next day, and then basted and grilled; or it may be done in one day as follows. It's very simple.

GRILLED LEMON DUCK Yield: 6 servings	1 duck (4½ to 5 pounds)	⅔ cup dark brown sugar
	2 tablespoons peanut oil	6 tablespoons fresh lemon juice
	2 dried red chili peppers	
	Zest from 1½ lemons, finely shredded	2 tablespoons fish sauce
		1 tablespoon dark soy sauce
	2 stalks lemon grass (bottom third only), coarsely chopped	1½ teaspoons salt
		½ teaspoon freshly ground white pepper
	4 cloves garlic, smashed	
	6 thick slices ginger, smashed	½ cup chopped fresh coriander (leaves and stems)
	3½ quarts water	

Rinse the duck. With a chef's knife or poultry shears, cut along either side of the backbone and remove it. (Save the backbone for stock or discard it.) Spread the duck open on a work surface and press on the breast bone so it will lie flat. Parboil for 5 minutes and rinse the duck.

In a pot large enough to hold the duck, heat the oil. When it is hot, add the chilis, lemon zest, lemon grass, garlic, and ginger. Stir-fry just until fragrant, about 30 seconds. Add the water and bring to a boil. Add the duck, and when the water comes to a boil again, reduce the heat to medium. Add the brown sugar, lemon juice, fish sauce, dark soy sauce, and 1 teaspoon of the salt. Cover, and simmer the duck for 35 to 40 minutes.

Remove the duck to a cooling rack. Skim most of the fat from the cooking liquid, then turn the heat to high and reduce to a thin syrup. Pour the syrup into a bowl and allow to cool slightly.

With a basting brush, paint the duck all over with the syrup. Allow it to sit for 1 hour, preferably in a cool breezy place. After the hour is up, paint the duck again. Then sprinkle it with the remaining ½ teaspoon salt and the pepper.

Meanwhile heat a charcoal fire, and allow it to cook down to medium. Place the duck on the rack, skin side down, and grill for 5 minutes or so; turn and grill for another 8 minutes or longer. When you remove the duck from the fire, sprinkle it with the coriander and allow to sit 10 minutes. While the duck is resting, reheat the reserved syrup slightly. Cut the duck into ten to twelve pieces, and serve with the syrup on the side as a dipping sauce.

NOTE: If a grill is not available, the duck can be roasted on a rack in a 450°F oven for 20 minutes.

One of the world's great duck dishes, this is best served on a bed of watercress that has been tossed with a little sesame oil and a very few drops of light soy sauce. The juices from the duck as it's cut—it slips right off the bone—act as a delicious dressing.

SICHUAN CRISPY-SKIN DUCK

Yield: 6 to 8 servings

1 *fresh duck (about 4½ pounds)*

3 or 4 *star anise*

2 *teaspoons Sichuan peppercorns*

1 *2-inch cinnamon stick*

1½ *tablespoons coarse salt, preferably kosher*

1 *1-inch cube fresh ginger, smashed*

1 *scallion*

1 *teaspoon dark soy sauce*

1 *tablespoon dry sherry or Shaoxing wine*

1 *tablespoon cornstarch*

½ *teaspoon sugar*

1 *egg white, beaten until foamy*

Oil for deep-frying

Rinse the duck and dry it thoroughly. Combine the star anise, Sichuan peppercorns, cinnamon stick, and salt in a dry skillet, and heat, shaking, until the spices begin to smoke and the salt starts to turn a light gold. Allow to cool.

Sprinkle some of this seasoning mixture into the cavity of the duck, including all the star anise and the cinnamon stick. Add the ginger and scallion to the cavity, and close it with a skewer. Rub the outside of the duck with the rest of the seasoning mixture. Hang the duck by a string—around the neck if the duck has a head or under the wings if not—overnight in a cool, airy place.

The next day, steam the duck for 1 to 1¼ hours on a plate in a large steamer or in a covered wok fitted with a rack. Allow it to cool, then rub all over with the dark soy sauce. Wrap the duck in foil and refrigerate until ready to use. (It's fine to leave it this way for a day or two.)

Several hours before cooking, take the duck out of the refrigerator. Make a light batter by mixing the sherry with the cornstarch and sugar until well blended. Stir in the egg white, and then rub the batter thoroughly all over the duck. Allow it to sit at room temperature for at least 1 hour.

In a wok at least 16 inches in diameter or in a large deep-fryer, heat a large quantity of oil until nearly smoking. Immerse the duck in the hot oil and fry until golden, about 15 minutes, continuously spooning the oil over the exposed part of the duck. You might want to turn the duck during this time. If so, carefully remove it with a large slotted spatula or skimmer, and drain the cavity into a bowl before adding it again to the hot oil. When the duck is done, drain it on paper towels.

Allow the duck to rest 5 to 10 minutes, then carve it Western-style or cut it into pieces Chinese-style.

TEA-SMOKED DUCK: Follow the steps above, steaming the duck just 1 hour. Before refrigerating the duck, line a large wok with aluminum foil and spread over the bottom 1 cup uncooked rice, 1 cup sugar, and ½ cup Chinese black tea leaves. Put the duck on a metal rack suspended over the tea mixture, and cover the duck with the wok lid. Moisten paper towels and press them around the edge of the lid, forming a seal. Turn the heat to medium-high and allow the duck to smoke for 15 to 20 minutes. Turn off the heat and allow the duck to sit for another 45 minutes. Uncover, wrap, and refrigerate, proceeding as in the rest of the recipe. The tea-smoked duck may be served at room temperature.

These little birds, best eaten at room temperature,
should sit for 8 hours or overnight in a cool place (not the refrigerator)
before they are served.

4 *squabs, with heads and feet*	2 *teaspoons Sichuan peppercorns*	**TEA-SMOKED SQUABS**
2 *tablespoons coarse salt*	6 *star anise*	Yield: 8 to 10 servings
	2 *2-inch cinnamon sticks*	
FOR SMOKING		
½ *cup uncooked rice*	2 *teaspoons dark soy sauce*	
½ *cup light brown sugar*		
¼ *cup black tea leaves*	*Oil for deep-frying*	

Cut the feet off the squabs, and rinse and dry the birds thoroughly. Toast the salt and spices in a dry skillet, shaking over medium heat until they begin to smoke and the salt begins to brown. Allow to cool. Discard the star anise and cinnamon, and rub the salt and peppercorns over the squabs, inside and out. Hang the squabs by strings in a cool airy place for 8 hours or overnight.

Place the squabs, breast side down, on a heatproof plate, and steam them for 30 minutes in a steamer or a covered wok fitted with a rack. Allow to cool, then rub each squab with ½ teaspoon dark soy sauce.

Cover the bottom of a wok with aluminum foil and add the rice, brown sugar, and tea. Put a rack in the wok, and arrange the squabs breast side up on the rack. Cover the wok, and ring the edge of the cover with dampened paper towels to keep the smoke from escaping. Turn the heat to medium-high and when you smell smoke, leave the heat on for 15 minutes. Turn the heat off and allow the birds to stay in the covered wok for another 45 minutes.

In a large wok or deep-fryer, heat a large amount of oil to nearly smoking. Add the squabs one at a time and fry them, continuously spooning the oil over them, for about 5 minutes. Remove and drain. Pat dry with paper towels. (The frying gives the skin an interesting texture.)

You can of course eat these warm, but the smoke and spice flavors seem to mellow and permeate the birds after they sit for 8 hours, or preferably overnight. Serve Chinese-style, chopped into bite-size pieces.

A fragrant and irresistible
appetizer from Singapore, to be served hot
or at room temperature.

QUAIL EGGS WITH SPICY LAMB CRUST

Yield: 12 servings

12 quail eggs
1 tablespoon coriander seeds
1 teaspoon cumin seeds
1 teaspoon fennel seeds
3 small dried red chili peppers
½ teaspoon ground turmeric
½ pound finely chopped lamb
3 egg yolks

2 small fresh green chili peppers, finely chopped
¼ cup chopped onion
½ cup fresh bread crumbs
2 tablespoons water
½ cup chopped fresh coriander (leaves and stems)
1 teaspoon salt
Peanut oil for deep-frying

Hard-boil the quail eggs, 4 to 5 minutes. Peel and set them aside.

Over medium heat toast the coriander seeds, cumin seeds, and fennel seeds in a dry skillet until fragrant, and then grind them to a medium-fine powder in a mortar or spice grinder. Mix the ground spices with the remaining ingredients (except the quail eggs and oil).

Heat the oil for deep-frying in a heavy skillet or wok. Meanwhile, coat the quail eggs liberally with the lamb mixture. When the oil is hot, add the eggs and fry until golden, 1½ to 2 minutes. Drain, and serve cut in half, warm or at room temperature.

FISH AND FISH MARKETS

CHINESE

In Hong Kong, visitors encounter what would seem by Western standards to be a fetish regarding the freshness of seafood. The Chinese, if they can help it, prefer not to eat a fish that has been dead longer than it takes to cook it. Thus the entrances to Hong Kong restaurants are lined with aquariums, and if you buy a pound of shrimp at a seafood store, you can walk away with a seawater-filled bag in which swim twenty or thirty of the creatures. A fine French restaurant in Manhattan that cooks sole flown straight from Europe is using an ingredient long past its prime by the standards of the average Hong Kong eater.

Until now, Chinese seafood markets here have offered only a limited variety of live fish—mostly a few freshwater species that are farmed. Recently, some West Coast markets have had swimming saltwater fish for sale. According to West Coast wholesalers, this is the wave of the future.

Chinese fishmongers buy mostly what's available locally, so it's impossible to be specific about what you might encounter at a typical market, but some generalities can be made.

FISH

The Chinese prefer white-fleshed fish—black sea bass on the East Coast; Florida snapper and grouper; rock cod on the West Coast—to oily fish such as the Eastern bluefish, mackerel, or tuna. A Chinese fish market, for example, although they may carry it, is not the place to buy salmon.

The Chinese aren't big fish filet eaters; fish are sold cut up only if they are too large to fit into a steamer. It's felt, with good reason, that the head and bones lend important flavor to the fish, and a fish cooked intact will be flakier and juicier. Thus the majority of the fish sold are whole and under 3 pounds.

You can request that a fish be fileted, but the standard cleaning job is to scale the fish, remove the gills from the head, and remove all or some of the innards. For Chinese customers, any roe the fish has will be left, as will its liver and the air bladder, referred to as the "maw" when sold dried. In New York's Chinatown, though I haven't seen it on the West Coast, a stalk of scallion and a knob of ginger will be tossed in the bag with your whole fish.

There is a one-to-one ratio between quality and price in a Chinese market, and if you are bewildered by the variety, you can trust that a fish selling for $3 a pound will be 50 percent better than one selling for $2. Heavy competition—next door in some cases—and high volume in Chinese communities ensure a good buy and fresh fish.

FRESHWATER FISH. Traditionally the Chinese have prized freshwater fish above those that swim in salt water, considering the latter to have been partially processed or "salted" by their environment. Freshwater fish are sold alive in Chinese markets, and the species don't vary much regionally. Common varieties include carp (thought to be native to China, and the first fish cultivated by man), catfish, and eel, all of which are farmed. On the West Coast, the blackfish or "black trout," called a "steelhead" by the Chinese, commonly shares the tank with catfish and carp. It's a sweet, delicate fish, much beloved, but rarely suggested to Caucasians because of its boniness.

When you order a freshwater fish, it will be scooped from the tank and stunned with a little truncheon before it's cleaned. Since carp live a while out of water, these species may be fresher than you want when you get them home.

SALTWATER FISH. These will be among the best local fish, available in astonishing array, albeit mostly dead on ice.* Species show up from time to time out of their locale—Florida red snapper in New York or even in San Francisco, or a whole Louisiana redfish, as in "blackened redfish," almost anywhere. Frozen Asian fish, such as the angel fish-like pomfret, which swims in the Indian Ocean and South China Sea, or the yellow croaker from off the coast of Shanghai, are usually available. They must be cleaned after thawing.

CRUSTACEANS

In the fall, the famed *Shanghai freshwater crabs* are flown directly to some Chinese communities in the United States to be steamed or pickled in Shaoxing wine.

*There is a burgeoning movement on the West Coast to keep high-grade types of rock cod alive in tanks à la Hong Kong.

On or near the East Coast, there are *blue crabs,* mostly females with their prized orange roe. On the West Coast there are the larger Dungeness, although the blue crab is flown west a couple of times a week to Chinese markets.

The *American lobster* from the North Atlantic can be purchased live in Chinese seafood stores throughout the country, and "spiny" or "rock" lobsters are sold regionally, as are live crayfish.

When they can be gotten, *fresh shrimp*—with their heads, which sometimes contain roe—are on display. The Chinese favor shrimp cooked with the shells, even with a sauce; they're peeled and deveined in Chinese restaurants in deference to non-Asian palates. Frozen shrimp of various sizes are always for sale and may be purchased in 5-pound boxes.

In regions that have them, live freshwater shrimp find their way to Chinese markets, where they squirm and snap in tubs. Large, dead, bluish *freshwater prawns,* close to 1 pound apiece, known in parts of Southeast Asia as "Mekong Delta crustaceans," are aquacultured in Hawaii and shipped to some Chinese markets.

BIVALVES AND UNIVALVES

Since raw *oysters* have marginal appeal to the Chinese palate, a Chinese market is not the place to get the best for shucking. However, large oysters, mostly to be steamed with black beans, ginger, scallions, and a light sauce, are available. Local *mussels* and *clams* of various sorts are readily displayed, and some Chinese markets carry the large *green mussels* shipped from farms in New Zealand.

On the West Coast the giant *geoduck clam,* with its 12-inch elephant trunk-like neck is for sale (the neck is skinned, sliced, pounded, and stir-fried), as are live *abalone.* East Coast Chinese fish stores are more apt to carry *conch* and *periwinkles*—the latter to be cooked with garlic and black beans, and sucked from the shell. *Scallops,* not as favored among the Chinese (except dried) as some other seafood, are sold, although almost always frozen on the West Coast.

SQUID

A standard food in the Chinese repertoire, these are on display fresh or frozen—squid freeze quite well—in all Chinese markets. The Chinese favor a brief parboiling, usually after the squid are scored, before they're stir-fried, tossed in a salad, or deep-fried in a batter. *Cuttlefish,* sometimes babies, show up on the market, usually frozen.

AMPHIBIANS

Large live *frogs* (*Rana catesbeiana* "bullfrogs") sit blinking in terrariums—they're grown on farms—and a wide variety of soft- and hard-shelled *turtles* are offered for sale. The most-prized turtles are loaded with clear, round golden eggs, the size of small marbles. While frogs are enjoyed by the Cantonese, Southeast Asians (Vietnamese, Cambodians, Laotians) count them as a staple, and it would seem the restaurants here would have at least one frog dish on their menus but they don't. They're popular grilled, sometimes stuffed first.

JAPANESE

Seafood is the foundation of Japanese cuisine, and an enormous amount of it is consumed raw. Above any other, you can trust a Japanese fish market to have sparkling fresh fish, and you'll pay for it. Unfortunately, not all of us have access to these markets because there aren't many in this country. Most, in fact, are fish departments within Japanese grocery stores, and the selection isn't as large as that of a Chinese fish market.

The Japanese prize oilier, darker-fleshed fish than the Chinese, such as tuna and mackerel, and a Japanese market, if it has little else, will have a selection of these. The Japanese are less apt to have the same variety of fish every day, as they will pass up what's not gleamingly fresh at the market.

DARK OR RED-FLESHED FISH. Sold in whatever size slice you want, up to a half dozen varieties of tuna may be available, as well as relatives such as the Pacific yellowtail (hamachi or buri) and the bonito (katsuo). These are most popular for sashimi. Tuna varies in price, the highest being the fattiest, known as toro or "white" prime tuna. Next in preference is the chu-toro. The maguro, or red-meat tuna, is the most common and is chosen by most Westerners who eat sashimi. Any of this tuna is of course delicious cooked. Japanese markets carry mackerel of whatever sorts are locally available. They're an excellent source for fresh salmon, and they usually have trout on hand.

WHITE-FLESHED FISH. Like Chinese markets, Japanese markets carry whole white-fleshed fish, but the selection is much smaller. You'll find flounder and other flatfish; porgies and black sea bass on the East Coast; red snapper, grouper, and pompano in warmer waters; and top-grade rock cod on the West Coast.

OTHER SEAFOOD. Also available is a familiar assortment of squid (ika), shrimp (ebi), crab (kani), and clams (hamaguri). Special to the Japanese market, and usually on display, is the delicious tenderized and parboiled octopus known as tako. Occasionally fresh sea urchin (uni) appears (to be eaten raw only), and there are various pickled fish.

This fish is sublime. The sauce, loaded with chopped ginger and lemon grass, may be made ahead and reheated. Topped with golden fried shallots and coriander fried to look like seaweed, the dish is also beautiful.

STEAMED FISH WITH COCONUT SAUCE AND FRIED SHALLOTS

Yield: 4 servings

- 1 *whole white-fleshed fish such as red snapper or sea bass (2 to 2½ pounds), cleaned, scaled, gills removed*
- 1 *teaspoon salt*
- ½ *cup peanut oil*
- 15 *large shallots, thinly sliced*
- 1 *cup whole coriander leaves*
- 1 *cup chopped fresh ginger*
- 1 *stalk lemon grass (bottom third only), finely minced*
- 2 to 4 *tiny fresh red chili peppers, finely minced, including seeds*
- 1½ *cups coconut milk (fresh, frozen, or canned)*
- 1 *cup water*
- ¼ *cup Thai or Vietnamese fish sauce*
- *Lots of freshly ground black pepper*

Score the fish lightly at 1-inch intervals on each side. Sprinkle the fish outside and inside with the salt, and set aside on a heatproof plate.

Heat the oil in a small skillet over medium heat, and add the shallots. Cook, stirring occasionally, until golden brown. (This will take a while; reduce the heat to prevent burning). Remove the shallots with a slotted spoon and drain on paper towels. Turn the heat to high and add the coriander to the same oil; fry 10 seconds, stirring. Remove the coriander with a slotted spoon and drain with the shallots. Strain the oil and reserve 3 tablespoons.

Heat a larger skillet or wok over high heat and add the reserved oil. Add the ginger, lemon grass, and chilis, and stir briefly. Add the coconut milk and 1 cup water. Bring to a boil, stirring. Reduce the heat to medium, add the fish sauce, and cook, stirring from time to time, about 8 to 10 minutes, until the sauce has reduced by one third or is slightly thickened. Set aside.

Bring the water in a steamer to a boil. Put the fish on its plate in the steamer, cover, and steam for about 12 minutes (more or less depending on the thickness of the fish). When it is done, transfer the fish to a serving platter, pour the sauce over it (reheated if necessary), decorate it with the fried shallots and coriander, and serve with the black pepper on the side.

A filet of fish spread with chopped shrimp, fresh water chestnuts, black mushrooms, and fresh coriander, then dipped in tempura batter and fried, this makes a delicate first course. It's full of flavor and texture, and for a fried food is curiously refreshing.

TEMPURA FRIED FISH WITH SHRIMP

Yield: 6 to 10 servings

2 dried black mushrooms

½ pound shrimp

3 ounces fresh pork fat

5 fresh water chestnuts

3 tablespoons minced coriander leaves and stems

2 tablespoons minced scallions

1 tablespoon minced fresh ginger

1 egg white

2 tablespoons Shaoxing wine

¾ teaspoon salt

¼ teaspoon sugar

½ teaspoon white pepper

1 teaspoon sesame oil

6 thin fish filets, preferably sole

Cornstarch

½ pound caul fat (lace fat)

BATTER

¾ cup flour

1½ tablespoons cornstarch

1½ teaspoons salt

½ teaspoon sugar

2 teaspoons baking powder

¾ to ⅞ cup water

Peanut oil for deep-frying

Soak the mushrooms in hot water for 30 minutes. Meanwhile, shell the shrimp, chop them coarsely, and put them in a mixing bowl.

In a small saucepan, simmer the pork fat for 3 minutes. Then allow it to cool, and chop finely. Measure out 2 tablespoons chopped fat and add it to the shrimp.

Peel and chop the water chestnuts, and add them to the shrimp along with the coriander, scallions, ginger, egg white, wine, salt, sugar, white pepper, and sesame oil.

Squeeze the liquid from the mushrooms, and cut off and discard the stems. Chop the mushrooms coarsely, and add them to the shrimp. Mix all these ingredients well. You may have to moisten the mixture with a little more wine.

Dust one side of each fish filet with some cornstarch, and cover that side with a thin layer—no more than ¼ inch thick—of the shrimp mixture. Rinse the caul fat in warm water and dry it with paper towels. Wrap the filets in the caul fat and set aside.

To make the batter, simply mix all the ingredients together, but don't stir too much.

Heat the oil for deep-frying to about 375°F in a wok or large skillet. Dip each filet in the batter and then fry until golden, turning it in the oil, about 3 to 4 minutes. Drain on paper towels. To serve, cut the filets into wedges about 1 inch wide.

NOTE: These may be served on spinach or mustard green leaves that have been fried briefly in the hot oil and drained. The leaves will have a crinkly texture similar to seaweed.

Perhaps the best way to enjoy crab, this can be made with the blue crabs of the East Coast (also lively and available in Asian markets on the West Coast), or with the large West Coast Dungeness crab.

CANTONESE-STYLE CRACKED CRAB WITH BLACK BEANS

Yield: 8 servings

6 large live blue crabs, or 1 Dungeness crab

Flour for dredging

2 tablespoons salted and fermented black beans

2 tablespoons chopped fresh ginger

1½ tablespoons chopped garlic

2 tablespoons Shaoxing wine

⅔ cup chicken stock

2 tablespoons light soy sauce

1½ teaspoons sugar

½ teaspoon salt

2 eggs

3¼ cups Peanut oil

5 to 6 ounces ground pork, lightly hand-chopped

2 teaspoons cornstarch mixed with 2 tablespoons water

3 scallions, cut into 1½-inch lengths (green part included)

Put the crabs in a basin of salted water and let them swim around for 15 minutes or so. Drain and rinse. To clean blue crabs: With a cloth or cotton gloves, carefully pull off the large claws and set them aside on a plate. Snip off the legs with kitchen shears and discard. Pull open and remove the apron on the underside of the shell, and then force the top shell away from the body, remove it, and set it aside. Snip away and discard the finger-like lungs. Cut the bodies of the crabs in half; dip the cut side in flour and set them on a plate. Gently crack the large claws. (For instructions on cleaning Dungeness crab, see Note on page 138.)

Lightly chop the black beans; combine them with the ginger, garlic, and wine in a small bowl and set aside. Mix the chicken stock with the soy sauce, sugar, and salt, and set aside. Beat the eggs lightly and set aside.

Add 3 cups of oil to a wok and heat it. When it is very hot, add the top shells of the crabs and cook just until they turn red, then remove to drain. Add the bodies of the crabs to the hot oil, and cook for 1 to 2 minutes. Then add the claws and cook for another 30 seconds. Remove all the crab pieces to drain.

Pour off all the oil, wipe the wok clean, and reheat. Add about ¼ cup oil. When it is hot, add the pork and cook, stirring, just until the grains have separated. Add the black bean mixture and stir until fragrant. Add the seasoned stock, and bring to a boil. Stir the cornstarch mixture, and add it. Cook, stirring, until the sauce has thickened and is clear and bubbling. Add the scallions and crab bodies and claws, and cook until piping hot, about 1 minute. Turn off the heat and stir in the beaten egg. Pour the contents from the wok into the center of a large platter, arrange the shells around the outside, and serve.

NOTE: Dungeness crabs—more docile than blue crabs—may be cleaned by first grasping all four legs and the claw on each side of the body from behind and cracking the underside of the crab against the sharp edge of a sink or cutting board, stunning the crab. Holding all the legs in one hand, pull off the top shell. Remove and discard the mouth parts of this crab, and snip off and discard the lungs. Cut the body of the crab in half; then cut each half into sections with one leg attached to each section. Crack each leg, dip the exposed parts of the body in flour, and set aside. Gently crack the large claws. A Dungeness crab should be presented with the large shell upside down, like a bowl, and the remaining ingredients on top of it.

This elegant offering is actually all seafood, with some bright green celery added for crunch. The pasta is a shrimp purée in the form of noodles, and it's not as difficult as it might seem. The idea came from the late Virginia Lee.

SHRIMP PASTA WITH SCALLOPS AND CELERY

Yield: 6 servings

PASTA

½ pound shrimp

1 teaspoon salt

2½ tablespoons cornstarch

1 egg white

2 tablespoons milk

1 tablespoon Shaoxing wine

2 tablespoons water

TOPPING

½ pound sea scallops

1 cup fresh chicken stock

1½ teaspoons salt

½ teaspoon sugar

½ teaspoon white pepper

¼ cup freshly rendered chicken fat (see page 320)

1 cup diced celery (¼-inch dice)

¼ cup finely minced fresh ginger

1½ teaspoons cornstarch mixed with 2 tablespoons water

⅓ cup chopped coriander leaves and stems

1 teaspoon sesame oil

Peel the shrimp and cut them into cubes. Place them in the container of a food processor along with the remaining pasta ingredients, and blend to a fine paste. If stiff, add a little more water.

Spoon the mixture into a pastry bag fitted with a number 6 tip. Squeeze the noodles into a large saucepan containing 2 quarts cold water. Heat the water, and when the noodles turn white and are set, turn off the heat and drain off the water. Pour fresh cold water over the noodles and gently scrape up any that are stuck to the bottom of the pan. Drain the noodles into a colander and set aside.

Cut the scallops into rounds about ¼ inch thick, and cut these in half. Mix the chicken stock in a saucepan with the salt, sugar, and white pepper, and heat.

Heat the chicken fat in a wok or skillet, and add the celery and 2 teaspoons of the ginger. Cook, stirring, over medium-high heat for 1 minute or so. Add the scallops and cook gently, stirring, just until they change color. Add the hot seasoned chicken stock and the noodles, and bring to a boil. Stir the cornstarch mixture, and add it. When the mixture is slightly thickened and glistening, turn off the heat and stir in the coriander. Transfer to a shallow serving bowl, dribble the sesame oil over it, and serve with the remaining ginger on the side.

A delicious hybrid of East and West,
this is a perfect first course. It's a little time-consuming,
but worth it.

SHRIMP QUENELLES WITH LEMON GRASS AND BASIL

Yield: 8 servings

FISH STOCK (FUMET)

4 *pounds fish trimmings: bones, heads (gills removed), shrimp tails and shells (see below)*

2 *tablespoons peanut oil*

¼ *cup lightly crushed coriander seeds*

3 *stalks lemon grass (bottom third only), coarsely chopped*

1 *onion, coarsely chopped*

4 *cloves garlic, smashed*

¾ *cup Shaoxing wine*

QUENELLES

4 *ounces pork fat*

1 *pound fresh shrimp, shelled (reserve shells for stock)*

1 *teaspoon finely minced fresh ginger*

2 *egg whites*

¼ *cup chopped coriander leaves and stems*

1 *tablespoon cornstarch*

1 *tablespoon sesame oil*

1 *teaspoon salt*

SAUCE

2 *tablespoons peanut oil*

1 *bunch scallions (white part only), sliced*

4 *cloves garlic, minced*

2 *small fresh red or green chili peppers, finely minced*

4 *large ripe tomatoes, peeled, seeded, and diced*

Salt and pepper to taste

⅓ *cup Asian basil, cut in thin strips*

1 *tablespoon fresh lemon juice, or more to taste*

MAKE THE FUMET: Rinse the fish trimmings (you should have enough to fill two-thirds of an 8-quart stock pot). Heat the oil in an 8-quart stock pot, and add the coriander seeds, lemon grass, onion, and garlic. Stir-fry briefly, until fragrant. Add the fish trimmings and stir over medium-low heat for 5 minutes or so. Add the wine and enough water to cover, and bring to a boil. Skim, lower the heat, and simmer uncovered 30 minutes. Turn off the heat and allow to sit for 15 minutes. Strain.

MEANWHILE, MAKE THE QUENELLES: Simmer the pork fat in a small skillet for 5 minutes, until translucent. Drain, and allow to cool. Then chop the pork fat and shrimp together to form a coarse paste. Mix in the ginger, egg whites, coriander, cornstarch, sesame oil, and salt. Blend thoroughly.

When the fumet is done, set aside 3 cups and heat the rest. When it is hot, take a serving spoon (you'll need two), dip it in water, and scoop out a spoonful of the shrimp paste. Dip the other spoon in water and use it to form the quenelle by scooping the shrimp paste from one spoon to the other. Poach the quenelles in the simmering stock for 3 to 4 minutes. Remove them with a slotted spoon to a warmed shallow terrine.

When all the quenelles are done, prepare the sauce: Heat the peanut oil in a large skillet or wok, and sauté the scallions, garlic, chilis, and tomatoes about 1 minute. Add the reserved fumet and bring to a boil. Add salt and pepper to taste, and turn off the heat. Sprinkle in the basil and lemon juice, and pour the sauce over the quenelles. Serve.

Scallops and water chestnuts complement each other in shape and texture. A meal can be made of this rich, spicy dish with the addition of just rice and a simple green salad.

SCALLOPS AND WATER CHESTNUTS IN THAI-STYLE PORK SAUCE

Yield: 6 to 8 servings

6 to 8 fresh water chestnuts (or canned if necessary)

1 pound sea scallops

2 teaspoons cornstarch

Few drops sesame oil

1 teaspoon cumin seeds

1 teaspoon fennel seeds

2 teaspoons coriander seeds

1 tablespoon minced fresh ginger

1 teaspoon minced fresh turmeric (if available)

4 garlic cloves, minced

4 small fresh red chilis, minced (including seeds)

1 stalk lemon grass (bottom third only), finely minced

¾ cup unsweetened coconut milk

½ cup water

Juice of 1 large lime

3 tablespoons fish sauce

1½ teaspoons sugar

Pinch of salt

1 cup + 3 tablespoons peanut oil

½ pound ground pork

¼ cup coriander leaves

Wash the mud from the water chestnuts, peel them, cut them in half, and put them in a bowl of cold water until ready to use.

Rinse the scallops and cut them in half. Toss with the cornstarch and sesame oil, and refrigerate until ready to cook.

Toast the seeds in a small dry skillet until fragrant; then grind them in a mortar or spice grinder and set aside. Combine the ginger, turmeric, garlic, chilis, and lemon grass in a small bowl and set aside. Mix the coconut milk, lime juice, fish sauce, sugar, and salt together, and set aside.

Heat 3 tablespoons of the oil in a skillet and add the pork. Cook, stirring to separate the grains. When the meat has changed color—it shouldn't brown—add the ground spices and stir for 30 seconds. Add the ginger mixture and cook, stirring, for another 30 seconds. Add the seasoned coconut milk, stir to blend, then add the water and bring to a boil. Turn the heat to medium-low and cook for 8 to 10 minutes, stirring from time to time, until it just begins to thicken. Add more water if necessary while you cook. Turn off the heat, cover, and set the sauce aside. (It may be prepared an hour or so ahead.)

Heat the remaining 1 cup oil in a wok, and when it is hot add the scallops, stirring to separate. Cook for 30 seconds, then remove with a slotted spoon and drain. Drain the water chestnuts and cook them in the hot oil for 15 seconds; remove with a slotted spoon.

Reheat the pork sauce. Add the scallops and water chestnuts and stir over high heat just until hot. Turn off the heat, garnish with the coriander, transfer to a serving platter, and serve.

Although there's evidence that "cooking" raw fish in lime juice originated in the South Pacific, I don't know how authentically Tahitian this is. It's based on a recipe from Time-Life's *Pacific and Southeast Asian Cooking,* and it's tasty and attractive. I like it with the tuna raw in the center.

TAHITIAN CEVICHE WITH TUNA AND CHILIS		
Yields: 6 to 8 servings	1 *pound raw, preferably fatty, tuna* ½ *cup fresh lime juice* 1½ *teaspoons salt* ¼ *cup chopped red onion* 2 *tablespoons chopped fresh red chili peppers (seeded)* ¼ *cup sliced scallions*	2 *small very ripe tomatoes, peeled and seeded* ⅓ *cup coriander leaves (packed)* 1 *hard-boiled egg, chopped* ½ *cup coconut milk* ½ *teaspoon freshly ground black pepper*

Slice the tuna into pieces ¼ inch thick and ¾ × 1½ inches. Toss the pieces in a bowl with the lime juice, 1 teaspoon of the salt, and the onion. Marinate for 1 hour if you want the tuna rare in the center, 2 hours or so if you want it "cooked."

When the tuna has marinated, drain off all the lime juice. Combine the remaining ingredients, toss them with the tuna, and serve.

PRESERVED AND PROCESSED INGREDI- ENTS

DRIED INGREDIENTS

To appreciate the dried ingredients of Asia, we have to leave our "fresh is best" mentality behind. While Asians enjoy the freshest of fresh foods—seafood is alive until just before it's cooked, and produce is picked twice a day to supply vegetable stalls that set up in the morning and late afternoon—dried foods must be appreciated in their own right.

Not simply what you use when you can't get the fresh version, certain foods have been found over the centuries to have a texture, an essence of flavor, or a medicinal quality when dried that they don't have in the fresh state, and they're often caught, harvested, or bred for that purpose. Fresh scallops are a mundane seafood to the Chinese, whereas dried scallops are a luxury sold in gift packaging and used with discretion. In fact some foods are rarely if ever eaten fresh because the process of drying makes them what they are; these include those quintessential delicacies bird's nest, shark's fin, and sea slug.

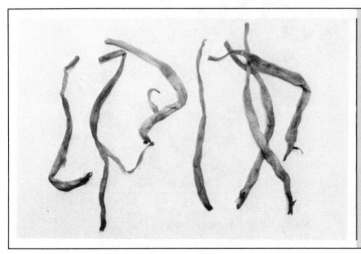

LILY BUDS
(Hemerocallis spp.)

OTHER NAMES: Golden needles, Tiger lily buds, Dried tiger lily stems, Dried lily flower

REGION OF USE: China

Despite their various names, these are not the buds of the tiger lily, *Lilium tigrinum*, but are the dried unopened flowers of yellow and orange day lilies, which at one time were worn around the waist by pregnant Chinese women in hopes of having a boy. Called "golden needles" simply because they are thin and golden in color, they're a popular vegetarian ingredient. Buddhists cook with them, perhaps because their earthly fragrance contrasts with garlic and onion, the more odoriferous members of the lily family, which some Buddhists won't eat.

Medicinally, dried lily buds are thought to be a mild pain reliever, and for reasons I can't track down, are often used in conjunction with tree ear fungus, most familiarly in Hot and Sour Soup and Mu Shu Pork.

Available in 8-ounce plastic packages, lily buds should be light golden in color and flexible when you buy them, not brown and brittle. Transfer them to a tightly covered jar, and if they're going to sit for months, store them out of the light.

Dried lily buds should be soaked in warm water until soft—20 minutes will do. Then cut off the hard tips of the stems, and cut the buds in half. To release their subtle fragrance, especially for soup, shred them coarsely by hand, which means tearing each stem once or twice lengthwise.

NOTE: The starchy bulbs of the tiger lily and other true lilies, which look like garlic bulbs with flattened cloves, are eaten fresh in China, Japan, and Korea; they're available dried in the United States.

BEANS

Left to right:
black and green mung beans;
red azuki *beans; yellow and black soybeans*

Plainly cooked beans were more a staple of the Chinese diet in ancient times than they are now. Unlike India, where many species of legume were first cultivated, Chinese cooking evolved away from eating them unprocessed. In the case of the soybean, the Chinese converted the nutrients into more digestible forms such as bean curd and protein-rich fermented bean sauces, and these techniques spread to Japan. Sprouting beans also improved them nutritionally, and in the case of the mung bean, they were made easier on the stomach by converting them to a starch that's made into noodles and wrappers.

A variety of dried beans are sold in Asian markets, generally in 1-pound plastic bags or in bulk.

OTHER NAMES: Cowpea REGION OF USE: Southeast Asia, China	**BLACK-EYED PEAS** (Vigna sinensis)

Usually labeled "Blackeye Beans" in Asian markets, it's always a surprise to see this staple of the Deep South on the shelves, but in fact they've been eaten in Asia for millennia. Black-eyed peas and rice is an old dish in Southeast Asia. Black-eyed peas are the mature seed of a variety of long bean, those foot-and-a-half-long legumes sold fresh in Asian markets (see page 88).

OTHER NAMES: Fava, Horsebean, Sora mame (Japanese) REGION OF USE: China, Japan, Korea	**BROAD BEANS**

Found, often unlabeled, in 1-pound packages in Chinese markets that specialize in northern goods, in Asia dried broad beans are usually soaked, braised, and eaten either warm or cold. In Shanghai they're cooked until soft with dark soy sauce, Shaoxing wine, sugar, salt, and sometimes star anise, then tossed with chopped scallions.

The Chinese very often cook the dried bean just after it has been sprouted. Unlike mung or soybean sprouts, the bean in this case is relished more than the sprout. If stir-fried, the soft bean is sucked out of the hull, which is spat out; if braised, the hull is soft enough to eat.

TO SPROUT: Spread a single layer of dried broad beans on a rimmed tray and soak them, changing the water daily, for 3 days. Once little sprouts appear, the beans can be kept for up to a week in the refrigerator; wrap them in a clean damp towel, and rinse the towel out daily. Chinese stores that carry northern goods often carry sprouted broad beans in plastic bags in the refrigerator case. (For more information about the bean and its use fresh, see page 87.)

MUNG BEANS	OTHER NAMES: Mung pea, Green gram
(Phaseolus aureus)	REGION OF USE: China, Southeast Asia, Japan, Korea

Next to the soybean, the mung bean, originally from India, is the most important in Asia. It comes in several colors, but green is by far the most widely used. Husked, the green mung bean becomes the yellow mung bean, cooked primarily in Southeast Asia as a result of Indian influence.

When watered, the green mung bean becomes the common bean sprout (see page 85). Starch processed from the bean is made into the wispy noodles known as cellophane or pea starch noodles, which are a staple of China and Southeast Asia (see page 293). Mung beans also have been used, though much less so than soybeans, for bean curd and fermented bean sauces.

In Southeast Asia, the beans themselves are cooked and eaten; in Malaysia they're the base for a gruel. In Thailand and elsewhere, sweetened pastes of ground mung beans are stuffed into pastries of glutinous rice flour, much like red beans in China and Japan (see below). Whole green mung beans are sold in 1-pound plastic packages in all Asian markets. Yellow (shelled) mung beans, split or whole, and split green mung beans are available in Southeast Asian and Indian markets.

Beautiful black grams *(P. mungo),* India's most prized bean (when hulled, they're called *urad dal*), are used in Southeast Asia. You'll find them in some Thai and Vietnamese markets in 14-ounce packages from Thailand, labeled "Black Bean."

RED BEANS	OTHER NAMES: Adzuki or azuki beans, Tiensin red beans
(Phaseolus angularis)	REGION OF USE: China, Japan, Korea, Southeast Asia

Since Han times in China (206 B.C. to A.D. 220), red beans, because of their color, have meant good fortune and are eaten without fail on festive occasions, one of the few times they're cooked whole. This tradition was adopted in Japan, where a steamed glutinous rice and red bean dish, tinted red by the bean-soaking liquid, is consumed in lieu of regular rice at birthdays, weddings, and on New Year's—at which time the bean is also scattered around the house to keep away bad spirits. They're also cooked with a syrup and served with shaved ice and condensed milk in Hong Kong and in Chinese outposts in the tropics.

Most often the red bean, which looks like the mung bean, is cooked, mashed, and mixed with sugar for use in sweets, usually in combination with sweet rice or sweet rice flour. In Japan it's safe to say most sweets contain a paste of this sort. Called *an*, the paste, like peanut butter, is made smooth or chunky.

Prepared sweet red bean pastes are sold canned in Chinese and Japanese food stores; the common Chinese brand is Companion. The Japanese also sell an instant "red bean flour" *sarashi-an*, which, requiring a couple of steps, isn't as instant as you would guess. It's not terribly difficult to make your own sweet red bean paste, and it's far more flavorful.

Red beans are available in some Asian markets in bulk and in all Asian markets in 14-ounce bags. Occasionally next to the red beans in some Chinese markets you will see a tiny thin bean called "red small beans" for use in savory dishes. For sweet bean pastes, however, you'll want the commonly available *azuki* or plain "red bean," or the variety called Tiensin red beans.

TO MAKE CHINESE SWEETENED RED BEAN PASTE: Soak 1 cup of red beans in water overnight. The next day, put the beans in a stainless steel or enamel saucepan, cover with an inch of water, and simmer on the stove for about 1 hour or until soft. Press the beans and the liquid through a sieve or food mill into a wok or heavy skillet. Cook over high heat about 30 minutes, stirring. (Be careful, as this sputters like hot lava.) Add ¾ cup sugar and a pinch of salt, and continue to cook for 10 minutes or so, until the mixture has the consistency of a thick bean soup.

Dribble 5 tablespoons freshly rendered lard (or peanut oil) around the edge of the mixture, and stir it in until it's thoroughly incorporated. The paste will keep refrigerated in a jar for a week or so.

TO MAKE JAPANESE CHUNKY SWEET RED BEAN PASTE, *tsubushi-an*: Put 1 cup of red beans in a saucepan, and add water to cover. Bring to a boil, then drain and discard the water. Return the beans to a saucepan with fresh water to cover, and simmer until the beans are very soft and most of the water has evaporated. (Add more water if necessary during the cooking.) When the beans are done, add 1 cup sugar and a pinch of salt, and stir with a wooden spoon until the seasonings are well incorporated and the beans half crushed. Use as directed or store in the refrigerator, where it will keep for a week or so.

SOYBEANS (Glycine max)	OTHER NAMES: Daizu ("Great bean," Japanese)
	REGION OF USE: China, Japan, Korea, Java, other areas of Southeast Asia

There are two dried soybeans sold in Chinese, Japanese, and Korean markets, in bulk or in 1-pound plastic bags: a straw-colored bean (yellow bean) whose shape has been likened to pearls; and a dusty-looking black soybean whose shape, while still roundish, is slightly more beanlike.

Most useful are the light-colored beans, from which soybean milk, bean curd, miso, soy sauce, and soybean sprouts are produced. They're occasionally cooked, but first must be soaked overnight, drained and rinsed, then boiled for about 10 minutes and drained and rinsed again, before they're finally seasoned and cooked. Toasted beans are cooked with rice gruel or ground into a flour, which is most popular in Japan.

Black soybeans, labeled (if at all) "Dried Black Beans" in Asian markets, are more likely to be just cooked and eaten. Koreans simmer them with soy sauce and sugar until the sauce disappears, at which point they're tossed with a little sesame oil, garnished with toasted sesame seeds, and served. In Korean Five-Grain Rice (*ogopap*), black soybeans are combined with glutinous rice, sorghum, millet, and red beans. The Chinese cook and mash black soybeans into pastes, which are sweetened and stuffed into pastries called black bean cakes.

FUNGI

BLACK MUSHROOMS
(Lentinus edodes)

OTHER NAMES: Black winter mushroom (*dong-gu*, Mandarin), Fragrant mushroom (*xiang-gu*, Mandarin), Shiitake (Japanese), Black Forest mushroom, Brown oak mushroom, P'yogo (Korean), Hed hom (Thai)

REGION OF USE: China, Japan, Korea, and some areas of Southeast Asia

The oldest cultivated mushrooms, sold in all Asian markets, these come with brown or black caps that range from 1 to 3 inches in diameter and are either thin and smooth or thick with white fissures. (The latter are the best.) The Japanese and Koreans eat these mushrooms both fresh and dried; the Chinese prefer them dried. The best in fact are always dried. (The fresh shiitakes suddenly for sale throughout the United States, as tasty as they are, are of inferior quality as far as these mushrooms go.)

Ancient Chinese *materia medica* describe these "winter" or "fragrant" mushrooms in terms of the kinds of fallen trees they grow on, which include chestnut and oak. The Japanese, who supply Chinese markets with them, cultivate them on the *shii* tree, an oak-related species, and thus refer to all of them, no matter what size and quality, as *shiitake*.

Whether the mushrooms come from Japan or Korea (source of some of the best), the widest variety of grades and sizes, and the best price per pound, can be had at Chinese herbal shops since, beyond the specific ailments these mushrooms are thought to remedy, they have long held the title of a "plant of immortality." A classic Buddhist dish featuring them is called Soft Immortal Food. The best may sell for over $30 a pound, and in Asia even costlier grades are offered.

The simplest way to reconstitute these mushrooms is to put them in a bowl, pour boiling water over them, then cover and allow to sit for 30 minutes. Some people hold that they are better when soaked for 6 hours in tepid water, or overnight in cold water. After soaking, squeeze the mushrooms over the soaking bowl—reserve the liquid for the next time you need water or stock—and then cut off the woody stems (which may be reserved for future stock) and rub a little oil or freshly rendered fat into the mushrooms. Set them aside until you are ready to use them.

Don't skimp when you buy these mushrooms. The over-$20-a-pound variety are full flavored, have a wonderful meaty texture, and are more than twice as good as the $10 kind. Herbal shops and a few other stores sell them in bulk, but most package their own in plastic bags weighing between 4 ounces and 1 pound. I store them in the freezer, because once in a great while, hundreds of tiny moths will hatch in one of the plastic bags, apparently from larvae that aren't included in the purchase price.

NOTE: The Japanese divide dried black mushrooms into four grades: Number one, naturally enough from Japan, is the thickest and has the deepest fisures; it is called *hana,* or "flower" mushroom. Number two, from Korea, is called *jyo,* or "superior"; it is thick but without as much white cracking. Grades three and four, both Japanese (*nami* and *nami koshin*), are "ordinary" mushrooms, thin and undistinguished.

中國川耳
BLACK FUNGUS
NET WT. 2 OZ

TREE EARS
(Auricularia auricula-judae)

OTHER NAMES: Black fungus, Black tree fungus, Mu-er (Mandarin), Cloud ear, Wood ear, Mouse ear fungus (Malay), Jew's ear

REGION OF USE: China, Korea, Southeast Asia

In the May 22, 1980, issue of the *New England Journal of Medicine,* a University of Minnesota scientist, Dr. Dale Hammerschmidt, reported a discovery—if you can call it that when Western medicine stumbles across the curative properties for which an ingredient has been heralded in China for centuries—involving the atherosclerosis-combatting properties of the tree ear mushroom. It seems a patient at a clinic in Minnesota, where the disease was being studied, showed marked improvement in the clotting properties of his blood after eating a Sichuan bean curd dish laced with these fungi. Not news to me: My cooking instructor, the late Virginia Lee, talked constantly about these fungi being "good for circulation," and the sixteenth-century *materia medica* of Li Shih-chen says the mushroom "has the reputation of rendering the blood fluid."

These mushrooms, which are sold dried in large and small sizes, and in gradations within those two categories if you look carefully, grow on rotting wood around the world. Alan Davidson, the English food authority, reports finding them growing 200 yards from his apartment in London. The Chinese, who are the biggest consumers of *mu-er,* have long cultivated them by cutting down a small kind of oak, which they cut into poles about 8 feet long and allow to rot for a year on the ground. The poles are erected into a kind of shed, and during the next two years the tree ears grow over them, at which point they're harvested, as the wood becomes too rotten to act as a host.

These fungi, which have little flavor but a pleasing crunch, dry easily and in fact live for quite some time in that state. It's best to buy the smallest of the small tree ears, which look like tiny gnarled black flakes, as the large ones, two-toned in color—called "cloud ears" by the Chinese—need their tough, gritty stems plucked off after they're soaked and must be sliced before they're used.

To reconstitute tree ears, pour boiling water over them, and let them soak for 30 minutes. When softened and enlarged, they should be rinsed thoroughly and drained. (A little goes a long way: Three heaping tablespoons of the dried will yield practically a cup softened.)

Tree ears are standard in Hot and Sour Soup and Mu Shu Pork, and they're wonderful in cold dishes in harmony with cucumbers and seafood. Included in Buddhist vegetarian dishes, they're often combined with dried lily buds to enhance their medical effectiveness. The Vietnamese chop them and stuff them into their spring rolls, *cha gio.*

Usually sold as "Black Fungus," tree ears are available in Chinese and Southeast Asian food stores in packages of 2 to 8 ounces. Herbal stores may carry them in bulk. They keep indefinitely in a covered jar on the shelf.

According to the Chinese pharmacopoeia,
this dish is superb for the circulation; it's also
delicate and tasty.

BONELESS FISH WITH TREE EARS

Yield: 4 to 6 servings

2 heaping tablespoons dried tree ear mushrooms

1 pound boneless white-fleshed fish, such as sole

¼ cup Shaoxing wine

Cornstarch for dredging

1 cup chicken stock

1½ teaspoons salt

1 teaspoon sugar

1 cup peanut oil

½ teaspoon white pepper

1 tablespoon melted chicken fat or sesame oil

2 tablespoons finely chopped coriander leaves

Pour boiling water over the tree ears and soak for at least 30 minutes.

Cut the fish into 2 × 1-inch strips and toss with 1 tablespoon of the wine. Dredge each piece in cornstarch and set aside. Combine 1 tablespoon cornstarch, the chicken stock, 1½ teaspoons salt, and the sugar; stir well.

Drain and rinse the tree ears, dry by squeezing them in a towel, and set aside.

Heat the oil in a wok or heavy skillet. When it is very hot, add the fish pieces, a few at a time, and cook briefly, just 15 seconds or so—they shouldn't brown—and drain them. Pour off all but 1 tablespoon oil from the wok and reheat.

Stir the chicken stock mixture again, and add it to the wok. Cook, stirring, until the sauce is bubbling hot and slightly clear. Add the remaining 3 tablespoons wine, and tree ears, and the fish, and cook until just hot.

Transfer the contents to a serving dish, sprinkle with the pepper, dribble with the fat or oil, and serve garnished with the coriander leaves.

WHITE TREE FUNGUS
(Tremella fuciformis)

OTHER NAMES: White fungus, White tree ear, Silver fungus, Silver ear, White jelly fungus, Tremella, Dried snow fungus*

REGION OF USE: China

White tree fungus, which in its dried state looks like a golden, crinkly sponge about 3 inches in diameter, is closely related to the black fungus or tree ear, except that it's more highly prized: It's a food for long life; after soaking it turns an auspicious "silver" (by a slight stretch of the imagination); and it's a little harder to come by. The tasteless crunch is very similar.

It's an exaggeration, however, to describe white tree fungus as expensive and rare; it's more like an affordable bird's nest, used much the same way, and sometimes in combination with it. A clear chicken stock is the common foil for it, as the fungus absorbs flavor. It can be used as a garnish, and it adds its texture to an unusual version of Chicken Velvet. Unlike black tree fungus, it is served sweetened as soup—warm or cold—made by simmering or steaming it in water and rock sugar.

To soak white tree fungus, pour warm water over it and let it sit. After 15 to 30 minutes, the spongy base of the fungus and any dirt clinging to it should be pulled or snipped away, leaving flowerettes that can soak until you're ready to use them.

White fungus is sold in bulk in herbal shops, or in 4-ounce cellophane-wrapped gift boxes. The price will depend on the size of the fungus, the largest (of three size categories) being the most expensive. At no more than $4 a box, your 4 ounces will go a long way. You can see the fungi in the box, which is fortunate, as some are terribly mislabeled in English, for example "Agar-agar" or simply "Dried Vegetable."

NOTE: The Romans enjoyed tree fungus, according to *The Roman Cookery Book* credited to Apicius, boiled and seasoned with crushed black pepper and *garum*, their fermented fish sauce.

*True "snow fungus" is a medicinal ingredient sold dried in herbal shops. White and gelatinous when soaked and used much the same way as the tree fungus, it is actually the reproductive glands of the male Beijing snow frog. Needless to say, it's more expensive. It should be soaked overnight in cold water before it is used.

FISH AND SHELLFISH

With some exceptions, if it swims and is edible, the Chinese long ago dried it to preserve it. No mere substitute, the most popular of these protein-rich foods, such as dried shrimp, squid, and scallops, have achieved status as foods unto themselves with their own highly regarded flavor—usually a fishiness that, once gotten used to, is delicious—and are eaten whether or not the fresh species is available. Some, such as shrimp, are used exclusively as seasonings rather than as the main item in a dish.

Fish are the most prevalent dried seafood in Chinese and Southeast Asian markets. The selection is vast from, anchovies—often just deep-fried and eaten like a snack—to large fish, small portions of which are used at a time. Some are salted and dried, others just dried. Some are dried quickly in the sun; others, which the Cantonese call *mui heung*, ferment slightly and are sold in a quasi-moist state. Dried fish typically are softened in warm water, sometimes rice-rinsing water, and this liquid may be added with the fish to a dish. Depending on what's to be done with the fish, as little as 30 minutes soaking time may do; for slow-cooked dishes, pieces of dried fish may be added unsoaked.

Dried fish may be simply cut up and cooked over rice. Some species are cut into pieces and deep-fried. (Be warned, the aroma will fill your kitchen.) A simple Singapore dish calls for dried fish to be crumbled, rinsed, and fried until crisp in a small quantity of oil. The fish is then removed with a slotted spoon, and a combination of bean sprouts, scallions, chili peppers, and garlic is added to the same hot oil and tossed quickly over high heat. When the vegetables are just cooked, the fish is returned, tossed, and the dish is served.

Squid is an extremely popular dried food, often served in conjunction with fresh squid in a Chinese dish. With its fishy flavor and chewy texture, it's a letdown to first-time eaters who compare it to fresh squid. But if one accepts it as a food unto itself, it's a taste well worth acquiring. Dried squid is softened for 24 hours in cold water to which a few teaspoons of baking soda have been added. The purple membrane is then peeled off and the squid picked over. It should be soaked again in fresh cold water for another hour or so before it is used. The bodies, like fresh squid, should be scored with a sharp knife on the inside in a crosshatch pattern with cuts ¼ inch apart, taking care not to slice through the squid. Depending on their size, the bodies should be cut into about six pieces and parboiled for 30 seconds before using.

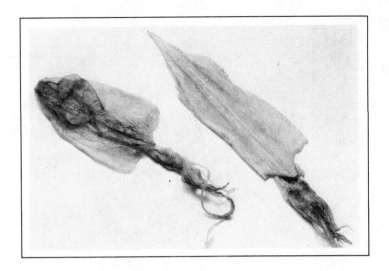

It's interesting to note that among those seeking fortunes in California in the 1800s, the Chinese alone appreciated abalone, most of which they dried and shipped back to China. And dried oysters from California's coast sustained the Chinese railroad workers in the latter part of the century. Sold in gift boxes, dried abalone is expensive. After an overnight soak in cold water and simmering for a few hours, abalone must be sliced thinly before it is used. The full flavor of dried oysters can be appreciated only after they are soaked in cold water, washed, and soaked again in changes of warm water until they are satisfactorily softened. Cleaning them of sand is the final step.

Certain dried sea oddities have become popular along the way, such as the fleshy lips of large groupers and the soft rim of turtle shells. More mundane items such as sea cucumbers, fish maw, shark's fin, and jellyfish are discussed individually in this chapter, as are other dried seafoods of particular interest.

FISH MAW

OTHER NAMES: Fried conger
pike maw, Pike maw

REGION OF USE: China

Not really the maw of the fish but rather the air bladder—a balloon-like organ that acclimates the fish to different water pressures—these are sold in 4-ounce packages that, because of their bulkiness, sometimes hang from overhead racks in grocery stores. The bulkiness results from frying the maw after it's cleaned and dried, which breaks down its tough fiber and puffs it up. Popularly from a fish called a conger pike, the maw is large and cream-colored; it's one of the few foods that shrinks when soaked. Although it gives off a kind of a low-tide smell, soaked maw has little flavor to speak of, but its spongy, soft, gelatinous texture absorbs rich stocks and sauces. It has been eaten upon occasion soaked in honey, but the concept might take some getting used to; soup is more common.

Fish maw isn't terribly hard to soak. One method (among several) is to soak it, weighted down by a plate, for 3 hours in cold water. Once it begins to soften, squeeze it occasionally to get rid of air bubbles (it will crackle softly). At the end of 3 hours, squeeze it once more and soak it for 10 minutes in hot water to which a little vinegar and Shaoxing wine have been added. Drain, rinse, squeeze again, and cut into inch-wide strips.

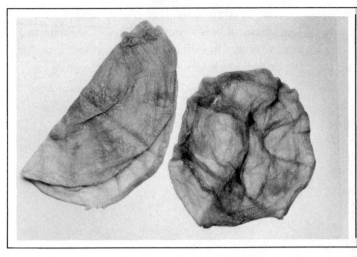

JELLYFISH
(Rhopilema esculenta)

OTHER NAMES: Dried jellyfish skin

REGION OF USE: China

"It's like eating rubber bands" is the typical judgment of a first-time consumer of jellyfish, which is usually served at room temperature in a light sesame oil dressing. It's thoroughly flavorless, and such is the Chinese appreciation of texture that the crunch of those "rubber bands" determines its price.

The fish itself, a gelatinous mass with tentacles (which are removed before it's dried), is a species harvested throughout southern Asian waters, much of it coming these days from Chinese packers in Malaysia and the Philippines. Large and round, when dried, the top edible part of the body or "skin" is thin, golden in color, and up to 18 inches in diameter. Before soaking, the texture is like plastic.

As the fish grows older, unlike most creatures, the top of the body grows thinner and more desirable. A well-stocked Chinese market, especially those handling Shanghai foods, may have three or four grades of jellyfish, the best of which is sold in bulk out of large decorative crocks; $6 to $8 a pound is usually tops.

Dried jellyfish also comes in 1-pound plastic bags, whole or sliced—or rather, hacked into shreds. Since the presentation of jellyfish can be beautiful in a cold banquet-style "salad" (see page 160), it's better to slice it yourself. Buy the top grade since you won't be using tons of it.

Why is this eaten? Besides being a fat-free protein (related to albumen, the egg white protein) that provides A and B vitamins, with a reputation for lowering blood pressure, it's another of those tasteless, crunchy, gelatinous delicacies—which include tree fungi, sea cucumber, and bird's nest—that will prevent your bones from getting brittle as you age, that is, it keeps you young. And you grow to appreciate the crunch, like a fine wine.

To soak and prepare dried jellyfish, unfold the pieces, cover them with cold water, and soak overnight, changing the water a couple of times. Before using it, parboil the skins briefly, 15 seconds or so, then immediately run them under cold water. Roll them up one at a time and slice as thinly as you can.

This Shanghai banquet dish, with its white threads of chicken and daikon, golden threads of jellyfish, and flecks of bright green scallion, is beautiful to look at—it gleams. It is also crunchy and flavorful, and makes an exotic buffet dish since it can be made ahead and is served at room temperature.

JELLYFISH, DAIKON, AND CHICKEN BREAST SALAD

Yield: 8 servings

½ pound dried salted jellyfish

1 daikon (Asian radish; about 1 pound)

2 teaspoons coarse salt

½ large chicken breast

½ egg white

1 teaspoon cornstarch

1 teaspoon sesame oil

3 cups water

SCALLION OIL DRESSING

½ teaspoon salt

1½ teaspoons sugar

2 teaspoons Shaoxing wine

3 tablespoons peanut oil

2 tablespoons sesame oil

3 scallions, chopped (green part included)

Soak the jellyfish sheets in a large bowl of cold water for 24 hours, changing the water a few times.

Peel the daikon with a swivel-bladed vegetable peeler. Cut it into thin slices; stack the slices and cut into matchstick-size shreds. Put the shreds in a large mixing bowl, toss with the coarse salt, and let stand 1 hour.

Meanwhile, drain the water from the jellyfish bowl. Pour boiling water over the jellyfish, and let it stand 15 seconds. Then drain, run under cold water, and set aside.

Bone and skin the chicken breast, slice it thinly, then cut the slices into shreds. Mix the chicken with the egg white, cornstarch, and sesame oil. Refrigerate for 30 minutes.

While the chicken is marinating, cut the jellyfish into shreds by rolling up each sheet and slicing it thinly. Place these in a large bowl. In a towel or with your hands, wring most of the moisture from the daikon shreds, and add them to the bowl with the jellyfish.

Heat the water in a saucepan. When it boils, turn off the heat and add the chicken shreds, stirring to separate the pieces. Once the pieces are separated, turn the heat back on and simmer them for 1 minute. Drain, and rinse under cold water to stop the cooking. Drain again, and add to the bowl with the jellyfish.

Make the scallion oil dressing: Blend the salt and sugar with the wine until they dissolve. Heat the oils in a saucepan, and add the seasoned wine. (It will sputter and evaporate.) When the oil is hot—don't let it smoke—turn off the heat and add the scallions. Allow the dressing to cool, then toss it with the jellyfish, daikon, and chicken shred mixture right before serving. Transfer to an attractive platter.

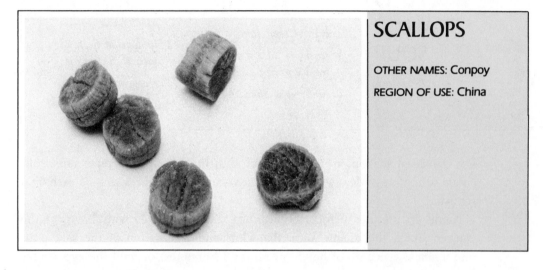

SCALLOPS

OTHER NAMES: Conpoy

REGION OF USE: China

Not exactly the sea scallop we know, but close, this 1-inch golden round is called a conpoy by the English, a transliteration of the Chinese *ganbei*. Rarely if ever eaten fresh, the dried scallop is a prized ingredient, sold in bulk in Chinese apothecaries and fine markets, and also in 8-ounce plastic gift boxes. In this country, large whole scallops cost around $40 a pound.

Used prudently to flavor soups, congee (sometimes called "rice porridge"), or sauces for delicate ingredients such as winter or fuzzy melon, dried scallops usually are first steamed a few at a time in a little bowl of water and/or Shao-xing wine for 30 minutes, or until they can be pulled apart into shreds. The liquid they sit in should be reserved and added to the sauce or soup.

At special occasions, however, dried scallops can be the main attraction of a dish, usually a soup, in the manner of shark's fin or bird's nest. My former cooking teacher, the late Virginia Lee, would spend days pulling apart dried scallops into fine strands for a dish she called "golden hair," which turned ou' to be a golden fried mass dribbled with a light sauce.

The place to buy dried scallops for a reasonable price and, although they keep almost indefinitely, to guarantee they haven't sat for years, is a well-appointed Chinese herbal shop. You can also save money by purchasing them in halves or even pieces. Dried scallops the size of bay scallops are also for sale, but lack the flavor of the larger ones.

Store dried scallops in a covered jar on a shelf.

Actually a steamed egg-white custard topped with soup, this dish, loaded with dried scallops—far more desirable to the Chinese than the fresh—is authentic and unusual.

CHINESE FRESH AND DRIED SCALLOP SOUP

Yield: 8 servings

6 *dried scallops*

½ *cup water*

8 *ounces sea scallops*

6 *egg whites*

2½ *cups chicken stock*

1 *teaspoon juice from freshly grated ginger*

1 *tablespoon Shaoxing wine*

1½ *teaspoons salt*

½ *cup chopped scallions*

1 *tablespoon cornstarch mixed with 3 tablespoons water*

1 *tablespoon freshly melted chicken fat*

1 *teaspoon sesame oil*

½ *teaspoon white pepper*

Put the dried scallops in a small bowl with the water, and steam until soft, about 30 minutes. Meanwhile, cut the sea scallops into three rounds each, and set aside.

About 15 minutes before serving, mix the egg whites with 1 cup of the chicken stock, the ginger juice, the wine, and 1 teaspoon of the salt; pour into a shallow heatproof bowl. Steam for 10 minutes, or until the egg whites have set.

While the egg whites steam, crumble the softened dried scallops and add them, with the liquid they steamed in, to a saucepan. Add the remaining 1½ cups stock, bring to a boil, season with the remaining ½ teaspoon salt, and lower to a simmer.

When the egg whites are done, remove the serving bowl from the steamer. Raise the heat under the stock to high, add the sea scallops and the scallions to the stock, and return to a boil. Give the cornstarch mixture a quick stir, and add it to the stock. Cook, stirring, until the stock thickens. Pour this gently over the egg whites. Dribble with the fat and sesame oil, sprinkle with the pepper, and serve.

SHRIMP

OTHER NAMES: Kung haeng (Thai)

REGION OF USE: China, Southeast Asia

The fishiness of dried shrimp puts some people off, but the flavor they add, which is worth getting used to, is the reason they're a staple seasoning throughout tropical Asia. These tiny pink crustaceans also flavor the food of West Africa and Brazil.

They're tossed whole into Chinese vegetable dishes, soups, and congee; chopped, they're mixed with pork and stuffed in wontons and dumplings. Used in Burma, Thailand, and environs almost like salt and pepper in the West, ground dried shrimp seasons salads such as green papaya or cucumber, soups, spring roll stuffings, and noodle dishes including the sweet Thai *mee krob*.

To prepare dried shrimp for Chinese cooking, they're ordinarily soaked, but there are no hard rules. They may be softened in warm water or steamed briefly. The liquid surrounding them can be added to the dish or discarded, depending on how much flavor you want. Shaoxing wine may be used as a soaking liquid to further mitigate their taste. Since I'm of the eat-them-like-peanuts school, I don't think a lot of soaking and rinsing is necessary. To flavor broths, they needn't be soaked at all.

For Southeast Asian cooking, buy the shrimp whole and grind them yourself with a mortar or in a food processor. "Shrimp powder" or "Ground Dried Shrimp" is sold in jars in Southeast Asian markets, but the quality isn't high. Surprisingly good is "Shrimp Powder w/Chilli," packaged in 3.5-ounce jars by the Pantainorasingh company in Thailand.

Sold mostly in 8-ounce plastic packages, and in bulk in Chinese and Southeast Asian food stores, dried shrimp are imported from Thailand, China, and elsewhere. The most prized in Asian markets here, and also the largest—they're over an inch in length—come from Louisiana and average $12 to $15 a pound. Dried shrimp for most purposes can be purchased for half that. Look for those that are pinkish orange, as they brown with age and lose or sometimes change flavor. Unlike other dried foods, they do not keep indefinitely on the shelf, but rather should be kept in a covered container in a cool place out of the light. Refrigerate if you expect to keep them for more than a month.

SHRIMP EGGS. These delicately flavored little grains, also called shrimp roe, are sold by the ounce in Chinese markets that carry foodstuffs from Shanghai. They're delicious sprinkled over soup, congee, or in stirred (scrambled) eggs. Dried shrimp roe is bottled with soy sauce in Shanghai; this makes a tasty condiment for dip sauces or for cooking.

If you haven't tried dried shrimp, this refreshing salad is a tasty introduction; you may want to use more than the recipe calls for. This salad can be made ahead; in fact it benefits from sitting at least 15 minutes.

THAI CUCUMBER SALAD		
Yield: 6 to 8 servings	2 heaping tablespoons dried shrimp	3 tablespoons fresh lime juice
	2 cucumbers	1½ tablespoons fish sauce
	¼ cup round, thin fresh red chili pepper slices (with seeds)	2 tablespoons sugar
		1 tablespoon sesame oil
	3 tablespoons chopped red onion	¼ cup chopped roasted or fried peanuts

Using a mortar or food processor, grind the shrimp to a coarse powder.

Peel the cucumbers. Cut off the ends, cut them in half lengthwise, and scrape out the seeds. Slice them thinly into half-moons. Place the cucumbers in a bowl along with the chili slices and onion. Add the ground shrimp, lime juice, fish sauce, sugar, and sesame oil, and toss well. Allow to sit or serve immediately, sprinkled with the peanuts.

SEAWEED

It's not news that seaweed is gastronomically vital to the Japanese diet, a fact pretty much determined by geography. By the same token a lot of seaweed is consumed or sometimes just chewed on by the Irish, Scotch, and Welsh who live on the North Atlantic coast. In Asia, seaweed is important to the Korean diet as well. And while it's not quite so closely associated with Chinese food, kelp, fresh and dried, and "laver," or *nori* as the Japanese call it, are staples along the Eastern coast and in the north of China; and the Chinese alone eat a kind of seaweed-like moss called "hairlike vegetable." The popular gelatin agar-agar, used in food throughout East Asia, is made from various seaweeds.

	KELP
OTHER NAMES: Konbu, Kombu, Sea tangle	**KELP**
REGION OF USE: Japan, Korea, China	**(Laminaria spp.)**

The main culinary use for kelp is in combination with dried bonito flakes to make the all-purpose Japanese sea stock *dashi*. The kelp's purpose is as a flavor enhancer; in fact it was from kelp that MSG was first extracted by the Japanese.

The kelp for dashi is gathered off the northern Japanese island of Hokkaido. The endlessly long olive-brown leaves, which average 5 or 6 inches in width, are dried in the sun, and packaged cut and folded. Sold as "Dashi Konbu," a 6-ounce package will be enough for making six batches of stock for four to six people. The whitish coating on konbu is perfectly okay. The kelp should never be washed, or it will lose flavor. Some Japanese chefs score it to help release its flavor-enchancing glutamic acid into the stock.

Used dried or fresh, kelp may also serve as a vegetable. On the eastern coast of China, it's simmered with other ingredients such as chicken. Perhaps because of its supposed cooling properties—it's very *yin* and too much of it is thought to be debilitating—it's cooked with a lot of fat or oil, which is considered warming. Chinese markets carry 8-ounce plastic packages of kelp simply labeled "Dried Sea Weed."

The Japanese package a couple of cuts of kelp for eating. As threads, it's soaked briefly and eaten sautéed or as a salad vegetable. It is not as tasty as *wakame* (see page 167), but vinegar cuts some of its unpleasant tidal-pool qualities. A kind of thin konbu is used as a wrapper for meat, fish, or vegetable rolls known as *konbu-maki*, which are served in soup. For the popular Japanese stew *oden*, thin kelp is cut into strips, tied in knots like little bow ties, and tossed in.

LAVER

(Porphyra spp.)

OTHER NAMES: Nori, Asakusa nori, Purple laver, Purple seaweed

REGION OF USE: Japan, Korea, China

Most familiar as the wrapping for sushi rolls, this is any of a few related species of seaweeds, or more correctly, marine algae.

According to food authority Shizuo Tsuji, nori has been produced in Japan since the seventeenth century by planting bamboo stakes in shallow offshore waters and letting the algae accumulate against them. It was then rinsed in cold water and dried on wooden frames, forming thin sheets. Today the process is highly mechanized, as the Japanese consume billions of sheets. This laver is also harvested and processed in Korea, and experiments in production have begun on the northwest coast of the United States.

By far, the most common use of nori is as a cylindrical shell for vinegared, sweetened rice, or sushi. Nori also may be used chopped in tempura batter; and in Korea strips are sometimes coated with a paste of glutinous rice flour and sesame seeds, and deep-fried. The eastern Chinese use it in soups; for example, the stock for authentic wonton soup in Shanghai contains nori, dried shrimp, pickled vegetable, dark soy sauce, and a little fresh pork lard.

Japanese markets, naturally, have the largest selection of nori, which ranges from dark green to purple and is sold in sheets measuring about 7 × 8 inches. Chinese markets, especially those that carry northern or Shanghai goods, offer a small selection, usually of packages of ten folded dark purple sheets.

To bring out its flavor and keep it from becoming tough and gummy, nori should be toasted before it is used, by passing one side over a gas flame a few times until crisp. Toasted or "roasted" nori (*yaki-nori* or *yaki sushi nori*) is sold in Japanese markets, and it makes sense to use these, particularly if you have an electric stove; these sheets are sold flat rather than folded.

You get what you pay for with nori sheets; for sushi, buy the best, which may run over $3 for ten sheets (7/10 ounce). Nori also is sold in packages of 50 and 100.

NOTE: A minced green nori, one of the flavorings in *shichimi* (see page 237), is sold in shakers in Japanese markets, to be used for seasoning food. Japanese snacks such as potato chips are sprinkled with it.

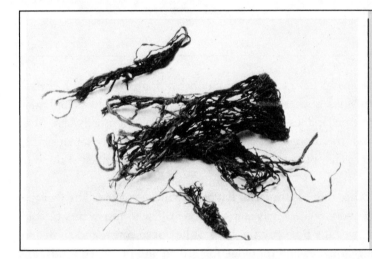

WAKAME
(Undaria pinnatifida)

REGION OF USE: Japan, Korea

If you have a sudden craving for seaweed, *wakame* should be your choice. After they are soaked, the leaves of the plant are briefly cooked in soups or used to make a delicious salad, even by themselves in a light vinegary dressing. In Japan wakame is eaten fresh in the spring. Here, it's found only dried, usually packaged in narrow plastic bags sometimes labeled *ito-wakame;* and it's expensive, around $2.50 an ounce.

Wakame can be reconstituted by soaking it in hot water for a few minutes; but it's better to pour tepid water over it and let it stand for 20 minutes, to maintain its flavor and high nutritional value. If the stem of the seaweed is present, it should be discarded.

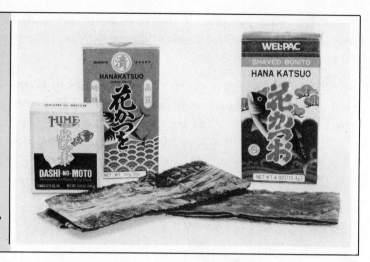

DASHI
(Japanese Sea Stock)

Left to right: instant dashi, bonito flakes, and konbu (kelp)

Japanese cooking seems to have an unusual number of ingredients that it doesn't share with other cuisines, such as *wasabi,* the green horseradish-like condiment for sushi, and *sansho,* or Japanese pepper, the dried berry of a prickly ash. Most uniquely, rather than traditional meat, chicken, or fish stock, the Japanese use *dashi,* made from kelp (konbu) and flakes of dried bonito, a member of the tuna family.

More than any other ingredient, dashi flavors Japanese cuisine. The fact that it's called for in so many recipes may put someone off who just wants to cook a Japanese dish or two. It's not only the base of Japanese soups and simmered dishes, it's used in marinades and toppings for grilled and pan-fried foods, and it's standard to many dipping sauces and salad dressings.

The problem with dashi is that there is no substitute; you must have access to a Japanese food store to get the ingredients. Once purchased, however, the ingredients keep (they're dried), and the stock is easy to make.

It's especially easy if you use instant dashi, *dashi-no-moto,* as many Japanese home cooks do. It isn't bad, and it's available in Japanese food stores in large tea-type bags, packaged in various size boxes. For a single cup of dashi, individual bags are also available. And Kikkoman puts out a liquid concentrate, with wine as a preservative, in 6.7-fluid-ounce bottles.

What's better, however, is to buy the bonito flakes (*katsuo bushi*), and the konbu (see page 165) and make your own fresh stock. (Though rarely done, what's even better is to buy the dried woodlike filets of bonito and shave them yourself, as needed, with a tool called a *katsuo-kezuri-ki,* which looks like a carpenter's plane.)

1 *4 × 6-inch piece (or the equivalent) konbu*

4½ cups cold water

About ⅓ loosely packed (1 package) dried bonito flakes

Place the konbu and water in a saucepan and bring to a boil over medium-high heat. As soon as the water boils, remove the pan from the heat and let it stand for 3 minutes. (You don't want the konbu to boil; it gives off a strong odor.) Take out the kelp and bring the stock to a boil again; then turn off the heat and immediately stir in the bonito flakes. Let them sit until they sink, and then strain the stock through cheesecloth or a coffee filter. Dashi will keep 3 to 4 days refrigerated.

HAIR VEGETABLE

(Nostoc commune)

OTHER NAMES: Black moss, Black sea moss, Hairlike vegetable, Fat choy (Cantonese)

REGION OF USE: China, Japan

Not a true seaweed, but related, this alga, dried, indeed looks like matted black hair and, once soaked, like something yanked from a tidal flat. What's a revelation, even to Chinese who have been eating it for years, is that hair vegetable is not even gathered from the sea, but rather grows in the Mongolian desert in water from mountain springs. The alga is a prized medicinal—like seaweeds, considered very cooling. And as a Chinese pharmacologist explained to me, "It's fiber that cleans out your system." The Chinese *materia medica* advises to eat it when "your guts are knotted up." It looks in fact like a scouring pad for your insides, which is perhaps why it's popular at New Year's, when everyone cleans house, so to speak, and starts anew.

Unusual culinary effects can be achieved with this alga. At a Sichuan banquet I attended, it served as the fur of small lifelike pandas made of minced fish in a dish called Pandas at Play. However, it's usually eaten more simply, for example as part of a vegetable/mushroom platter.

Before it is used, the hair vegetable should be soaked in cold water for 30 minutes or so, and rinsed well. Some dishes call for steaming it—5 to 10 minutes will do—with simple seasonings such as salt, sugar, and wine, and then pouring a light chicken stock sauce over it. It also may be deep-fried. Expensive, it's sold in Chinese markets in 1.3-ounce packages for around $3; Chinese pharmacies sell it in bulk.

AGAR-AGAR

OTHER NAMES: Kanten (Japanese), Japanese or Chinese gelatin

REGION OF USE: China, Japan, Southeast Asia

The slippery, gelatinous sweets flavored with almond, coconut, and black soy-beans that are wheeled around on *dim sum* carts, as well as garishly colored little molded jellies flavored with jasmine, pandan, and even creamed corn—popular in Southeast Asia—all owe their solidity to this gelatin processed from seaweed. Originally from a kind of red alga the Japanese call *tengusa*, agar-agar is now extracted from a number of seaweeds by boiling, filtering, and freeze-drying.

Known mostly in the West as a culture for bacteria (agar-agar is sold in pharmacies), its use as a gelatin has yet to be exploited by Western cooks. Its advantages include setting and melting at a higher temperature than regular gelatin (useful in the days before refrigeration) and gelling quickly, thus seal-ing in fresh flavors if fruit or other foods are used with it.

Agar-agar is carried in almost all Chinese, Japanese, and Southeast Asian food markets in two forms: 2- to 4-ounce packages of 14-inch strands that look like crinkled cellophane, and packages of two feather-light rectangular sticks, 10 inches long. The strands, after a 30-minute soaking in cold water, are cut and used like noodles in Chinese salads with such ingredients as chicken and shredded radish. They also may augment bird's nest in soup, thus cutting its cost.

Generally, ⅔ ounce of agar-agar will gel 1 quart of liquid, but the propor-tions are best learned by experience since the liquid may include other ingre-dients, such as sugar, that affect its gelling properties.

To use agar-agar as a gelatin, cut the strips or tear the sticks into pieces and soak in cold water for 20 minutes. Wring the pieces out and add to cold water in a saucepan. (Sugar may be added at this point.) Bring to a boil over medium heat without stirring. Simmer—do not boil—stirring occasionally, until the agar-agar dissolves. Strain, and stir in the other ingredients required by your recipe. Heat again just to a boil. Pour into a mold or dish, and refrigerate (not necessary to gel agar-agar, but it speeds up the process).

THE CHINESE DELICACIES

More than just their expense, these foods, which would seem to have nothing in common, are gastronomic soul brothers. All are tasteless, depending on the food they're served with for flavor; all are gelatinous, savored mostly for their textural subtleties; all are credited with extraordinary tonic properties; all are processed by drying, and are time consuming if not difficult to prepare; all come in differing grades, which in the case of bird's nest and shark's fin, especially, require knowledge and experience (in other words, a connoisseur) to appreciate; and, at least in recent centuries, all have become status foods, served on special special occasions or to impress.

Bird's nest, shark's fin, and sea slug are in fact part of a larger family of flavorless, gelatinous oddities the Chinese have developed an inordinate appreciation for over the centuries—one of the first being the pad of a bear's paw. These include other rarities such as snow fungus (the reproductive glands of a kind of frog) and the more common white tree fungus, jellyfish, fish "maw," fish lips, and tendons of deer and beef shin.

BIRD'S NEST

OTHER NAMES: Swallow's nest

REGION OF USE: China (and by the Chinese throughout Southeast Asia)

A certain prefect once served large bowls of plain boiled bird's nest. It was completely tasteless. Others praised it, but I said with a smile, "I just came to eat bird's nest, not to get it wholesale." We were each served several ounces of it, to do us honor. Had he given us each a bowlful of pearls, we would have valued them as much, and found them quite as inedible.

—Yuan Mei, eighteenth-century renaissance man and
writer about food (as quoted in *Chinese Gastronomy*)

If, as has been suggested, the first person to eat an oyster was brave, how about the person who first sampled the regurgitated spittle, sometimes peppered with feathers and twigs, of a swift, called "bird's nest"? However it came to be that this person imagined it edible, the Chinese who now eat it dole out a small fortune to get it.

The birds responsible, three species of the genus *Collacallia,* live in the East Asian tropics and build their nests in colonies in huge caverns where it's often precarious to gather them. During the breeding season, the salivary glands of both male and female birds secrete a gelatinous liquid for nest-making. The nests crafted by certain of these swifts are practically all saliva; the most desirable, they're called "white nests." The top grade of these on the market may be nearly complete white cups. Those sold in broken pieces are called "dragon's teeth" and, while expensive, are much less so.

Less esteemed are the "black nests" containing moss, feathers, and grass to augment the saliva. Commonly for sale and least expensive (shunned by serious cooks) is precleaned bird's nest in varying grades that looks somewhat granular. Not cheap, at last check at a well-appointed store in San Francisco's Chinatown, the best of this was $34 for 3½ ounces—enough for about six servings. At the same store, a 12-ounce twine-wrapped bundle of "white nest" from Thailand, complete with a few feathers to be picked, sold for $550.

Bird's nest is considered an elixir of the first order. Like all the gelatinous delicacies, it is thought to stave off the brittleness of age. In the case of bird's nest, its predigested protein and nutrients are easy on the stomach, good for the very young or the very old. For anyone, it's thought to preserve the complexion and is prescribed for those recovering from a long illness.

Usually Chinese cookbooks give matter-of-fact methods for soaking and preparing bird's nest, as if it were just another ingredient like zucchini. However, like shark's fin, bird's nest is very difficult for the unexperienced home cook to make any sense of. It's a good idea to have tasted different grades in the company of someone who understands it. Instructions on buying it, and on soaking and picking the nests, from a chef who knows the ingredient would help.

That said, there are different opinions about soaking bird's nest for cooking. Some feel it's best to soak it overnight in cold water, then clean it, removing feathers and other foreign matter with tweezers, and finally to simmer it for 10 minutes in water or stock, and drain it before using it. A quicker method calls for soaking it for 1 hour in warm water, cleaning it, then soaking it for 5 minutes in a bowl of hot water in which a little baking soda has been dissolved; it should then be rinsed thoroughly in cold water and squeezed dry.

Bird's nest is not traditionally overadorned. Classically it's swimming in a clear rich stock surrounded by steamed pigeon eggs that are garnished with minced ham and coriander leaves. This is of course a soup, but the term doesn't do it justice. A bird's nest soup made with finely minced chicken, egg white, and wine, and garnished with ham, is also prized. The most spectacular version I've ever seen (or sampled) was baked in a pumpkin that had been lightly carved and deep-fried to look like an antique urn. Bird's nest also is often steamed with water and rock sugar to make a sweet soup.

To cut its expense, bird's nest is sometimes supplemented by white tree fungus or agar-agar.

SEA SLUG
(Holothurioidea)

OTHER NAMES: Sea cucumber, Bêche de mer

REGION OF USE: China, Japan

One of the earliest references to the sea slug, the boneless and shell-less Chinese gastronomic prize that creeps along the ocean floor, is in a pre-fifth-century fragment of a work scholars call *The Canon of Gastronomy*, which no longer exists. The name of the sea slug at the time was *hai-shu*, or "sea rat," and it was described simply as "looking like a leach, but larger."

Somewhere between that time and the Ming period, about a thousand years later, the creature's status had been upgraded considerably. Its name had become, as it's called today, *hai-shen*, or roughly, "ginseng of the sea." A Ming period writer explaining the etymology said that it was named by the people who caught the sea slug in the North China Sea. They felt that this flabby sea animal had the same wondrous medicinal properties as ginseng, which was native to their region.

The Chinese have harvested the sea slug for centuries, along the length of their own coast and beyond. A thousand years ago they ventured as far as East Africa in search of it. In 1415 the king of what is now Sri Lanka, annoyed at the hundreds of Chinese ships fishing for sea slugs right off his shore, ordered them away. The Chinese sent an army after him, captured him, and continued to fish.

The Chinese have culled the waters for this creature east to Fiji and south to the tropical waters off Australia, which by the beginning of this century were nearly fished out. An article in the May 19, 1986, *Wall Street Journal* described a modern shortage of sea slugs in China that has led to soaring prices and black market sales.

When caught, sea slugs are dried as hard as a rock and shipped to market. After soaking them for several days, boiling them in changes of stock or water, and cleaning them, one is left with a spongy, translucent seafood that when finally cooked has a tasteless crunch reminiscent of boiled pork fat. In spite of centuries of enjoyment, the Chinese have not managed to spread their love for this creature much beyond their borders.*

According to a Ming period description, the sea slug is "warming and restorative." Modern dietary experts might praise the fact that pound for pound, it has almost four times the protein of beef and zero cholesterol. But above all else was its supposed ability to enhance male virility. In an era when appearances counted, the sea slug was a phallic-shaped creature that swelled to the touch. A 16th-century Chinese work reported that people in North China who couldn't get the sea slug "take the penis of a donkey and use it as a substitute."

Usually, but not necessarily, featured in a dish, sea slugs are often cooked with other ingredients that give it a little flavor, such as pork, chicken, or mushrooms; they may be part of a seafood conglomeration in a dish called Happy Family; or they're added to soups. Sea slugs are most distinguished by the time involved in preparing them, which literally takes days. There are practically as many soaking and cleaning methods as there are cooks who cook them, but the goal is always a certain gelatinous resilience.

Sea slugs are sold in a variety of sizes. The prices vary from $5 a pound for large black, spiny sea slugs to $30 a pound for small (2-inch-long) black, spiny sea slugs from Korea. The small slugs are valued because they can be served whole, but there's more cleaning involved. For around $15 a pound very good smallish (4-inch) sea slugs can be purchased. Some stores carry them presoaked, but that eliminates the fun of working with this animal. Half a pound of dried sea slugs will yield about 1 pound soaked.

SEA SLUG PREPARATION METHOD #1. Place the sea slugs in a large bowl with warm water to cover, and soak them for 3 days, changing the water every day. At the end of 3 days they should be softened; if not, continue another day or two. When they are soft, cut the sea slugs open lengthwise, and while rinsing them under cold tap water, clean the insides of debris and sand: Using your hands, pull out and rub away as much as you can. Rinse and then simmer the

---

*The Japanese sometimes eat them sliced raw in vinegar at sushi bars.

sea slugs in light chicken or pork stock for 10 minutes. Discard the stock, rinse the sea slugs in cold water, and scrape away the inside membrane of the animals. Simmer them again in fresh stock, which again should be drained and discarded at the end of 10 minutes. Rinse the sea slugs, picking over them a final time if necessary.

SEA SLUG PREPARATION METHOD #2. With heatproof tongs, hold the sea slugs over a gas flame, turning them from side to side for about 1 minute. (They will singe slightly.) Put them in a large bowl, cover with warm water, and soak overnight. Then drain, place them in plenty of fresh water, and simmer, covered, for 1½ hours. Let cool in the liquid, then drain and rinse. Soak overnight in fresh warm water once more. Drain the sea slugs and rinse. Then slit open their abdomens and clean out whatever happens to be inside, scraping it away with your fingernail. Simmer the sea slugs a final time in a large quantity of water with a bunch of scallions tied in a bundle and 5 or 6 slices of peeled fresh ginger.

SHARK'S FIN
(Mustelus manazo,
Carcharias dussumieri,
and others)

REGION OF USE: China

The term "soup" doesn't adequately convey the luxuriousness of a shark's fin dish. An exquisitely rich stock is often the medium for what turns out to be clear, amber-colored gelatinous strands that have little flavor save a hint of the sea; the "soup" may include crabmeat and/or crab roe as well. Shark's fin may also be stuffed into a duck and steamed, or scrambled in eggs; and there's a beautifully pleated shark's fin dumpling that's offered in *dim sum* houses. Shark's fin restaurants in Hong Kong list a page or more of shark's fin dishes, some costing hundreds of dollars for a small bowl.

A symbol of the world's most extravagant banquet fare, shark's fin on a Chinese menu, as some are surprised to learn, is indeed shark's fin, meaning the dorsal "comb fin," or the two ventral fins of any of a variety of sharks, most of which swim in warm Asian waters. Considering Chinese food history, eating shark's fin isn't an ancient practice; it didn't come into vogue until the Song Dynasty (960–1279).

Aside from its status as a general tonic, shark's fin "opens the stomach," according to the sixteenth-century *materia medica,* meaning it's an appetite stimulator. It may start a meal, or served at the peak of a banquet, it readies you for the onslaught of dishes to follow.

Sold only dried, it's not meat that's eaten from these fins, but rather the needles that make up the interior. To prepare them involves an elaborate process of soaking and boiling in changes of water and richly seasoned stock, a chore not tackled by many home cooks. Available at Chinese herbal shops and fine groceries, shark's fins are typically skinned, simmered, and scraped clean of most of their unwanted mucilaginous material before they come to market. The price ranges from $40 a pound for strands to $70 a pound and up for the whole fin, the finest of which are dorsal fins, thick and pale yellow in color. In the most lavish presentation, the fin is served intact, which involves wrapping the fin while it's prepared, traditionally in a special silver net.

Chefs each have their own procedure for preparing shark's fin. The goal is to achieve a soft yet resilient texture while eliminating any fishy smell.

TO PREPARE SHARK'S FIN: Soak 1 pound fin (whole or "needles") in a generous amount of cold water for 24 hours, changing the water three or four times. Drain, and scrub the fin as best you can with a brush. Add the fin to a wok or large pot filled with cold water, and slowly heat to boiling. Drain, and put the fin in cold water again.

When the fin has cooled, rinse it and put it into a heatproof bowl. Heat 3 to 4 tablespoons oil in a wok and add 6 scallions and 12 slices of ginger. Stir until fragrant; then add 1 tablespoon Shaoxing wine and 2 cups rich stock (made from ¼ duck and 1 whole chicken), and bring to a boil. Strain the stock and pour it over the fin, put the bowl with the fin in a steamer, and steam for 3 hours. Remove the fin, discarding the cooking liquid, and carefully rinse it in three changes of hot water. It is now ready to use in most shark's fin recipes. Most simply, it may be again put into a heatproof bowl, covered with 3 cups of a rich chicken-duck stock that has been seasoned, including a little soy sauce for color, and steamed for another hour or more. Before serving, it may be dribbled with some freshly rendered chicken fat and garnished with minced or slivered Smithfield ham.

NOTE: Strands of shark's fin already soaked, simmered, and softened are found for sale frozen in 8-ounce packages in some Chinese and Southeast Asian stores. Rather than use these, I would start from scratch; but if you must, these should be simmered for 15 minutes or so in stock, which should then be discarded, before using in whatever dish you like.

SALTED AND
CURED INGREDIENTS

Chinese-restaurant-goers, especially non-Asians, rarely get to taste them—they're considered too "home-style." Nevertheless preserved vegetables have added rich flavor and nutrition to Chinese braised foods, soups, stews, dumplings, and stir-fried dishes for centuries. Members of the cabbage family—most are mustards or radish—they're cured primarily with salt.

Sometimes referred to or even labeled "Plum Vegetables," ancient curing directions specified that they be set in salt or brine in the twelfth lunar month (around January), when the winter plum blossoms first show, and removed from their pickling bath in the late spring, when the plums are ripening, to dry in the sun. The finest, after pickling and drying, are steamed and dried two times. Dark and richly flavored, the very best of these are sprinkled with sesame oil during the second steaming, for example *gan-cai-sun* (dried fermented mustard), which is traditionally cooked with pork belly.

Preserved vegetables are often cooked with pork or duck. The early Chinese found that they cured the meat somewhat, keeping it from spoiling for a week or more. The provinces on China's east coast—Anhui, Zhejiang, Jiangsu—are famous for this sort of product.

Preserved vegetables come in a variety of packaging. Some are sold out of large decorative crocks; on the shelves they are found in small crocks or cans. Plastic packages of 1 pound are the most common. The label "Preserved Vegetable" almost always means mustard green. Next to mustard in popularity, golden-colored "Preserved Turnip" (radish) comes minced for use in congee and dumpling stuffings, in small lumps ("Turnip Pulp") for braising with meat, or you can buy the whole pickled plant, including leaves.

Preserved vegetables should be rinsed, as some are sandy.

SICHUAN PRESERVED VEGETABLE (also Sichuan Preserved Mustard Stem, Sichuan Preserved Radish). Widely available and popular—sold in cans and in bulk from crocks—these rubbery green lumps are cured in ground chili pepper and salt. From a variety called "swollen stem mustard," native to Sichuan, the vegetable, sliced and cooked in plain water, makes one of the richest vegetarian stocks imaginable. Chopped, the vegetable is added to dumpling stuffings and dip sauces, or it may be cut into matchstick shreds and stir-fried with pork. It keeps indefinitely in a covered jar. If you can, buy it in bulk. The next best choice is a 12-ounce can labeled "Szechuan Preserved Vegetable," from Shanghai.

Most salted and cured or "preserved" vegetables aren't totally dried. Dried bamboo shoots (expensive and delicious in braised dishes) and lotus root are two of the more common vegetables that are completely dried. The most intriguing, with a heady aroma like a fine black tea, is mustard greens with bits of bamboo shoot, known as *gan-cai-sun*. (It's in the family of "plum-dried" vegetables discussed in this chapter.) It's used in soups, and braised or steamed with fatty meats such as duck or pork, most classically with pork belly (fresh bacon). It must be rinsed before using. The brand to look for is Yue Jin, which comes in a blue box holding 250 grams.

1½ -pound strip of fresh bacon (pork belly), with rind	¼ cup peanut oil	**FRESH BACON WITH DRIED, FERMENTED MUSTARD GREENS**
Approximately 2½ tablespoons dark soy sauce	8 cloves garlic, smashed	
	3 ounces gan-cai-sun, rinsed thoroughly and drained	(Mei-gan-sun Rou)
1 tablespoon sugar	Fresh coriander sprigs for garnish	Yield: 6 to 8 servings
½ cup Shaoxing wine		

Put the bacon in a large pot with water to cover, and bring to a boil. Turn the heat to low and simmer for 45 minutes. Then drain and rinse the meat, and dry it with paper towels. Rub the rind with a little dark soy sauce and set aside.

Combine 2 tablespoons soy sauce, the sugar, and the wine, and set aside.

Heat a wok over high heat for a minute or so. Add the oil and swirl it around so it coats the bottom of the wok. Add the bacon, rind side down (be careful; it will sputter), and cook, shifting the meat in the oil until the rind is browned, 2 to 3 minutes. Turn off the heat and remove the bacon with two slotted spoons. Set it aside to drain.

Over high heat reheat the oil in the wok, and add the garlic. Stir-fry briefly, until fragrant. Add the mustard greens, and cook, stirring, for 20 seconds. Add the soy sauce/wine mixture, bring to a boil, stirring, and turn off the heat.

Cut the meat into ¼-inch-thick slices, and keeping the slices together, place them in two rows in a 10-inch Pyrex or other heatproof plate. Spoon the mustard greens and sauce over the slices.

Start water boiling in a steamer large enough to hold the plate of bacon, place the plate in the steamer (or in a wok with a rack and cover), cover it, and steam the meat 2½ hours, until it is tender.

To serve, spoon the mustard greens onto a serving platter. Arrange the bacon rind side up on the greens, and pour the sauce over. Garnish with the coriander sprigs.

The garlicky-sour-salty flavor of Tientsin preserved vegetable
is a fine foil for sweet young green beans. Fresh snow
peas will also work well in this recipe.

YOUNG GREEN BEANS WITH TIENTSIN PRESERVED VEGETABLE Yield: 6 servings	1 *pound fresh young green beans* 3 *tablespoons chicken stock* 1 *tablespoon Shaoxing wine* 1 *teaspoon sugar*	¼ *cup peanut oil or freshly rendered chicken fat (see page 320)* 2 *tablespoons Tientsin preserved vegetable*

Pinch off and discard the tips of the green beans. Mix together the stock, wine, and sugar, and set aside.

Over high heat heat a wok or skillet and add the oil. When it is hot, add the green beans and cook, stirring, until well coated with the oil. Add the preserved vegetable and stir briefly. Toss in the seasoned stock, cover, and steam until the beans are nearly tender. Uncover, and stir over high heat until most of the liquid is gone. Serve.

RED-IN-SNOW (also Preserved Snow Cabbages). A cold-resistant mustard, this vegetable is grown only to be salted. The name is said to come from the sight of its red root appearing just above the snow in the spring. A specialty of

Ningbo in Zhejiang province, it's chopped, salted, and canned without the elaborate curing of some of the other preserved vegetables. Red-in-snow is delicious in fried rice or with minced pork or chicken.

The bean curd is mashed up in this dish, and its soft granules contrast nicely with the fresh hot peppers, the pork, and the briny pickle known as "Sichuan preserved vegetable." If you make this once, you'll make it a lot. Serve it hot or at room temperature.

HOME-STYLE BEAN CURD WITH PRESERVED VEGETABLE AND HOT PEPPERS

Yield: 6 to 8 servings

6 to 8 cakes bean curd, about 1½ pounds

½ pound ground pork

1 tablespoon dark soy sauce

6 to 10 small fresh hot chili peppers (red or green)

½ cup chopped scallions (green part included)

2 tablespoons chopped Sichuan preserved vegetable

2 tablespoons light soy sauce

1 tablespoon Shaoxing wine

½ teaspoon sugar

3 tablespoons peanut oil

2 teaspoons cornstarch mixed with ¼ cup water

½ cup chopped coriander leaves

1 tablespoon sesame oil

Mash the bean curd into a pulp with your hands, and set aside in a bowl. Mix the pork with the dark soy sauce and set aside. Seed and chop the peppers, combine them with the scallions and Sichuan vegetable, and set aside. Mix the soy sauce, wine, and sugar.

Over high heat, heat a wok or skillet and add the peanut oil. Add the pork and cook, stirring, until the grains are separated (do not brown). Add the pepper mixture and stir another 30 seconds. Add the soy sauce mixture and stir another 15 seconds. Drain any liquid that has accumulated around the bean curd, and add the bean curd. Cook over high heat until the mixture bubbles. (If the bean curd is dry, add a little water.) Give the cornstarch mixture another stir, and add it. Cook, stirring, for at least 1 minute, or until the mixture thickens and shines. Turn off the heat. Stir in the coriander, dribble with the sesame oil, and serve.

TIENTSIN PRESERVED VEGETABLE. A specialty from around Beijing, this is Chinese celery cabbage pickled with salt and garlic. Available in small shreds in a squat 21-ounce crock, it is used as a condiment for the Chinese rice porridge called congee, and it adds flavor to stir-fried fresh vegetables such as bok choy.

CHINESE CURED MEATS

Left to right: duck liver sausage, sweet sausage,
and winter-cured pork

It may surprise some people to learn that pork products such as ham, bacon, and sausage are as Chinese as chopsticks; they are ancient foods in China. Ham and bacon, in fact, were probably eaten there first.

HAM. *Huo-fu,* or "fire-dried meat," was how the Chinese first referred to ham —or to any meat they cured by soaking in a soy sauce marinade and drying over a slow fire. Ham became specifically *huo-tui,* or "fire thigh," and while we know it as an American food, it has been beloved in certain regions of China for centuries. This is no surprise, considering that the Chinese have a lengthy history of salt curing and that they domesticated the barnyard pig so long ago it has no known ancestor.

China's most famous ham is cured in the southwestern province of Yunnan. The cooking of nearby Hunan also employs ham; one of the signature dishes of that province is a kind of honeyed ham. Another world-class ham comes from Jinhua, south of Shanghai. In that whole eastern region, ham is such a staple that people keep small pieces of it on hand to mince and sprinkle like salt over vegetables and other dishes. One of the hams closest to a hard, dried Chinese ham—which cannot be imported—is our own Smithfield. That's why you'll find these smoked country hams whole and by the piece in Chinese markets that carry Shanghainese goods. This ham keeps indefinitely refrigerated; if mold appears, just scrape it away.

I've always disliked even the idea of those Chinese corn soup recipes that call for canned creamed corn. This version requires fresh-shucked corn, which ideally should be picked within 30 minutes of making the soup. Silver Queen or another white corn variety tastes best and is the most visually appealing.

4 ears very fresh corn	3 tablespoons cornstarch	**FRESH-SHUCKED CORN AND HAM SOUP**
4 egg whites	3 tablespoons water	
3 tablespoons milk	½ teaspoon sesame oil	
4 to 5 cups fresh chicken stock	½ cup minced ham (preferably Smithfield or similar type)	
2 teaspoons salt, or to taste		Yield: 6 to 8 servings

Slice the kernels of corn off the cobs into a bowl. In another bowl, beat the egg whites until they begin to froth, then beat in the milk.

Heat the stock until boiling. Add the salt, then add the corn and bring the stock to a boil again. Blend the cornstarch, water, and sesame oil, and add it to the soup. Stir until the soup is thickened and clear.

Turn off the heat and immediately but slowly pour in the egg white mixture while you stir the soup gently in a circle. Transfer to a tureen, garnish with the ham, and serve.

WINTER-CURED PORK (also soy sauce pork). The world's first bacon, these cured strips of pork belly, dark golden in color, hang by strings in Chinese meat markets. The name "winter cured" comes from an ancient prescription that meats and vegetables be cured in the twelfth lunar month, and this strip is a remnant of the oldest kind of Chinese curing. Traditionally these are soaked in a soy sauce marinade and dry-cured over a slow fire. Diced winter-cured pork is delicious in glutinous rice stuffings, fried rice, turnip cake, stir-fried with vegetables, or any way you might use a full-flavored bacon. A strip will keep for over a month refrigerated. The tough rind must be cut away before the pork is used.

SAUSAGES. Hard red 6-inch-long Chinese sweet sausages (lop chong in Cantonese), made of pork and pork fat, are available in 1-pound packages in Chinese markets or, better, hanging by strings in meat markets or sausage stores in Chinese communities. A darker, grainier duck liver sausage can be purchased in some Chinese markets, which may offer a beef sausage as well.

Before stir-frying, or if they're to be eaten plain, Chinese sausages should be steamed for 15 minutes. If they're to be steamed anyway, for example on rice as it cooks or over chicken as it simmers in a casserole, the sausage needn't be cooked. Chinese sausages will keep for weeks in the refrigerator.

Similar to a French country dish, this Chinese casserole is best cooked and served in a Chinese clay pot. However, any heavy pot that can withstand a direct flame will do.

CHICKEN AND CHINESE SAUSAGE CASSEROLE

Yield: 6 to 8 servings

6 *large dried black mushrooms*

1 *chicken (3½ pounds), cut Chinese-style into small pieces*

2 *tablespoons Shaoxing wine*

1 *teaspoon salt*

1 *tablespoon cornstarch*

1 *tablespoon sesame oil*

2 *pounds celery cabbage (napa)*

2 *tablespoons peanut oil*

4 *links Chinese sweet sausage (lop chong)*

2 *teaspoons sugar*

2 *tablespoons dark soy sauce*

Put the mushrooms in a bowl and cover them with boiling water. Let soak 30 minutes or longer. Meanwhile mix the chicken pieces with the wine, salt, cornstarch, and sesame oil, and set aside.

Remove the core of the cabbage and cut the leaves across into inch-wide strips. Heat a wok and add the peanut oil. When it is hot, add the cabbage and cook, stirring, until it is thoroughly wilted and noticeably reduced in bulk, 5 minutes or so.

Put the cooked cabbage in a clay pot or other flameproof casserole. Arrange the chicken pieces, with the marinade, over the cabbage. Wring the moisture from the mushrooms, reserving the liquid, and cut off and discard the stems. Cut the caps in half and wedge the pieces between the chicken pieces. Cut the sausages diagonally into thin oblong-shaped slices, and spread these over the chicken. Combine ⅓ cup of the reserved mushroom liquid with the sugar and soy sauce, and pour this over the sausages.

Cover the pot and bring the casserole to a boil over medium heat. When it is bubbling and steaming, turn the heat down and cook for 40 minutes. (Toward the end check to make sure all the liquid hasn't evaporated; if necessary add a little water.) When it is done, uncover, and allow the dish to cool 5 minutes or so before serving.

2 links Chinese sweet sausage (lop chong)	2 cups uncooked long-grain rice Water	CHINESE SWEET SAUSAGE WITH RICE Yield: 8 servings

Cut the sausages on the diagonal into slices ⅛ inch thick. Rinse the rice and put it in a heavy pan or rice cooker. Cover it with water to one knuckle joint above the rice. Bring to a boil and cook for a few minutes uncovered. Then turn the heat to low, spread the sausage slices over the rice, cover, and cook for 18 minutes. When it is done, let the dish sit covered for 8 to 10 minutes. Serve.

ASIAN "DAIRY":
THE SOYBEAN AND THE COCONUT

Except for a brief two hundred years around the fifth and sixth centuries in northern China, when butter and cheese were in vogue because of the intermarriage of Chinese and northern invaders, true dairy products have had little place in East Asian cuisine. In fact many Asians lack a physical tolerance for them, and cheese is generally abhorred. What takes their place is the soybean in China, Japan, and Korea, and the coconut in the countries in the tropical south. The milk both produced from the soybean and extracted from the coconut has properties remarkably similar to cow's milk.

SOYBEAN CURD

OTHER NAMES: Tofu (Japanese), Dou-fu (Chinese), Bean cake, Soybean cheese, Tubu (Korean)

REGION OF USE: China, Japan, Korea

Soybean milk and bean curd

Unfortunately, those of us who didn't grow up eating bean curd think of it as a health food or a meat substitute (and now an ice cream substitute). It's indeed high in protein and low in saturated fats and cholesterol; babies and the elderly can digest it; it's inexpensive; and it's ecologically sensible (you can get twenty times the usable protein from an acre of soybeans that you can from cattle grazing on the same land). But bean curd is also a food that should have a pleasant, lightly creamy texture and a springwater-fresh taste; and on this score, most of the bean curd available in small plastic containers in supermarkets and in many health food stores is mediocre at best.

Originally made in China from a variety of beans and peas—some bean curd is still made from mung beans—the techniques were passed on to the

Japanese in the tenth or eleventh century. Some attribute its invention to Lin An, a Chinese ruler who lived around 160 B.C., but it's more likely to have been eaten in any great quantity first during the Song Period (960 to 1270), when we have the first records of its use. Bean curd is enormously important in Asia. Without a lot of meat available to the average person, in South China for example, a huge bowl of rice mounded with bean curd and some cabbage, fresh or pickled, is a typical and ample meal. In Japan, bean curd, along with seafood, is a major protein source.

Bean curd is soybean milk to which a coagulant has been added; the curds, separated from the whey, are molded into a cake. It's a fresh product, not fermented, which keeps for a few days in changes of water although it begins to deteriorate in flavor and texture immediately. Several bean curd products are also staples in Asia. These include "bean brain" (*dou-fu nao*, a humorously derogatory term in China), which is lightly coagulated soy milk; fermented bean curd (*fu-ru*), the closest thing to a cheese in China (see page 209); molded bean curd (*chou dou-fu*), a moldy, smelly substance not available in the United States, which when wheeled down a Chinese street on a vendor's cart causes Westerners to flee; dried bean curd (*dou-fu gan*), brown cakes processed with soy sauce and sometimes spices; and bean curd skin, a skinlike wrapper for various stuffings to be fried or fried and steamed (see page 306).

To make bean curd, yellow soybeans must be first soaked and then ground between granite millstones. The resulting purée is dropped into boiling water and cooked. The soy milk is strained out, and a coagulant such as calcium sulfate (a natural gypsum) or *nagari* (magnesium chloride extracted from seawater) is stirred into it. The milk, like cheese, divides into curds and whey. The curds are strained out, put into a mold, and compressed for 10 to 20 minutes, depending on how firm a bean curd is desired.

Bean curd that is larger and softer is said to be Japanese-style, and the firmer cakes are considered Chinese. However, large creamy cakes as well as small firm cakes are available, at least on the East Coast, in Chinese markets. It's best to buy bean curd from large tubs (preferably where it's made, the day it's made) rather than in small plastic containers, although some health departments require that it be purchased that way.

SOYBEAN MILK. Bean curd shops throughout Asia carry this fresh, and it can be found, refrigerated, in plastic bottles in Asian markets here. You can also make your own: The process involves soaking yellow soybeans for about 10 hours, then puréeing them in a blender with about twice the quantity of boiling water. This is strained and squeezed through a clean cloth. Finally the milk is brought to a boil and simmered for 7 to 8 minutes. Soybean milk is nutritious, digestible—it's the basis for some baby formulas—and inexpensive. It's served like soup for breakfast throughout northern China—sweet or salty, often with dumplings—and drunk throughout Japan and Korea.

COCONUT MILK

REGION OF USE:
Southeast Asia

Young and mature coconuts with Thai coconut milk

Coconut milk is fundamental to soups, stews, roasts, beverages, puddings, candies, and cakes in tropical Asia—and everywhere else in the tropics for that matter. For a third of the world's population it's more important than cow's milk is here. It sometimes even takes the place of water for making rice. Where its use originated is hard to tell. There is only one species of coconut, and since coconuts float, they implanted themselves around the tropical beaches of the world a long time ago.

Coconut milk is not the liquid inside the coconut, but is rather the liquid wrung from the grated and soaked meat. It has many properties of cow's milk: The cream rises to the top when it sits, it must be stirred as it comes to a boil, and the fat is chemically closer to butterfat than to vegetable fat. While there are many canned coconut milks on the market, and I'll get to them, you can make your own. Ever fresher husked coconuts are available in Asian and Latin markets.

TO MAKE YOUR OWN COCONUT MILK: Puncture two of the three eyes of the husked coconut, and drain and reserve the liquid. Bake the coconut at 375°F for 15 minutes, the split it with a hammer. The meat should fall away from the shell. (Stubborn pieces may be pried loose with a knife.) Pare off the brown skin, break up the large pieces of meat, and blend them with the reserved liquid in a blender or food processor. Add 1 cup of boiling water and allow the gratings to soak for 1 hour. Then strain the liquid through cheesecloth, twisting it tightly to extract every last drop. The milk can be kept in a jar in the refrigerator for up to a week. (Where coconuts are a staple, cooks often reinfuse the gratings with hot water to use in dishes, such as rice, where only a light flavoring is called for.)

If you can't imagine yourself bothering to make your own, there are good, reasonably priced brands of canned coconut milk on the market, imported from the Philippines, Thailand, Singapore, and Samoa; and some Southeast Asian and Indian markets carry frozen grated coconut and frozen coconut milk. Among the canned, those from Thailand, such as Chaokoh brand, are inexpensive (under 80 cents for 14 ounces), rich, and quite good—often better in fact than the milk you can make from the average "fresh" coconut available at American produce stands. For most dishes you'll want to blend the milk and cream (which will have risen to the top), although some desserts call for only the cream. Store unused canned coconut milk in a jar in the refrigerator as you would the fresh.

RECOMMENDED: Chaokoh, from Thailand, available in 14- and 7-ounce cans. Chef's Choice, from Thailand, available in 14-ounce cans. Thep Padung Porn Coconut Co. (Thailand), available in 14-ounce cans.

NOTE: Look for *unsweetened* coconut milk.

Steamed custards made with coconut milk are popular in Southeast Asia. This one, laden with crunchy fresh water chestnuts, is topped with golden brown palm sugar and finished like a *crème brulée*.

3½ *cups coconut milk, cream included*	8 *fresh water chestnuts, peeled and chopped*	**COCONUT "CRÈME BRULÉE"**
7 *tablespoons granulated sugar*	1 *teaspoon vanilla extract*	Yield: 8 servings
¼ *teaspoon salt*	⅓ *cup palm sugar (or brown sugar)*	
8 *egg yolks*		

Pour the coconut milk into a saucepan placed over simmering water or into the top of a double boiler. Stir in the granulated sugar and the salt. Continue to stir until the milk is piping hot and the sugar has dissolved.

Stir the egg yolks until well blended, and slowly pour the hot coconut mixture over them, continuing to stir vigorously. Stir in the water chestnuts and the vanilla.

Pour the mixture into a 6-cup soufflé dish and steam in a covered pot or steamer over boiling water for 30 to 40 minutes (the center may still be a little runny). Refrigerate for at least 3 hours. When you are ready to serve the custard, preheat your broiler and spread the palm sugar as best you can over the top of the custard. Place the custard directly under the broiler and cook until the sugar is caramelized, 30 seconds to 2 minutes. Serve.

The elegance of this preparation belies the fact that it's a simple Laotian country dish. The sauce, with its creamy anchovy flavor—essentially coconut milk and fish sauce—seems almost northern Italian. It's meant to be eaten with generous sprinklings of coarsely ground black pepper and coriander leaves, which are served on the side.

CHICKEN WITH SHALLOTS AND BLACK PEPPER

Yield: 6 servings

1 whole fresh chicken (4 to 5 pounds)

1 teaspoon salt

1 cup peanut oil

10 large shallots, peeled and left whole

16 scallions, trimmed to 6 inches (including a few inches of green)

16 1-inch cubes fresh red chili pepper

1 14-ounce can unsweetened coconut milk

1¾ cups water

¼ cup fish sauce

½ cup coarsely ground black pepper

1 cup whole coriander leaves

Cut the chicken into sixteen or so pieces (or have your butcher do it). Sprinkle the pieces with the salt, and set aside for 30 minutes.

Heat the oil in a wok or skillet, add the shallots, and cook until very lightly browned. Remove the shallots with a slotted spoon, and set aside to drain. Add the scallions to the same oil, which should be very hot, and cook until bright green and just wilted. Remove with a slotted spoon, and set aside to drain. Repeat with the chili peppers, cooking them just briefly. Then brown the chicken pieces, a small batch at a time, 2 to 3 minutes. Remove these to drain.

Pour off all but 3 tablespoons of the oil. Over high heat, reheat the wok, and add the chicken and the coconut milk. Stir briefly, and when it is piping hot, add the water and shallots, and bring to a boil. Reduce the heat to medium, add the fish sauce, cover, and cook for 10 minutes. Uncover, add the chilis, and cook 10 to 15 minutes longer, stirring from time to time. (If the sauce evaporates too quickly, you may have to add a little water; more likely, you'll have to turn the heat up a little during the last few minutes to reduce it to a creamy consistency.)

Arrange the scallions on a serving platter, and pour the chicken and sauce over them. Serve with the black pepper and coriander in small bowls on the side.

Diane Elwyn, an excellent young cook who tested the recipes for this book, created this tropically flavored tart. With its macadamia nut crust and carefully arranged ripe mangoes, it's delicious and attractive.

MANGO AND COCONUT CREAM TART

Yield: 10 servings

MACADAMIA NUT CRUST
1¼ cup flour
¾ cup finely chopped salted macadamia nuts
¼ teaspoon salt
2 teaspoons sugar

4 tablespoons (½ stick) unsalted butter, chilled
½ teaspoon fresh lime juice
¼ cup ice water

COCONUT PASTRY CREAM
1½ cups (1 can) coconut milk with cream
¼ teaspoon vanilla extract
3 tablespoons sugar

2 tablespoons cornstarch
4 egg yolks
Pinch of salt
1 tablespoon palm sugar (or brown sugar)

FINISH
3 mangoes, peeled and sliced

2 tablespoons lychee or other honey
1 teaspoon orange liquer

MAKE THE CRUST: Combine the flour, macadamia nuts, salt, and sugar in a mixing bowl. Cut the butter into ½-inch cubes and quickly mix it into the flour mixture, until it resembles coarse meal. Using two forks, mix in the lime juice and ice water, 1 tablespoon at a time, until it forms a crumbly mass. Put the dough in a plastic bag and shape it into a ball. Refrigerate for 1 hour.

Turn the dough out of the bag and roll it out; then press it into a 9½-inch tart pan with a removable bottom.

Preheat your oven to 375°F, refrigerating the dough while the oven heats. Then cover the dough with aluminum foil weighted down with beans or pie weights, and bake for 15 minutes. Remove the foil, reduce the heat to 325°F, and bake another 20 to 30 minutes, until the crust is light golden brown. Allow it to cool while you make the pastry cream.

MAKE THE PASTRY CREAM: Combine the coconut milk and vanilla in a medium-size saucepan. Bring to a boil, reduce the heat, and cook at a low boil for 3 minutes. Turn off the heat.

Whisk together the sugar, cornstarch, egg yolks, and salt. Whisk 3 tablespoons of the hot coconut milk mixture into the egg yolk mixture; then whisk that back into the saucepan. Place the pan over medium heat and whisk constantly until very thick, 5 to 8 minutes. Sprinkle with the palm sugar, cover with plastic wrap, and refrigerate until well chilled, 1 hour or more.

TO FINISH: When the tart shell is completely cooled, fill it with the pastry cream. Stir the honey and liqueur together until well blended and heat in a saucepan until warm. Arrange the mango slices tightly together on top of the pastry cream, brush with the honey mixture, and serve.

CONDI-MENTS AND SAUCES

SOYBEAN SAUCES, CONDIMENTS, AND PASTES

According to early records, the northern Chinese, the probable originators of soybean sauces, also salted and fermented other protein sources such as fish and shellfish (as is done in Southeast Asia today)—even mutton, venison, hare, and other animal meats—as a means of preserving them before soybeans were ever considered. It's conceivable that some early Chinese cooks mixed their food, millet, for example, with a certain rabbit paste they preferred; others, with a paste made from fermented freshwater crab. In China today, because of its practicality, the soybean is the base of all these sauces.

A sixth-century agricultural encyclopedia, the *Qi Min Yao Shu*, which contains the world's oldest collection of recipes to have survived intact, describes methods for making a number of these salty condiments, two of which are ancestors of today's soybean sauces: a runny bean sauce called *jiang*, literally "bean pickle," and the familiar salted and fermented black beans called *shi*, which were prepared and used 1,500 years ago pretty much the same way they are now. It is hard to know when these two soybean condiments were first used, but records of their use were recovered from a Han period tomb dating to around 165 B.C., and they must have been used well before that. The liquid soy sauces we know today came later, although they too have been used for centuries.

SALTED AND FERMENTED BLACK BEANS

OTHER NAMES: Preserved beans, Salted beans

REGION OF USE: Southern China

Called *shi* in early texts, these soybeans—partially decomposed by a special mold, then dried and sometimes salted—predates soy sauce and perhaps any other soy food. Because they're cheap and easy to make, they have long been a favorite of rural people who could not afford another type of condiment. Once the only soy seasoning, they were used throughout China, but are now more widely used in the south and are a fixture of Cantonese cooking. The chili pastes of southerly Hunan province will often have a sprinkling of black beans, whereas the nearly identical pastes of Sichuan province will not.

Black beans have a pleasing winy flavor, and when used properly are a wonderful complement to seafood. (Unfortunately, in restaurants they often end up in gloppy, musty-tasting brown sauces.) Meats and poultry can also be delicious when seasoned with black beans, and among vegetables, asparagus and broccoli have an affinity for their special flavor.

Rinsing black beans, as some recipes suggest, is unnecessary and in fact diminishes their flavor slightly. When buying the salted kind, just take their saltiness into account when adding other seasonings. Depending on the dish, black beans should be chopped lightly or crushed a little with the side of a cleaver to release their flavor, then tossed with a tablespoon or two of Shaoxing wine or dry sherry, and chopped garlic and ginger if the dish calls for them, and set aside until ready to use.

Fermented black beans, often flavored with bits of ginger and sometimes orange peel, are usually sold in 8-ounce plastic packages. Mee Chun, the most common brand, is an acceptable product, as are the black beans of the Koon Chun Sauce Factory. Earthier and probably more classic are the Yang Jiang Preserved Beans (with ginger) from Kwangtung, China. After the package is opened, black beans should be transferred to a covered jar and stored away from light and heat. They will keep indefinitely.

RECOMMENDED: Mee Chun, available in 8-ounce plastic packages. Koon Chun Sauce Factory, available in 8-ounce plastic packages. Yang Jiang Preserved Beans, available in 17-ounce cylindrical boxes.

This is not a traditional Chinese way
of using salted and fermented black beans,
but it's delicious.

		ROAST CHICKEN WITH BLACK BEANS STUFFED UNDER THE SKIN
1 *whole chicken (4 pounds)*	½ *cup chopped coriander leaves and stems*	
1 *teaspoon dark soy sauce*	1 *tablespoon rice wine*	
2 *tablespoons salted and fermented black beans*	1 *teaspoon sesame oil*	
	¼ *teaspoon sugar*	
½ *tablespoon chopped garlic*	*Salt and freshly ground black pepper to taste*	
1½ *tablespoons chopped fresh ginger*		Yield: 6 Servings

With a French chef's knife inserted in the cavity, cut along either side of the backbone of the chicken and remove it, so the chicken will lie flat. Rub the chicken all over with the soy sauce.

In a mortar, pound together the black beans, garlic, ginger, coriander, wine, sesame oil, and sugar to form a lumpy paste. Spread this mixture underneath the skin of the chicken as best you can. Salt and pepper the outside of the chicken, and let it sit while the oven heats to 500°F.

When the oven is hot, place the chicken on a rack in a roasting pan and cook for 15 minutes. Reduce the heat to 350°F and cook for 25 minutes more. Serve.

This is a wonderful Chinese solution to the American soft-shell crab.
A friend who has traveled around the world, after tasting this dish made
with crabs barely out of the water, remarked that it was the
best dish he ever had, period.

SOFT-SHELL CRABS WITH GINGER, LEMON, AND BLACK BEANS

Yield: 6 servings

6 soft-shell crabs, cleaned of their gills and ready to cook

½ cup + 1½ tablespoons cornstarch

¼ cup finely shredded fresh ginger

1 tablespoon shredded lemon zest (yellow part only)

2 small fresh red chili peppers, shredded

3 scallions, cut into 1-inch lengths

1½ tablespoons minced garlic

1 tablespoon salted and fermented black beans

1 tablespoon Shaoxing wine or dry sherry

1½ cups fresh chicken or fish stock

1 tablespoon grated lemon zest

2 tablespoons oyster sauce

1 tablespoon light soy sauce

1 teaspoon sugar

Pinch of salt

¼ cup water

Peanut oil for deep-frying

¼ cup peanut oil

Coriander sprigs for garnish

Cut the crabs in half through the top of the shell. Put about ½ cup cornstarch in a bowl, and dip the cut part of each crab into it. Set them aside.

Combine the ginger, shredded lemon zest, chili peppers, and scallions and set aside. Combine the garlic, black beans, and wine and set aside. Blend the stock with the grated lemon zest, oyster sauce, soy sauce, sugar, and salt, and set aside. Combine 1½ tablespoons cornstarch with ¼ cup water, and set aside.

Heat the frying oil in a wok or deep skillet until very hot but not smoking, and add half the crab pieces. Cook for 2 to 4 minutes, turning them in the oil until red and crisp. Remove and drain. Repeat with the other pieces.

Over high heat, heat a clean wok or skillet and add ¼ cup oil. When it is hot, add the ginger combination and cook, stirring, until just fragrant, about 10 seconds. Add the black bean mixture and cook, stirring, another 20 seconds. Add the seasoned stock and bring to a boil. Give the cornstarch and water a quick stir and add it to the sauce. When the sauce is thickened and glossy, turn off the heat. Arrange the crabs on a serving platter, pour the sauce over, and serve garnished with the coriander sprigs.

OTHER NAMES: Yellow bean sauce, Brown bean sauce, Bean paste, Soybean condiment

REGION OF USE: China, Southeast Asia

An ages-old paste of fermented soybeans, favored in China's northern and western provinces (Sichuan and Hunan), bean sauce comes two ways: "whole," meaning that the sauce contains whole beans; and "ground," which is simply a purée of the same sauce. If it's labeled just "Bean Sauce," it means whole bean sauce. This is the more desirable of the two as it has a more pleasing texture—more like the original soy sauce of antiquity—and has a rounder flavor; ground bean sauce is bitingly salty.

Known originally as *jiang,* or "bean pickle," bean sauce is the oldest soybean sauce. *Jiang* has been translated as "soy sauce" from ancient texts, but these first soy sauces were actually runny versions of today's bean sauce, which has been thickened with a little flour. Japan's *miso* can trace its ancestry to these early northern Chinese bean sauces.

Bean sauce most frequently seasons meat dishes in North China, the most famous being the Peking noodle dish * za jiang mein,* which can lay claim to the title of the world's oldest surviving pasta dish. Bean sauce, not hoisin sauce, is the base of the traditional condiment served with Peking Duck, though the latter is what we commonly see.

Bean sauce is vital to authentic Sichuan and Hunan cooking. Usually added with chili peppers in some form, bean sauce—more than soy sauce—flavors many fiery country-style dishes, from Chicken with Peanuts, to "twice-cooked" fresh bacon and cabbage dishes, to whole fish smothered in ground pork, chilis, and bean sauce.

Whereas in China food stores might offer wonderful local bean sauces by the scoop, we're stuck with canned varieties, two of which are perfectly acceptable: Koon Chun Sauce Factory's "Bean Sauce," and "Szechuan Bean Sauce" from the Sze Chuan Food Products Company. If you buy bean sauce in a jar, just store it in the refrigerator; if it is in a can, transfer it to a jar and store in the refrigerator. It should keep indefinitely.

RECOMMENDED: "Szechuan Bean Sauce," from Sze Chuan Food Products Company, available in blue 6- or 16-ounce cans.

Koon Chun Sauce Factory's "Bean Sauce," available in 15-ounce jars (preferred) or 16-ounce cans.

Bean sauce family

| HOT BEAN SAUCE | OTHER NAMES: Hot bean paste, Soybean paste with chilli, Hot fermented soybeans, Kochujang (Korean) |
| | REGION: China, Korea |

Hot bean sauce is simply bean sauce (see page 199) made hot by the addition of chili peppers in paste or dried form. Other flavorings such as garlic, sesame oil, and sugar are sometimes added. While the quality of some ready-made hot bean sauces is very good—one is excellent—the sauce is not so much a staple, like soy sauce for example, as it is a mixture of ingredients that a true Sichuan chef might choose to add to a dish individually, in the quantities he likes. A good recipe is more likely to ask for bean sauce and chili paste separately than to ask for hot bean sauce, since the proportion of bean sauce to chili pepper as well as the quantities of other ingredients varies widely from brand to brand. Some, like Yeo's from Singapore, are incendiary and garlicky, while others are mild and contain no garlic at all.

A standard hot bean sauce is the widely available "Szechuan Hot Bean Sauce" packaged by Sze Chuan Food Products. Its quality is high, and it seems made for recipes that call for hot bean sauce. However, one of the finest canned condiments of any sort is Lan Chi brand "Soy Bean Paste With Chilli." Its ingredients are fermented soybeans, pieces of dried chili pepper, salt, sesame oil, and wine, and it has a delicious homemade quality.

NOTE: Some Hunan-style hot bean sauces contain salted black beans in addition to bean sauce and chili peppers. Other Hunan hot sauces contain no bean sauce, only chili paste and salted black beans; these are discussed under "Chili Pastes and Sauces," page 221.

HIGHLY RECOMMENDED: Lan Chi brand "Soy Bean Paste With Chilli," available in 8-ounce jars.

RECOMMENDED: Sze Chuan Food Products Co. "Szechuan Hot Bean Sauce," available in 6- and 16-ounce cans.

As a topping for fresh egg noodles, this simple ground meat dish makes a sort of Sichuan spaghetti. It also keeps for a few days and is delicious reheated and mixed with leftover rice.

GROUND PORK WITH HOT BEAN SAUCE

Yield: 4 servings

1 *pound ground pork*

¼ *cup peanut oil*

¼ *cup chopped fresh ginger*

3 *tablespoons whole bean sauce*

2 *tablespoons chili paste*

2 *teaspoons sugar*

½ *cup chopped scallions, green part included*

½ *pound fresh egg noodles*

1 *teaspoon sesame oil*

With a cleaver or French chef's knife, chop the pork for a minute or two into an even finer mince. Over high heat, heat a wok or skillet and add the oil. When it is hot, add the ginger and stir briefly, about 20 seconds. Add the pork and stir for 2 to 3 minutes to separate the grains (do not brown). When the pork grains have separated and changed color, add the bean sauce, chili paste, and sugar, and continue to cook, stirring, for 3 to 4 minutes. Then stir in the scallions and turn off the heat.

Bring a large quantity of water to a boil and add the noodles. Cook 3½ to 5 minutes—depending on how you like your noodles—then drain them thoroughly and toss with the sesame oil. Serve the noodles and sauce separately, or mix them together and serve. (Reheat the sauce if necessary.)

NOTE: Five tablespoons of a good Hot Bean Sauce (see page 200) may be substituted for the bean sauce and chili paste.

HOISIN SAUCE

OTHER NAMES: Hoi sin sauce, barbecue sauce (see page 202)

REGION: Southern China

This brownish-red member of the soybean sauce family is almost always sweet, garlicky, and spicy—it has the anise flavor of 5-spice powder and is peppered with a little dried chili. The texture ranges from a creamy jam to a runny sauce. Chinese restaurants in the West, recognizing that Westerners have taken a liking to it, sometimes offer it as a ketchup-like condiment, which is unfortunate since just a dash of its heavy, cloying flavor can obliterate the subtleties of many Chinese dishes.

Hoisin sauce mixed with sugar and thinned with sesame oil has become the standard accompaniment to Peking Duck practically everywhere outside of northern China, where the dish originated. Sweetened whole or ground bean sauce (which is the base of hoisin sauce anyway) mixed with sesame oil is the traditional condiment for this famous dish.

Hoisin is best as part of a paste to be smeared over meats for grilling or roasting. Since the best brands contain a natural red coloring called red rice (see page 283) and have the coloring qualities of dark soy sauce, spareribs and other meats get something of that red roasted look when they are cooked with hoisin.

CHEE HOU SAUCE. This hoisin family member has the same basic ingredients, but it's slightly spicier. It can be used just like hoisin.

BARBECUE SAUCE. Not to be confused with the "barbecue sauce" whose basic ingredient is dried fish (see page 219), this is a jazzed-up hoisin sauce specifically for roasting meats, bottled by Koon Chun and other companies. Containing a heavier dash of coloring, and sometimes tomato paste, it is redder than the average hoisin sauce. It's better to make your own marinade using hoisin and whatever else you choose to add—vinegar, bean sauce, sesame paste— than to rely on these all-purpose sauces.

HIGHLY RECOMMENDED: Ma Ling (China) "Hoisin Sauce," a thin but full-flavored natural sauce; the only one to use red rice; available in 16-ounce cans.

RECOMMENDED: Koon Chun Sauce Factory "Hoisin Sauce," available in 15-ounce jars (preferred) or 16-ounce cans; Wei-Chuan "Hoi Sin Sauce," available in 6-ounce jars.

SWEET BEAN SAUCE

REGION OF USE: Taiwan

This sauce, simply a mixture of ground bean sauce and sugar, is frequently confused with sweetened red bean paste, which is made with tiny azuki beans (see page 148), not soybeans. Sweet bean sauce seems to be called for mostly in one series of popular cookbooks, those published by the Wei-Chuan Foods Corporation of Taiwan. About the only available sweet bean sauce comes in cans from the Taiwan company Sze Chuan Products, and there's no real reason to buy it. If a recipe calls for it—and not many will—mix three parts bean sauce or ground bean sauce with 1 part sugar, and add it accordingly.

Soy sauce is a naturally fermented product made in several steps and aged up to two years. Typically, roasted soybean meal and a lightly ground grain, usually wheat, are mixed with an *Aspergillus* mold starter; the resulting culture takes a few days to grow. Brine is then added to the fermented meal, along with a *Lactobacillus* starter (bacteria like those that produce yogurt and sourdough bread) and yeast. The mash is then aged slowly. When the producer determines it's ready, the soy sauce is strained and bottled.

Supermarket varieties, like La Choy, made from quickly hydrolized vegetable protein, are not true soy sauces, and since the real thing, Japanese or Chinese, doesn't cost much and is readily available—they're now found in many supermarkets next to the La Choy—there's never a reason to buy the phony sauces. It also makes little sense to pay the money for health food store varieties (usually Japanese-style sauces) since they're no more natural and are truly exorbitant in price.

CHINESE SOY SAUCE

The Chinese invented soy sauce, and the Japanese learned the technology from them. A purely liquid soy sauce probably wasn't used until sometime around the sixth century, before which soy sauce was like a runny whole bean sauce. Soy sauce's first function was to preserve food and to keep it over the winter months. As a side benefit the Chinese produced a highly nutritious and easily digestible protein concentrate.

The Chinese, particularly in the south, use both light and dark soy sauce. The latter is aged longer, and toward the end of the processing is mixed with bead molasses, which gives it a darker caramellike hue. You can think of them as you would red and white wine, since as a rule, dark soy flavors (and colors) heartier dishes, particularly those with red meat, whereas light soy sauce is more appropriate with seafood, vegetables, soups, and in dipping sauces. Traditional northern Chinese cooks use only dark soy sauce.

HIGHLY RECOMMENDED LIGHT SOY SAUCE: Pearl River Bridge's "Golden Label Superior Soy," a premium-brand light soy to use for dipping sauces as well as cooking; it's a little darker, though clearer, than their standard Superior Soy (see below), but by no means expensive.

RECOMMENDED LIGHT SOY SAUCES: Pearl River Bridge's "Superior Soy" (not the dark "Soy, Superior," which also has a red label), a product of Guangzhou; available in 22-ounce bottles; Koon Chun Sauce Factory's "Thin Soy Sauce," a slightly lighter sauce, also acceptable for cooking.

RECOMMENDED DARK SOY SAUCES: Pearl River Bridge's Mushroom Soy, flavored by straw mushrooms; rich, full-flavored; to be used whenever dark soy sauce is called for. Koon Chun Sauce Factory makes a decent "Black Soy Sauce" and a double black soy, a little of which gives meats a deep, rich color.

JAPANESE SOY SAUCE

The art of making soy sauce was introduced to Japan by the Chinese about 1,000 years ago, and since that time the Japanese have developed distinguished varieties to meet the needs of their cuisine. Whether Japanese or Chinese, the aging and fermenting are the same, but as a rule, Japanese soy sauce (*shoyu*) contains more wheat and is thus a little sweeter and less salty. Standard to Japanese cooking is what they call "dark" soy sauce, which is labeled simply "soy sauce," *shoyu,* or *koi-kuchi shoyu.* This sauce, on a Chinese scale of dark to light, would fall on the light end, and in a pinch could be substituted for Chinese light soy. An even lighter Japanese soy sauce (*usu-kuchi shoyu*) is favored around Osaka, in southern Japan, where people like food free of what they feel is unwarranted color. Saltier than the standard Japanese soy sauce, it's available only in Japanese markets.

With a factory in Wisconsin, Kikkoman is the most widely available real soy sauce in this country. It's quality is high, but it contains sodium benzoate, a preservative. Japanese markets offer an array of good soy sauces.

The Japanese market low-sodium soy sauces here. Like salt, however, it's better to cut back on the amount of this most fundamental seasoning rather than to use an altered version of it.

TAMARI

Thanks to the macrobiotic food movement in the 1960s, the Japanese term *tamari* has been misapplied to Japanese-style soy sauces of varying quality, most of which are sold in U.S. health food stores for, in most cases, several times the price of a comparable product in a Japanese or Chinese market. True *tamari*, rare in Japan, is a rich, dark soy sauce brewed without wheat. It is a remnant of the ancient soy sauce methods learned from the Chinese.

MASTER SAUCE CHICKEN

One of the easiest and oldest methods of cooking a whole chicken is simply to poach it in water, wine, soy sauce, and rock sugar. Other seasonings are sometimes added, typically a cinnamon stick, star anise, or dried tangerine peels, but they aren't necessary.

With minimal attention the chicken turns out flavorfully succulent and deep golden in color. The intriguing thing about this method is that the sauce can be strained and saved for the next chicken. This "master sauce," in fact, becomes richer and more flavorful each time it's used, and for some reason, the older the sauce, the less cooking time required. You need only replenish it with a little of the original seasonings each time you use it.

Master sauce will keep in the refrigerator for two weeks, and if you bring it to a boil every ten days or so, you can cook chickens in it for years. Some master sauces supposedly have been kept for 200 years, passed down from generation to generation.

For even coloring and the tastiest results, it's important to use a fresh-killed chicken such as those available in Chinese poultry markets. The little yellowish chickens with the tags on them that have been raised in factory-like conditions and shipped on ice turn out with blotchy coloring when cooked this way, for some reason.

1 *whole fresh-killed chicken (4 pounds)*   Yield: 6 servings

1 *tablespoon + 2 teaspoons salt*

1 *cup dark soy sauce*

1 *cup Shaoxing wine or dry sherry*

   Approximately ¾ cup yellow rock sugar

5 *cups water*

   Sesame oil

Rinse the chicken and pat it dry. Sprinkle it inside and out with about 1 tablespoon salt and let it stand for at least 2 hours.

Heat a wok or large pot and add the soy sauce, wine, rock sugar, water, and another 2 teaspoons salt. Bring to a boil and cook, stirring, until the sugar has dissolved.

Add the chicken, breast side down, and when the sauce returns to a boil, reduce the heat to medium. Baste the chicken from time to time by pouring the sauce over it with a ladle. After 25 minutes, turn the chicken carefully, and continue to cook and occasionally baste for another 15 minutes.

Turn off the heat and let the chicken sit in the liquid for another 20 minutes. Ladle the sauce over the chicken two or three times as it cools.

Remove the chicken, and brush it with a little sesame oil. You may serve it warm, carved Western-style, or cooled to room temperature and cut into pieces; or you may refrigerate it until the next day.

Strain the sauce through a fine-mesh strainer, and store it in a jar or plastic container in the refrigerator. When the fat congeals, remove most of it. To keep the sauce indefinitely, bring it to a boil every 10 days. You may concentrate it by boiling it down before you store it. To reuse, simply bring it to a boil, add a small amount of sauce ingredients in approximately their original proportions, add as much water as necessary, and cook another chicken.

JAVA'S KETJAP AND OTHER SOY SAUCES

The tomato sauce we know and love, ketchup, although it would seem to be in the family of Asian pickled products, may or may not be an Asian invention; but the word "ketchup" was. It comes from the Maylay *kēchap,* which apparently derives from the *kôe-chiap* of a southern Chinese dialect (Amoy); both of these refer to the kind of briny liquid preserves that include fish and soy sauces. Whereas most everywhere in Southeast Asia various fish sauces are the standard condiment, in Java, because it has one of the few environments in the region hospitable to soybeans, soy sauce is used. Sometimes called *ketjap manis,* it's traditionally sweetened with palm syrup and seasoned with garlic, star anise, salam leaves (a tropical laurel-like tree, *Eugenia polyantha*), and galangal, and its use is fundamental to Javanese cooking.

Because of the Chinese population there, soy sauce is manufactured in Singapore and other pockets of Southeast Asia. Thailand, in fact, produces decent light and dark Chinese-style soy sauces, which are appearing on the shelves of some Southeast Asian markets here. Not staples of traditional Thai cooking, these soy sauces are made for the Chinese in Thailand and for Thai cooks to use in their Chinese dishes.

Decent soy sauce, light by Chinese standards, is produced in the Philippines by Silver Swan Manufacturing and others. A most interesting soy sauce called *toyo mansi* is rendered flavorfully sour by a lemon indigenous to the Philippines, called a *calamansi.* Carried in Philippine food stores, Mother's Best, which comes in 12-ounce bottles, is the brand to buy; it's worth experimenting with for many types of cooking. Citrus-flavored soy sauce is not unique to the Philippines, as the Japanese use *ponzu shoyu,* a lemon-flavored soy sauce found in Japanese markets.

Given a boost in this country by the macrobiotic food movement of a decade or so ago, the protein-rich soybean paste known as *miso* is consumed in small quantities by nearly everyone in Japan every day. For most Japanese, a warm bowl of miso soup, of the sort that is familiar to anyone who has been to a Japanese restaurant, is a morning ritual.

Miso is a paste of varying shades—from cream-colored to reddish brown to deep chocolate—and textures from chunky to smooth. It's made by salting and fermenting soybeans and a grain (usually rice or barley) with *Aspergillus oryzae* (a mold), in much the same way that other soybean sauces are made. Miso's ancestor is in fact the original runny Chinese soybean sauce, *jiang,* which was taken to Japan from China by Buddhist priests somewhere around the seventh or eighth century. From *jiang* evolved not only liquid soy sauces but also the numerous regional varieties of miso, of which there are about half a dozen basic types.

Like Chinese soybean sauce, miso was originally a food preservative; it is still a pickling medium. Along the way it has become a most important seasoning. Besides combining with Japanese stock, *dashi,* to make a soup that's drunk up to three times a day, miso adds its winy pungency to dressings for vegetables and to dip sauces. As the base of a marinade-paste, it's spread on foods to be grilled. Known as *dengaku,* these include snack-type skewered vegetables, seafood, and meat spread with pastes of miso and sometimes sake, dashi, ground sesame seeds, ginger juice, and lemon rind.

Like soy sauce, miso is aged, sometimes as long as three years. Miso is found in Japanese food markets and in health food stores, in plastic tubs, jars, squeeze tubes, plastic bags, and in bulk from crocks. Some types are better suited for specific purposes, in dressings for example, than others. But many are all-purpose, and it's recommended that a variety be sampled before settling on one or two.

YELLOW MISO (SHINSHU-MISO). A smooth-textured miso that ranges from light yellow to yellowish brown, this is the most widely available type in the United States and accounts for 20 percent of all miso consumed in Japan. Salty and protein-rich, it's aged quickly in Japan and is thus the least expensive. An all-purpose miso, it's used for dressings, dips, soups, and grilled foods.

WHITE MISO (SHIRO MISO). Also called *kyoto shiro miso,* or "sweet white miso," this is nearly two-thirds rice. Smooth and sweet, it's a tasty paste that's especially good in dressings. Mixed with red (azuki) beans, it's one of the few misos used in Japanese sweets. In Japan it is also used to pickle fish and vegetables, and is a favored topping for foods to be grilled.

RED MISO (AKA MISO). A common rice miso—in northern Japan it's the main "farmhouse" miso—the varieties range from light to deep red-brown and the texture from smooth to chunky. Because of its high salt content, red miso will keep practically indefinitely at room temperature, whereas other misos should be refrigerated. It may develop mold, which can be scraped off to no ill effect.

HATCHO MISO. The premier miso, made of only soybeans and aged for up to three years in cedar vats, *hatcho miso* has been enjoyed for centuries by connoisseurs. Coarse in texture, its deep, complex flavor and slight bitterness is reminiscent of chocolate. Historically it was fermented with its own mold, *Aspergillis hatcho*. To enjoy it at its most unadulterated (it's also a highly regarded tonic), hatcho is usually used in soups, occasionally mixed with yellow miso to soften its flavor.

BARLEY MISO (MUGI MISO). The most popular miso in Japan until fifty years ago or so, barley miso became fashionable among miso-users in this country in the 1960s and is found more readily in health food stores than in Japanese markets. Chunky, dark brown, earthy in flavor and well aged, this is an expensive miso not used much in modern Japanese cooking.

Japanese salads, *aemono* ("dressed things"), use a wide range
of vegetables, raw and parboiled, and seafood, cooked or uncooked.
The dressings are flavorful and often tangy, like the all-purpose one here,
which is tossed with asparagus. The white miso and
mustard combination is superb.

ASPARAGUS WITH MUSTARD-MISO DRESSING Yield: 4 servings	2 teaspoons mustard powder 2 teaspoons cold water 1 pound thin asparagus 1 egg yolk 2 teaspoons white miso 2 teaspoons Japanese soy sauce	1 tablespoon fresh lemon juice 1 tablespoon white rice vinegar 2 tablespoons minced scallions (white part only)

Mix the mustard powder and water together to form a thin paste. Allow it to sit for 10 minutes.

Cut the asparagus diagonally into thin slices about 1 inch long. Cook the asparagus slices in boiling water until barely tender, 1½ minutes or so. Then run under cold water to stop the cooking. Drain and set aside.

Vigorously mix the egg yolk with the mustard. Then stir in the remaining ingredients in order, and allow to sit at least 10 minutes before tossing with the asparagus. Serve at room temperature.

FERMENTED BEAN CURD

OTHER NAMES: Preserved bean curd, Wet bean curd, Bean cheese, Dou-fu ru or Fu-ru (Mandarin), Fu yu (Cantonese)

REGION OF USE: China

Unless they've learned to love it by living in the West, the best way to get a table of Chinese diners to quickly excuse themselves is to set down a platter of ripened, aromatic cheeses. Cheese is one of the least palatable foods to the Chinese. In the past few hundred years, however, the Chinese have made their own of sorts of cheese out of bean curd. Ironically they call it *fu-ru,* or "spoiled milk," a derogatory term they coined hundreds of years ago for the real cheese of their northern neighbors, the Mongols. In fact, knowledge of barbarian cheesemaking may have prodded the Chinese to ferment bean curd, perhaps to make it in the first place. Fermented bean curd comes in two colors, each with its own uses.

WHITE FERMENTED BEAN CURD (also White bean cheese, Wine-fermented bean curd). Cut into ¾-inch cubes, bean curd is innoculated with special mold spores and incubated for three days until it is covered with odorous white *mycelium* mold. The cubes are then submerged in a brining liquor that includes rice wine, salt, and sometimes red chili pepper and/or sesame oil. After ripening from four to six months to develop a creamy consistency and spunky flavor, it's ready, though it continues to improve with age. Whole, this seasoning commonly accompanies the rice porridge *congee.* Mashed with other seasonings, it's cooked with leafy vegetables such as spinach or *ung choy* (water spinach). Usually packaged in 16-ounce jars, variously seasoned types come from China, Hong Kong ("Wet Bean Curd," packed by Chan Moon Kee, is common), and Taiwan; and San Francisco's Quong Hop & Company has been making it for decades. Once opened, it will keep indefinitely in the refrigerator.

Cubes of fermented cheeselike bean curd (*fu-ru*)
lend a pungent, winy flavor to this sauce. This is a very popular
Chinese method of cooking spinach, and it's one of the
best in any cuisine.

SPINACH WITH WHITE BEAN CHEESE

Yield: 4 servings

2 bunches spinach (about 1 pound leaves)

2 squares fermented white bean curd

1 tablespoon chicken stock or water

Pinch of salt

½ teaspoon sugar

3 tablespoons peanut oil

1 tablespoon finely shredded fresh ginger

Rinse and dry the spinach thoroughly. Mash the bean curd with the stock, salt, and sugar, and set aside.

Over high heat, heat a wok and add the oil. When it is hot, add the spinach and stir quickly until just covered with oil. Add the ginger and stir 5 seconds or so, then add the bean curd sauce. Stir over high heat until most of the liquid has evaporated and the spinach is just cooked. Serve.

NOTE: Two bunches of water spinach (*ung choy*), the leaves and top third or so of the stems, may be substituted for the spinach. Cut stems into 2- to 3-inch lengths.

RED FERMENTED BEAN CURD (also red bean cheese). This is prepared like white fermented bean curd, except that red rice, a natural red coloring (see page 283), is added during the brining, which colors the bean curd and its liquid a deep red and gives it a thick consistency. Unlike the white variety, which seasons light foods such as vegetables, red bean curd seasons and colors pork, either as part of a marinade for meat to be roasted or as an addition to a braising sauce. Red bean curd is sold in 16-ounce jars, but the best comes from Zhejiang, China, in small 16-ounce crocks labeled "Preserved Bean Curd (Red)." It keeps indefinitely in the refrigerator.

This is a classic Chinese use of the cheeselike red fermented bean curd. Believing that Western palates cannot handle the combination of this strong-flavored seasoning and rich fresh bacon, this is one of those dishes, beloved by the Chinese, that a lot of restaurants offer, but not on the English part of the menu.

FRESH BACON STEAMED WITH TARO ROOT

Yield: 8 to 10 servings

1 pound taro root (1 root)

3 pounds fresh bacon (pork belly, about 2 strips)

5 teaspoons dark soy sauce

7 tablespoons peanut oil

6 large garlic cloves, smashed

2 cubes red bean curd mashed with ½ cup water or chicken stock

1 tablespoon Shaoxing wine

2½ tablespoons sugar

Pinch of salt

1 tablespoon minced fresh ginger

8 dried hot red peppers

Steam the whole taro root, with the skin, about 1 hour. Drain and set aside.

Meanwhile, place the pork in a large pot with water to cover and bring it to a boil. Reduce the heat to medium, and simmer the pork for 30 minutes. Drain, and rinse under cold water. Dry thoroughly and rub the rind with 1 teaspoon of the soy sauce. Set aside.

Over medium-high heat, heat a small skillet and add 1 tablespoon of the oil. Add the garlic and sauté briefly. Add the bean curd mixture, wine, 2 tablespoons of the sugar, salt, and remaining 4 teaspoons soy sauce. Cook, stirring, until it becomes a smooth sauce, 2 minutes. (Add a little more water if necessary.) Set aside.

Place the remaining 6 tablespoons peanut oil in a wok and heat until hot but not smoking. Add the pork, skin side down, and cook, shifting the pork in the oil until the skin is lightly browned, 2 to 3 minutes (be careful; it will spatter). Turn off the heat and remove the pork to drain.

Cut the pork into ½-inch-thick slices, and keeping the slices together, place them in rows in a 10-inch Pyrex or other heatproof dish. Peel the taro root, cut it in half lengthwise, and then cut it into slices no more than ½ inch thick. Arrange these in rows over the pork. Pour the sauce evenly over the taro slices. Sprinkle with the remaining ½ tablespoon sugar, the ginger, and the dried hot peppers.

Start water boiling in a steamer large enough to hold the plate of bacon (a wok with a rack and cover will do). Put the plate in the steamer and steam for 2½ to 3 hours, until the pork is tender.

To serve, remove the taro slices to a serving platter. Arrange the pork, rind side up, over the taro. Pour the sauce over and garnish with the scallions.

FISH AND SHELLFISH SAUCES
AND PASTES

Fish sauces, the product of salted and fermented fish, were known in the Western world long before the recent influx of immigrants from Southeast Asia, for whom these sauces are the main staple. The ancient Romans doused everything with *liquamen* (or *garum*), made from anchovies and other fish in much the same manner as Southeast Asian fish sauce. Anchovies packed in salt, which lend their heady fragrance to Italian dishes, are a remnant of this kind of ancient fish pickling.

Like soy sauce, the most common fish sauce is a clear, salty liquid, rich in protein. And like the soybean sauces that use whole or ground beans and that predate liquid soy sauce, some fish sauces—presumably of ancient origin—contain whole or ground fish.

FISH SAUCE

OTHER NAMES: Nu'ó'c mâ'm (Vietnamese), Nam pla (Thai), Tuk trey (Kampuchean), Ngan-pya-ye (Burmese), Fish gravy, Patis (Filipino)

REGION OF USE: Southeast Asia, principally Burma, Vietnam, Thailand, Laos, Kampuchea, the Philippines

Just as soy sauce is the fundamental ingredient in China and Japan, fish sauce is added to nearly every dish in Southeast Asia, and if it's not in the dish, it is served next to it as the base for a dipping sauce. Unlike soy sauce, fish sauce can take some getting used to for those who haven't grown up with it. Trying it has been likened to encountering Camembert for the first time. The aroma, fortunately stronger than the taste, is more like an odorous cheese than an aged fish.

Called *nu'ó'c mâ'm* in Vietnam, *nam pla* in Thailand, *tuk trey* in Kampuchea, and *ngan-pya-ye* in Burma, fish sauce is made by packing fish, usually anchovies, in barrels or crocks, covering them with brine, and allowing them to ferment in the tropical sun over a period of months. The resulting brown liquid is drained off and used. Highly nutritious (rich in B vitamins and protein), fish sauce and rice were the K-rations that sustained the Vietcong.

The finest fish sauce is said to come from an island off Vietnam, Phu Quoc, a name that is now generic for top quality. Like olive oil, the first pressing (in this case siphoning), from which flows a clear amber liquid, is the most highly prized and is usually reserved for dipping sauces. Sweet, watery versions of these sauces, with a scant drop or two of fish sauce, are served in Vietnamese and Thai restaurants here. (See page 214.)

Most fish sauces here come from Thailand; the rest come from Hong Kong, China, and the Philippines, where besides anchovies, mackerel, and other fish are used. For a little over $1 you can buy a decent fish sauce for cooking, such as the popular Squid brand from the Thai Fishsauce Company. For around twice the price you can have the very fine Flying Lion brand "Phu Quoc" or Viet Huong's "Three Crabs Brand," which is best reserved for dips and dressings. Avoid fish sauce, or any sauce, in plastic bottles. Fish sauce keeps indefinitely on the shelf.

HIGHLY RECOMMENDED: Viet Huong "Three Crabs Brand 'Fish Sauce'" from Thailand; for dips and dressings; available in 24-ounce bottles. Flying Lion brand "Phu Quoc" from Thailand; for dipping sauces and cooking; available in 24-ounce bottles. Viêt-Mỹ Corporation "Nuoc Mam 'Phu Quoc,'" packaged in Virginia; for dips and cooking; available in 10-ounce bottles.

RECOMMENDED (ALL IN BOTTLES OF AROUND 24 OUNCES): Dek Brand "Fish Sauce" from Thailand; for dipping sauce and cooking; Thai Fishsauce Company "Squid Brand" for cooking; Pin Dhian Fishgravy Company "Fish Sauce" from Hong Kong; for cooking; Pufina Batis from the Philippines; Narcissus "Fish Gravy" from China; for cooking.

A more substantial sauce than the sweet, insipid versions
set out in most Vietnamese restaurants here, a little of this goes a long way.
It's excellent with even non-Asian batter-fried foods, or with steamed
or boiled Chinese dumplings.

VIETNAMESE DIPPING SAUCE	¼ cup minced garlic	⅓ cup fresh lime juice
	½ cup fish sauce (for dipping; see page 212)	1 tablespoon sugar
Yield : 4 to 6 dip bowls		1 teaspoon chili oil

Mix the garlic, fish sauce, lime juice, and sugar, and stir until the sugar has dissolved. Stir in the chili oil. Serve in small bowls, for dipping with fried food (such as Cha Gio, page 304).

NOTE: This sauce is best made 1 hour ahead.

TOMATO SAUCE	1 small red onion, chopped	1½ tablespoons palm vinegar
	3 red ripe tomatoes, cut into ¼-inch dice	1 teaspoon sugar
	2 teaspoons "Tiny Shrimp" shrimp paste (bagoong)	½ cup chopped coriander leaves and stems

Mix together all the ingredients, and serve with *adobo*.

An extremely popular dish in the Philippines, *adobo* was originally a way of preserving meat, and sometimes fish, so it would keep in the tropical heat. The meat—usually chicken and pork—is marinated in tangy palm vinegar and other seasonings, simmered in the marinade until tender, and browned in lard or oil. The sauce is reduced, then stirred rapidly over high heat with the meat. Adobo may be served with a number of accompaniments, among them a kind of Philippine salsa with fresh tomatoes and *bagoong,* a paste of fermented tiny shrimp.

ADOBO
(Philippine Braised Chicken and Pork)

Yield: 6 to 8 servings

1 chicken (3½ pounds), cut into about 12 pieces	3 tablespoons palm sugar
2½ pounds boneless pork butt, cut into 2-inch cubes	1 teaspoon ground black pepper
1¼ cups palm vinegar	3 tablespoons Philippine soy sauce or patis (fish sauce)
¾ cup water	1 cup fresh lard or peanut oil
¼ cup well mashed garlic	
2 teaspoons salt	

Combine the chicken and pork with the vinegar, water, garlic, salt, palm sugar, and pepper in a stainless steel or enamel pot, and let stand for 30 minutes, turning the meat from time to time. Put the pot on the heat and bring to a boil. Then skim it, cover tightly, and simmer for 20 minutes. Add the soy sauce and simmer for another 30 to 40 minutes, or until the pork is tender. Remove the meat with a slotted spoon, and set it aside to drain.

Turn the heat under the sauce to high, and reduce the sauce by about two thirds. Allow it to rest, then skim off and discard half or more of the fat.

Meanwhile, heat a heavy skillet or wok and add 1 cup (or more) of lard or oil. When it is smoking hot, add the meat, half a dozen pieces at a time, and brown it, turning frequently. Remove the meat with a slotted spoon to drain. Heat a clean wok over high heat and add the reserved sauce. When it starts to get syrupy, add the meat and toss until almost all the sauce is gone. Transfer the meat to a platter and serve, with tomato sauce if you like.

GROUND FISH SAUCE

OTHER NAMES: Anchovy cream, Ground preserved fish, Mâ'm Nêm Xay or Mâ'm Nêm

REGION OF USE: Southeast Asia, principally Vietnam, Thailand, and Kampuchea

This sauce, expensive relative to fish sauce, is a suspension of ground anchovies in liquid fish sauce. "Creamed anchovies" is an apt description. The flavor and smell of this sauce is less the briny cheesiness of fish sauce and more like a fine anchovy paste we might use in Italian cooking. If you favor this sort of sauce, you should find it luxuriantly rich and delicious. It can be substituted for fish sauce, particularly in Southeast Asian curried dishes or other stewlike dishes made with coconut cream. In fact it seems ripe for experimentation in Western cooking.

RECOMMENDED: Viêt-Mỹ Corporation "Mâ'm Nêm Xay 'Phú-Quô'c,'" available in 10-ounce bottles; "Mâ'm Nêm Viet-Nam," available in 7-ounce bottles.

WHOLE FISH SAUCE

OTHER NAMES: Mâ'm nêm, Whole preserved fish

REGION OF USE: Southeast Asia, principally Vietnam, Thailand, and Kampuchea

Just as whole beans were to be found in the first soybean sauce, whole fish or fish pieces fermented in brine were undoubtedly the first fish sauces. As with liquid fish sauce, anchovies are the fish of choice—except away from the sea, in Laos for example, where freshwater fish are preserved this way. The result, called *padek,* is used in cooking by removing the fish and pounding it with other seasonings as a base for a stew; or the liquid alone may be used like fish sauce.

RECOMMENDED: Viêt-Mỹ Corporation "Mâ'm Nêm 'Phú Quô'c,'" available in 8-ounce jars.

NOTE: Various Southeast Asian fishes—such as gourami and mudfish—are sold "pickled" in jars in Southeast Asian markets. These condiments may be used to flavor sauces and stews.

OYSTER SAUCE

OTHER NAMES: Oyster flavored sauce

REGION OF USE: Southern China

A Cantonese staple made of oysters, water, salt, and, these days, cornstarch and caramel coloring, it was the flavor of this sauce that lent an exotic touch to the first Chinese-American food such as chow mein and chop suey. Depending on its quality, it can be an excellent all-purpose seasoning for noodle, meat, seafood, and vegetable dishes.

Originally the sauce was just oysters, water, and salt, and as such was a kind of gray suspension in liquid. It was extremely flavorful but it was none too appetizing looking, which explains the caramel and cornstarch. The cornstarch homogenizes the sauce, and in the case of cheaper sauces, fewer oysters can then be used.

The quality and corresponding price for a 14-ounce bottle of oyster sauce —the standard size for home use—varies widely, and you get what you pay for in terms of rich oyster flavor. The Hop Sing Lung Oyster Sauce Company of Hong Kong always makes a good product. The best is a new import from China labeled "Oyster Flavored Sauce," over a picture of oysters on the half shell. The small label near the top of the bottle says it's a "Product of Kwangtung."

Oyster sauce will keep indefinitely in the refrigerator. If you purchased it in a tin, transfer the unused portion to a covered jar after opening.

Most oyster sauces in the $2 range and up (for a 14-ounce bottle) are acceptable. Avoid the cheap sauces. If you find yourself using a lot of it, most companies offer theirs in large tins at considerable savings.

HIGHLY RECOMMENDED: Sa Cheng "Oyster Flavored Sauce" from China, available in 14-ounce bottles.

RECOMMENDED: Hop Sing Lung Oyster Sauce Factory "Oyster Flavored Sauce" (two qualities in 14-ounce bottles; choose the slightly more expensive).

STORAGE: Keeps indefinitely refrigerated; if bought in tins, transfer to a covered jar once opened and refrigerate.

SHRIMP SAUCE AND FINE SHRIMP SAUCE

OTHER NAMES: Shrimp paste, Kapee (Thai)

REGIONS OF USE: South coastal China and all of Southeast Asia

Shrimp sauce and dried shrimp paste

On Cheung Chau Island, a fishing habitat about an hour from Hong Kong, women make "fine shrimp sauce" by smearing a reddish-gray paste of pulverized shrimp and salt in round flat baskets and letting it bake in the sun. This dries to a toothpaste-like consistency before it's packaged.

To make plain "shrimp sauce" this extra drying step isn't necessary: Small shrimp are put in large jars and salted. They ferment by more or less digesting themselves with their own digestive enzymes, and the result is extraordinarily nutritious.

Probably the most difficult of the fish-type sauces for an unaccustomed Western palate, shrimp sauce, which is a staple throughout tropical Asia, is hardly used in restaurants here. The owner of a popular Thai restaurant in Berkeley, California, said simply that the smell of it cooking would drive away customers.

In Thailand, however, shrimp sauce—preferably the dried "fine shrimp sauce"—is an integral part of curry pastes, marinades, and *sambals*. In the Philippines this "preserved *alamang*" is used with abandon. The southern Chinese use shrimp sauce to flavor clay pot casseroles, noodle dishes, and fried rice, or put it out as a dipping sauce. It takes some getting used to, and English language cookbooks on South Asian cooking, if they call for it at all, do so in very timid quantities.

RECOMMENDED: Lee Kum Kee (Lkk) "Fine Shrimp Sauce" or "Shrimp Sauce" from Hong Kong; available in 8- or 13-ounce jars; Koon Chun Sauce Factory from Hong Kong, available in 8- or 13-ounce jars.

DRIED SHRIMP PASTE OR SHRIMP PASTE. Called *blachan* in Malaysia, this is fine shrimp sauce dried and sold in bricks, usually weighing 8 ounces. Used throughout Southeast Asia, it keeps better this way in the tropical heat. The color ranges from a pinkish to dark brown, and it's cut off in slices to be pounded with other seasonings into sauces, dips, and curry pastes. The slices are often toasted first or fried in a little oil to bring out their flavor.

NOTE: On the soy sauce shelf in stores specializing in Shanghai goods, a liquid labeled "Shrimp Sauce" may be found in soy-sauce-size bottles (21 fluid ounces). This is simply soy sauce with dried shrimp roe, a popular Shanghai condiment. It's favored as a dipping sauce.

REGION OF USE: Southern China	BARBECUE SAUCE

Not your everyday barbecue sauce, this intriguing oily paste called *sha zha jiang* consists of ground dried fish, chili peppers, garlic, dried shrimp, and ground peanuts spiced with coriander seeds, star anise, and Sichuan peppercorns. This is the closest the Chinese come to a curry paste.

Barbecue sauce may be smeared on meat just before broiling or grilling; or it may be used like a curry paste in stir-fried dishes. The flavor, which seems odd at first, quickly becomes addictive. It will keep indefinitely in the refrigerator.

NOTE: Once you've found "Barbecue Sauce," check to see if the ingredients are similar to those listed above. Barbecue Sauce may also mean a kind of hoisin sauce (see page 202).

HIGHLY RECOMMENDED: Lan Chi Brand "Barbecue Sauce," sometimes labeled "Sa Cha Chiang," available in 7-ounce jars.

RECOMMENDED: Sze Chuan Food Company's T.F. Brand "Barbecue Sauce," available in 8-ounce jars.

Sha zha jiang is a spicy sauce consisting predominantly of ground dried fish, not unlike a curry paste, and it makes an unusual stir-fried dish with flank steak, chili peppers, and shallots.

BEEF WITH SHA ZHA JIANG Yield: 4 servings	1 *pound flank steak* 2 *teaspoons cornstarch* 1 *tablespoon dark soy sauce* 1 *teaspoon sesame oil* ¼ *cup chopped seeded fresh chili peppers (green or red)* ¼ *cup finely chopped shallots* 1 *scallion, chopped (green part included)*	1 *cup + 2 tablespoons peanut oil* ½ *teaspoon salt, or to taste* 1 *teaspoon sugar* 3 *to 4 tablespoons Sha Zha Jiang (Barbecue Sauce)* 1 *tablespoon chicken stock mixed with 1 tablespoon Shaoxing wine*

Cut the flank steak as thinly as possible across the grain. Put the slices in a mixing bowl, add the cornstarch, soy sauce, and sesame oil, and mix well.

Combine the chili peppers, shallots, and scallion, and set aside.

Heat 1 cup of the oil to near smoking in a wok or heavy skillet. Turn off the heat and add the beef. Stir quickly to separate the slices. When the meat has begun to change color—some of it will be pink—remove it to a colander to drain.

Place a clean wok or skillet over high heat. When it is very hot, add 2 tablespoons oil and then the chili pepper mixture. Add the salt and sugar, stir for 20 seconds, then add the *sha zha jiang*. Stir until hot. Add the meat and the stock mixture, and cook, stirring, until well blended and hot, about 30 seconds. Serve with rice.

CHILI PASTES AND SAUCES

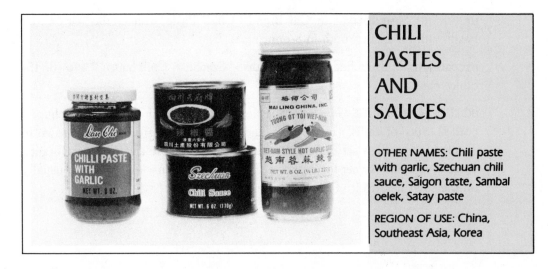

Chili peppers, a New World product, were quickly adopted in the western regions of China (Sichuan and Hunan), as they were in India and throughout Southeast Asia. They were—and still are—used both fresh and dried; but the Chinese, as they had done with soybeans, also ground them up, and salted and fermented them into richly flavored pastes.

Homemade or locally made in China for the most part, there are myriad bottled versions of these chili pastes on the market here. Available also are Korean pastes fermented like the Chinese pastes, and Southeast Asian sauces, crimson red and often bottled fresh, that is, without fermenting. Many of these are made locally. For example, Tia Chieu "Pepper Sa-te," a blazing hot Vietnamese-style sauce made in Los Angeles, advises that it goes with "pizzas, burritos, spaghetti, tacos, burgers and sandwiches."

The quality of the pastes runs from delicious to awful. The ingredients are fundamentally chili peppers, salt, oil, and often garlic, but they may include in addition, black beans, preserved radish, ginger, and, often, soybeans. If predominately soybeans, they're referred to as "hot bean pastes."

The Chinese and Koreans cook with chili pastes, whereas the Vietnamese use them frequently as condiments. Two brands, both Chinese (see next page), are excellent and can be used in either Southeast Asian or Chinese dishes. The Vietnamese-style pastes, taking up ever more shelf space in Southeast Asian markets, are incendiary; they're also preserved with potassium sorbate and the like, and don't have the character of the Chinese sauces. Many are packaged in plastic, which negatively affects the taste.

The Southeast Asian sauces also include some mixtures—*sambal oelek, sambal badjak* ("pirates sauce"), satay paste, and so on—which contain several ingredients such as peanuts, shrimp, sugar, or vinegar. These are best freshly made rather than bought. If called for, recipes can be found in cookbooks describing Indonesian or Malaysian dishes.

HIGHLY RECOMMENDED: Lan Chi Brand "Chilli Paste with Garlic" or "Chilli Paste with Soybean," both in 8-ounce jars.

RECOMMENDED: Sze Chuan Food Products "Szechuan Chili Sauce," in 6- or 15-ounce cans.

BOTTLED CHILI SAUCE. *Sriracha is* a table condiment on the order of ketchup, a bottled sauce of chilis, vinegar, salt, and sugar. Named after a seaside town in Thailand, and often set out on the tables of Vietnamese and Thai restaurants, sriracha is a little sweet for my taste. Better is the Louisiana hot sauce, usually on the shelf next to it in Southeast Asian markets.

VINEGAR AND SPIRITS
VINEGAR

A staple seasoning and ages-old medicinal throughout much of East Asia, vinegar, from the French meaning "sour wine," implies the use of grapes. With the exception of small quantities in China, however, grape vinegar has not played much of a role in Asian cooking. It's not all rice vinegar, though. The Chinese, who were the first in the region to make vinegar, used grains such as millet and barley, honey, fruits including peaches, dates, grapes, and cherries, and of course rice.

The Japanese learned about rice vinegar (as well as rice wine) from the Chinese in the fourth or fifth century, and rice vinegar is the staple vinegar of Japan. As you move into Southeast Asia, lime juice or tamarind is more apt to add sour flavor to food.

Palm vinegar, made from the sap of various palm trees (which also yield palm sugar and a kind of palm toddy), is popular in the Asian tropics and is imported here from the Philippines.

As a medicinal, vinegar was (and is) employed as an antiseptic, internally and externally. Thought to be cooling and beneficial for cleansing the system, its use is recommended in soups or stews—with pigs' feet, for example—to be eaten after childbirth. According to a sixth-century Chinese work, there were three methods for making vinegar: First, one makes a porridge of millet, barley, or glutinous rice, adds a wheat yeast, and allows it to ferment in a jar. Second, one adds a highly regarded wine of the time called "bitter liquor" during the brewing process, thus producing a fine black vinegar of the sort made today in Zhejiang. And third, one converts spoiled wine to vinegar.

In ancient China, there was also a curiosity called plum vinegar, which seems to have been more a method for storing fine vinegar or carrying it around. Dried and cured plums were soaked in "bitter liquor vinegar" for several days, then dried and pounded into chips. Anytime you wanted vinegar, you threw a few chips in water and let them soak.

NOTE: Palm vinegar, made from nipa palm sap, is sold in stores that carry Filipino foods. The best is Lorins, a lime-green, limelike flavored vinegar with a lively taste. Unlike most other vinegars, however, it loses some flavor a few weeks after the bottle is opened.

WHITE RICE VINEGAR	REGION OF USE: China, Japan, Korea, some areas of Southeast Asia

Much of the white rice vinegar produced by Chinese or Japanese manufacturers these days is made from rice wine lees and alcohol. In earlier times they started with rice that was cooked with water and then treated with a yeast, fermenting the sugar in the grain. This method of creating an alcoholic liquid, to be turned into vinegar via the action of acetic acid–producing bacteria, took an extra step but there was more aging involved, resulting in a complex, flavorful vinegar. Unfortunately these vinegars are hard to come by today.

The Japanese vinegars on the market, such as Marukan—sweetish and mild, diluted to a 4.3 percent acidity—are uniformly pleasant but undistinguished (some might say insipid). They're weaker in flavor than American white vinegar, comparable instead to cider vinegar less the fruitiness. Far more flavorful is the light golden Narcissus Brand rice vinegar from Fujian province, China, or the brand labeled "Swatow." Full-flavored also, though a little harsher, is the Taiwanese Kong Yen Rice Vinegar. All are widely available and good for any kind of cooking.

RECOMMENDED: Narcissus Brand "Rice Vinegar," or Swatow Rice Vinegar, both available in 19-ounce bottles.

Kong Yen Food Co.'s Kong Yen Rice Vinegar, from Taiwan, available in 20.2-ounce bottles.

Not all Chinese vinegars are rice vinegars; the fine dark vinegars of northern China are usually made from other grains. Wheat, millet, and sorghum are used, and the best, reminiscent of Italy's balsamic vinegar, are aged for years.

Zhejiang, on China's north coast, is known for its vinegars. They're aged and have a wonderfully complex, smoky flavor that is lightly and pleasantly bitter. Unlike fine vinegars from other regions, such as Shanxi, near Beijing, where chefs add vinegar to practically every dish (they even poach eggs in it), good Zhejiang vinegar is found here at Chinese food stores. The premier brand, made from glutinous rice and malt, is Gold Plum "Chinkiang Vinegar."

Other flavorful black vinegars on the market include Tientsin, a good all-purpose sorghum vinegar that's not as interesting as the Zhejiang, and Narcissus Brand "Yongchun Loagu," a fine aged vinegar. Both are from China.

Some black rice vinegars, such as Hong Kong's Koon Chun, are often diluted (meaning they have only about 2½ percent acetic acid) and have little depth.

HIGHLY RECOMMENDED: Gold Plum's "Chinkiang Vinegar," available in 19-ounce bottles.

RECOMMENDED: Tientsin Vinegar, available in 20-ounce bottles; Narcissus "Yongchun Loagu," available in 7-ounce bottles.

A little black vinegar is the perfect foil
for the slightly bitter, fibrous yow choy, my favorite
of the bok choy–type vegetables.

YOW CHOY WITH BLACK VINEGAR		
Yield: 6 servings	2 *pounds yow choy*	1 *tablespoon water*
	1½ *tablespoons black vinegar*	3 *tablespoons fresh lard or peanut oil*
	1½ *teaspoons sugar*	½ *tablespoon finely slivered fresh ginger*
	1 *teaspoon salt*	1 *tablespoon finely slivered Smithfield ham*
	1 *tablespoon Shaoxing wine*	

Cut off and discard the bottom 1 or 2 inches of the tough stems of the yow choy, and cut the remainder into 2-inch lengths, leaves and all. Set aside.

Mix the vinegar, sugar, salt, wine, and water, and set aside.

Over high heat, heat a wok and add the lard or oil. When it is hot, add the ginger and yow choy. Cook, stirring, until wilted. Add the seasoned vinegar and stir briefly. Cover, reduce the heat, and steam briefly. Take off the cover, turn the heat to high, and cook, stirring, until most of the liquid has been absorbed, another 2 minutes or so. Stir in the ham and serve.

A simple dish, good hot
or at room temperature, this makes good use of the
smoky Chinese black vinegar.

SAUTÉED EGGPLANT WITH BLACK VINEGAR		
Yield: 4 to 6 servings	1¼ *pounds Asian eggplants*	¾ *teaspoon salt*
	3 *tablespoons Gold Plum "Chinkiang" vinegar or other Chinese black vinegar*	⅓ *cup peanut oil*
		1 *teaspoon crushed dried red chili pepper*
	2 *teaspoons sugar*	2 *tablespoons finely chopped scallions, green part included*

Cut the eggplants in half and then into wedges no more than ½ inch wide. Cut the wedges into strips measuring 2 inches by ½ inch. Blend the vinegar, sugar, and salt, and set aside.

Heat a skillet over medium-high heat and add the oil. When it is hot, add the eggplant and cook, stirring constantly, about 5 minutes or until lightly browned and thoroughly wilted. Add the dried chili pepper and stir briefly. Add the vinegar mixture and cook another minute or two, until the liquid is thoroughly absorbed. Stir in the scallions and turn off the heat. Serve warm or at room temperature.

A traditional use for Chinese black vinegar,
this spareribs-in-caramel dish is like candy. It may be served warm
or at room temperature.

3 *pounds spareribs cut into 1½-inch lengths (see Note)* 6 *tablespoons Chinese black vinegar (undiluted and unsweetened)*	½ *cup sugar* 1 *tablespoon dark soy sauce* 1 *teaspoon salt (less if Chinkiang Vinegar is used)* *Peanut oil for deep-frying*	**SHANGHAI-STYLE SWEET AND SOUR SPARERIBS** Yield: 4 to 6 servings

Rinse the spareribs, pat them dry, and then cut between the ribs to separate the individual pieces.

Blend the vinegar, sugar, soy sauce, and salt. Set aside.

Heat a large quantity of oil in a wok until it's almost smoking. Add the ribs (about 1 pound at a time) and cook for 5 to 8 minutes, until well browned. Remove with a skimmer or slotted spoon to drain.

Remove the oil from the wok, raise the heat to high, and add the vinegar mixture. Let it cook until it becomes syrupy. Add the ribs and stir vigorously to coat them with the sauce. Transfer the ribs to a platter, allow them to sit for 10 minutes, and serve; or they may be served at room temperature.

NOTE: Have your butcher cut across the bones with his band saw.

| SHAOXING WINE | OTHER NAMES: Shao hsing, Shao-hsing, Hua tiao, Hua daio |
| | REGION OF USE: China |

China's most famous rice wine, from Shaoxing in Zhejiang province, has been made, it is said, for over 2,000 years. Blended glutinous rice, rice millet, a special yeast, and local mineral and spring waters give this amber-colored beverage its unique flavor. More like a sherry in color, bouquet, and alcohol content (18 percent) than a sake or a grape wine, it is aged about ten years in earthenware in underground cellars. The finest age for a century or more.

Shaoxing wine is also called *hua daio,* meaning "carved flower," after the design on the urns in which it's aged; also "daughter's wine," since traditionally some is stored at the birth of a daughter, to be drunk at her wedding.

Like sake, Shaoxing is drunk warm, and since it's rarely left out of a dish, it is vital to Chinese cooking. The only substitute is a good dry sherry. White wine or sake won't do.

A sprinkling of Shaoxing is standard to most stir-fried dishes, and a quarter of a cup or more may be used with braised foods. A bottle or two may be used in what the Chinese refer to as "drunken" dishes. In Drunken Crabs or

Drunken Shrimp, the live shellfish actually expire in a Shaoxing brine, where they pickle for a few days before they're eaten.

The real Shaoxing from Shaoxing is bottled under the Pagoda Brand in a blue-labeled bottle of 624 ml (not to be confused with the yellow-labeled bottle, which is sweetened) and a red-labeled bottle of 750 ml. A decent "Shaoxing" comes from Taiwan in a red-labeled bottle that resembles a bottle of Johnny Walker Red Label scotch.

HIGHLY RECOMMENDED: Pagoda Brand "Shao Xing Rice Wine" from Zhejiang, China, available in 750-ml bottles.

Pagoda Brand "Shao Hsing Hua Tiao Chiew" from Zhejiang, China, available in 624-ml bottles.

RECOMMENDED: "Shaoxing" from Taiwan, available in 21-ounce bottles.

OTHER NAMES: Sweet sake	**MIRIN**
REGION OF USE: Japan	

Although the Japanese don't cook with sugar much, use of the heavily sweetened rice wine *mirin* makes up for it. Typically, in small quantities, mirin seasons salad dressings; combined with dashi and soy sauce and heated, it's ladled over certain deep-fried foods; it seasons the stew known as *oden* and is added to the liquid for other simmered dishes; with dark soy sauce, it's responsible for the sticky brown glaze on teriyaki steak; and it's used in marinades for grilled dishes.

Mirins on the market include *hon-mirin*, or "true" mirin, meaning naturally brewed, and *aji-mirin*, or mirin with additives such as salt and corn syrup. The latter "new, improved mirin" (according to one manufacturer) falls into the category of seasoning mixtures that are more of a hindrance to a serious cook and are never quite the quality of the unadulterated ingredient. Mirin is sold in bottles from 10 ounces up to 1.5 liters (something under a half gallon).

RECOMMENDED: *Hon-mirin* (Kikkoman produces one) or other plain mirin.

NOT RECOMMENDED: *Aji-mirin* (Kikkoman produces one of these too).

FLAVORED OILS

SESAME OIL

OTHER NAMES: Sesame seed oil, Goma abura (Japanese)

REGION OF USE: China, Japan, Korea

Amber-colored sesame oil, used primarily as a flavoring, is a prime contender for the world's most seductively flavored oil. Besides lending its own nutty fragrance, it enlivens the other flavors in a dish—which is why the northern Chinese, who use it the most, sprinkle a few drops over almost everything they cook just as the heat is turned off. Soups such as Hot and Sour are dribbled with up to a tablespoon.

Sesame oil is used like a salad oil in dressing Chinese room-temperature dishes, and it's mixed with vinegar, soy sauce, and sometimes chili paste to make a dip for dumplings. Because of its expense, sesame oil isn't a standard table condiment in dumpling parlors, but you can request it.

Sesame oil comes by its enchanting aroma from sesame seeds that are roasted before their oil is extracted. Oil pressed from raw sesame seeds, though good for cooking, is not an acceptable substitute; in fact there is no substitute. By the same token the oil from the roasted seeds makes a poor cooking oil, as it burns easily and loses its fragrance over high heat. It's also expensive to cook with.

One notable exception is tempura oil, which is blended by Japanese chefs according to taste and may contain half sesame oil. The effect of frying batter-coated vegetables and seafood in part sesame oil (it's usually blended with soybean and rapeseed oils) is subtle though mandatory according to Japanese gourmets. Sichuan chefs make a seasoned oil by blackening dried chili peppers and Sichuan peppercorns in sesame oil, then straining it to use for cooking or dribbling over dishes. The slightly burned flavor is desired in this case.

Sesame oil, used both externally and internally, is sort of a cod liver oil of the East. It makes a luxurious massage medium when combined with fresh ginger juice to relieve aches and pains, and it's thought to facilitate childbirth if ingested.

There's no reason why sesame oil can't work its magic with Western dishes. A teaspoon beaten with eggs to be scrambled yields a more flavorful result. It's excellent for basting roasting fowl, and it goes especially well with mustard. A sesame oil vinaigrette is delicious.

Unfortunately sesame oil is increasingly packaged in plastic bottles, in which the oil seems to turn rancid more quickly than in glass bottles or cans. The most reliable brand is Kadoya of Japan, which comes in various-size bottles and a beautiful lavender tin of just under 2 quarts. The Taiwanese Kinlan Brand, with its red-labeled bottles, is also good.

HIGHLY RECOMMENDED: Kodaya Brand "Pure Sesame Oil," available in bottles or a tin of just under 2 quarts.

RECOMMENDED: Kinlan Brand; Dynasty Brand.

BLACK SESAME OIL. Although it's sold in Chinese food stores, this dark oil is used only medicinally, primarily as a postpartum restorative.

OTHER NAMES: Hot oil, Sa-te oil, Sesame chili oil	**CHILI OIL**
REGION OF USE: China, Southeast Asia, Japan	

If homemade and kept out of the light, a few drops of this fiery red oil— essentially chili pepper–infused cooking oil—is excellent in dipping sauces for dumplings or in dressings for Asian salads. With few exceptions, however, store-bought chili oil, particularly in plastic bottles, has a tendency to go rancid quickly, which is why it's often augmented with other flavorings such as Sichuan peppercorns, aniseeds, and garlic, or even preservatives.

TO MAKE CHILI OIL: In a spice grinder, coarsely chop 1 cup dried red chili peppers, preferably the small Thai variety. Place them in a stainless steel or porcelain saucepan with ¾ cup fresh peanut oil. Heat slowly until the peppers begin to foam. Keep cooking, and at the first sign that some of the smallest flecks on the side of the pan are blackening, turn off the heat, cover, and let sit 4 to 6 hours. Strain and bottle, and store out of the light.

RECOMMENDED IN A PINCH: Japan Food Corporation's Sesame Chili Oil (*chima rayu*), available in 3.5-ounce bottles.

SPICES, SUGARS, NUTS, AND SEEDS

SPICES AND FLAVORINGS

SPICES

The world has always looked to East Asia, especially the tropics, for the dried berries, bark, and roots we call spices, so it's ironic that most East Asians—the Chinese, Japanese, and Koreans—cook with very few of them. Southeast Asians cook with spices, but mostly as a legacy of Indian influence.

CHINA

Among the few spices employed with any regularity in this vast cuisine, two —cinnamon (actually cassia) and star anise—are used in certain meat and poultry dishes. Only one other indigenous spice is of any importance: the Sichuan peppercorn. White pepper and chili peppers were introduced. Cloves, called "chicken tongue spice," nutmeg, and a kind of cardamom—all of which grow in Southeast Asia—have been tried, but never caught on other than medicinally. Five-spice powder (for seasoning meats to be roasted) and curry powder are used in southern China (see below). However, when people write of "spicy" Sichuan and Hunan cuisines, they're confusing "spicy" with "hot." A Sichuan dish exploding with the fire and flavor of chilis, ginger, garlic, vinegar, and chili paste may contain not a single spice. In spite of millennia of exchange with India, even with the acceptance of spices for medicinal use, the Chinese is fundamentally a cuisine of simple fresh seasonings.

JAPAN

One of the most spice-free cuisines (traditionally without even the peppercorn), the spices the Japanese do use—sansho, mustard powder, wasabi powder, and dried chili pepper—they use with discretion.

KOREA

Korea, with its nearly overwhelming use of garlic and its heavy hand with ground chili pepper, does not have a timid cuisine. But with the exception of the chilis and plain pepper, Koreans use few spices.

SOUTHEAST ASIA

The use of spices (and herbs) distinguishes the cooking of Thailand, Indonesia, and Malaysia from their northern neighbors. Partly it's because this is where spices such as pepper, cloves, and nutmeg grow, but mostly it is India's influence in the region. Unlike China and Japan, in Southeast Asia there are slow-cooked dishes, or curries, which begin with the grinding of spices, often Umbelliferae seeds.

THE UMBELLIFERAE (coriander, cumin, caraway, fennel, and anise). India's influence in Southeast Asia shows up in the use of these seeds, all native to central and western Asia. The coriander seed is the most heavily used. Little distinction is made between cumin and caraway or anise and fennel; in Thailand all four seeds are just called *mellet*.

THAI RED CURRY PASTE

Yield: about 1½ cups

24 small dried red chili peppers	5 slices fresh galangal or fresh ginger
1 teaspoon coarse salt	6 garlic cloves
2 teaspoons cumin seeds	2 bunches coriander, roots and stems only
1 tablespoon coriander seeds	Zest of 1 lime
2 teaspoons black peppercorns	1 stalk lemon grass (bottom third only), cut into 1-inch lengths
2 medium or 6 small fresh red chili peppers	1 tablespoon fine shrimp paste
6 shallots	6 tablespoons peanut oil

Over medium heat, toast the dried chilis, coarse salt, cumin seeds, coriander seeds, and peppercorns in a dry skillet until fragrant. Grind to a coarse powder in a mortar or spice grinder, and set aside.

Put the fresh peppers, shallots, galangal, garlic, coriander, lime zest, lemon grass, shrimp paste, and 2 tablespoons of the oil in a large mortar or food processor, and grind to a paste. Add the spice powder and blend in. Remove the paste to a bowl and stir in the remaining oil. Transfer to a jar and store in the refrigerator. It will keep 1 month.

SPICE MIXTURES

The problem with spice mixtures is that like the spices themselves, they're best freshly ground. You're liable to run into several spice mixtures in Asian groceries, such as "Sweet Pork Char Siu Mix," "Philippine Adobo Pudding Mix," "Kim Chi Base Mix," and "Roasted Duck Mix," and most can be ignored.

CURRY POWDER. It's ironic that southern Chinese and even Japanese cooks, whose cuisines at their best are sparkling fresh, will occasionally resort to this tired powder, as do European chefs. Indians and Southeast Asians, who rely on spices, grind their own as needed. Turmeric makes curry powder yellow, and other common curry spices include coriander seeds, cumin, chili peppers, cloves, and cinnamon. The best comes as a paste, Daw Sen's from Calcutta, which is available in Chinese and some Indian food stores.

FIVE SPICES. This is a holdover from a time when medicinal uses of spices were as important as culinary. The number five had symbolic power, ensuring the healthfulness of this mixture. Not always exactly five spices, it commonly contains star anise, fennel or anise seed, cinnamon, cloves, licorice root, Sichuan peppercorns, and sometimes ground ginger. It's used in southern China and Vietnam to season meats and poultry to be roasted. Five spices comes in messy little plastic bags or small jars, and is sold in Chinese, Japanese, and Vietnamese grocery stores.

SHICHIMI. Also "seven spices," or more accurately "seven flavors," this Japanese mixture contains sansho, chili pepper, orange peel, poppy seeds, sesame seeds, black hemp (sesame) seeds, and bits of seaweed. Looking like the debris from the bottom of a bird feeder, and sometimes labeled just "Red Pepper," shichimi is available in ½-ounce jars in Japanese and Korean groceries. It's sprinkled over *udon* noodles, soups, and a variety of other dishes.

STAR ANISE
(Illicium verum)

OTHER NAMES: Chinese anise, Clove flowers, Badian

REGION OF USE: China, Vietnam, other areas of Southeast Asia

From a small evergreen that grows in southwestern China and northern Vietnam, this striking-looking eight-pointed pod is one of the few spices used in Chinese cooking. Star anise has been popular in Europe since the early 1600s. Having traveled there overland for trade via the China-Russia tea route, the pods used to be known as "Siberian cardamoms."

Star anise has a reputation as being mildly sleep-inducing, which is a blessing compared to others in its family, the Illiciaceae, all of which are toxic. According to the late Waverly Root, one close relative of star anise native to Japan is a narcotic that is taken in small doses as a prelude to committing hara-kiri. It was originally given the Latin name *Illicium anisatum,* and when the mistake was discovered, the real star anise was named *Illicium verum.*

Although it has the same essential oil, anethole, star anise is not related to the aniseed, a member of the parsley family (Umbelliferae). Because of its more intense flavor and higher essential oil content, star anise is used in the West as a licorice flavoring more often than aniseed—by the French in anisette, for example.

The Chinese use star anise in much the same way they use cinnamon, and sometimes in conjunction with it, whole, in meat and poultry dishes. It's also one of the six or seven components of five-spice powder. The Vietnamese add star anise pods to their beef soup called *phó*.

Star anise is sold in plastic bags, usually of 4 ounces, in Chinese and Southeast Asian markets. Stored in a jar away from light and heat, it will keep for months.

This a technique is unique to Chinese cooking, as far as I know.
Marinated strips of lamb are rolled in ground toasted rice and star anise
and steamed until succulent.

LAMB STEAMED IN RICE POWDER

Yield: 3 to 4 servings

¾-pound piece boneless lamb

2 teaspoons dark soy sauce

1 tablespoon light soy sauce

Pinch of salt

½ teaspoon sugar

5 slices fresh ginger

1 tablespoon ginger juice (see Note)

4 cloves garlic, crushed

2 scallions, cut in half and smashed (white parts only)

2 small dried hot chili peppers, ground

1 cup uncooked long-grain rice

2 star anise

Fresh banana leaves (optional, see Note)

Cut the meat into "butterfly" slices by making one slice not quite all the way through and the second slice all the way through. Pound the meat lightly.

Combine the two soy sauces, salt, sugar, ginger, ginger juice, garlic, scallions, and ground hot peppers in a bowl. Toss in the meat, mix well, and marinate for 30 minutes.

Meanwhile, make the rice powder by putting the rice and star anise in a dry skillet and cooking and stirring over high heat until the rice is brown. (It should be thoroughly browned but not scorched.) Spoon the rice and anise into a blender—a food processor won't work—and blend until it's the consistency of fine sand. (Don't blend it too finely.)

Line two steamer sections with banana leaves cut to fit. Put half the rice powder into a bowl, reserving the rest in a jar for future use, and dredge the lamb pieces in the powder, coating them generously. Arrange the lamb on the banana leaves and steam for 25 minutes. At the end of 15 minutes, sprinkle the lamb with a little water. Serve in the steamer.

NOTE: Ginger juice in this case is made by covering fresh crushed ginger in boiling water and letting it stand for 15 minutes or so, then straining the liquid.

If you can't get banana leaves, the lamb may be steamed on a plate.

CASSIA BARK
(Cinnamomum cassia)

OTHER NAMES: Cinnamon, Chinese cinnamon, Cassia

REGION OF USE: China, Vietnam, Korea

Fourth-century philosopher Bao-pu-zi, touting cassia, said that if it was taken with toads' brains for seven years, one could then walk on water and would never die. We have the chance to test this here in the United States, since what's sold as cinnamon is usually cassia, a first cousin and fellow member of the laurel family. Called "Chinese cinnamon," cassia was just about the first recorded spice used in Chinese cooking. It's native to China—forests of it once grew in Hunan—and is more pungent than true cinnamon, which comes from Sri Lanka these days.

While we tend to associate cinnamon flavor with sweets, it was first valued as a meat preservative, used in ancient China to make a kind of jerky from venison and other red meat. (In India, ironically, it's one of the few spices *not* used with sweets.) According to ancient texts, its culinary value lay with its ability to "eliminate the stench of raw flesh." It does contain phenols, which inhibit the bacteria responsible for putrefaction.

Rather than grinding cassia, the Chinese add the sticks, usually to braised meat dishes. The exception is five-spice powder, of which it's a component. The Vietnamese often add a stick to their famous beef soup known as *phổ*. The sticks yield more flavor, as the ground spice quickly becomes stale and dull. The freshest, most reasonably priced cinnamon (cassia) is to be found in small plastic packages in Chinese and Southeast Asian markets. The most pungent and full flavored is the inner bark of small, young branches; so look for the thinnest rolled "quills."

CASSIA BLOSSOMS. These are not the blossoms of the cassia (laurel) tree, but rather are plucked from a cliff-dwelling member of the jasmine family (*Osmanthus fragrans*). Cassia flowers, more properly called osmanthus blossoms, have been scenting Chinese tea and wines through the ages. The flowers sold here in small jars, preserved in a sweetened brine, are yellow—they also come in white and red—and are used to perfume sweets such as lotus seed soup, various pastries, and steamed pears. They're also sold embalmed in a sugary paste called cassia blossom jam.

	DRIED
OTHER NAMES: Galanga, Laos or Laos powder (Indonesian), Ka or Kha (Thai)	**DRIED GALANGAL**
REGION OF USE: Southeast Asia, especially Thailand, Laos, Kampuchea, Java	

Dried and ground galangal, often called *laos* (its Indonesian name, not derived from the country Laos, where it also happens to be a staple), is added by the teaspoonful to soups, stews, and curries in Southeast Asia. The ground powder in fact finds its way into spice mixtures as far west as Morocco.

The better way to buy dried galangal is in slices, though they are next to impossible to grind in a mortar. The slices are added without soaking to soups and stews. They're sold in plastic packages in stores that carry Thai and Vietnamese goods.

THREE "PEPPERS"

PEPPER (Piper nigrum)	OTHER NAMES: Pepper seed, Barbarian fagara (ancient China)
	REGION OF USE: Southeast Asia, China, Korea

First harvested in India from a native tropical vine, the peppercorn was introduced to Java as early as 100 B.C. by Hindus who created kingdoms there, and it was eventually used, if not cultivated, in most of Southeast Asia. The spice reached China in the first or second century, but never had the culinary impact it did in Ancient Rome and the West. The Japanese, who learned of pepper from the Chinese around the eighth century, accepted it as a medicine but never saw fit to sprinkle it over their food.

Called "barbarian pepper" by the Chinese (to the Chinese pepper was always *fagara,* the Sichuan peppercorn, which is unrelated), they wrote of it as native to Persia since it reached their shores via Persian traders. However it was used little, other than medicinally, until the Tang Period some 600 years later, when there was a fascination with "exotics" and Chinese gourmets took it up at the expense of their native pepper.

Today it's a staple in China, but mostly the white peppercorn—white pepper is the "hot" in Hot and Sour Soup, for example—which is processed differently from the black: The pepper berry is allowed to ripen to a bright orange-red, then soaked in water until the soft fruit sloughs off, leaving the inner seed, which is sometimes treated with a little lime water to bleach it. Black peppercorns occur when green (unripe) berries are picked, allowed to ferment, and then dried.

To the south—in Vietnam, Thailand, Indonesia—black peppercorns are integral to the cuisines. They're ground with other spices and fresh herbs to make curry pastes; or the ground pepper is sprinkled over dishes at the end, as we do in Western cooking. Southeast Asian markets in fact are an excellent source for "pepper seeds," black or white, sold in plastic packets, as they're shipped right from the source. Chinese markets carry white peppercorns as well as the ground powder.

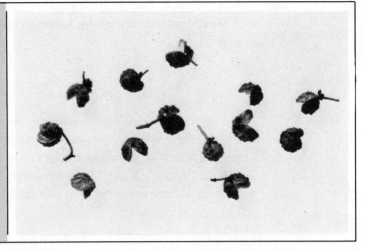

SICHUAN PEPPER-CORNS
(Zanthoxylum simulans)

OTHER NAMES: Fagara, Wild pepper, Anise pepper, Chinese pepper

REGION OF USE: China

The dried reddish-brown berries known as Sichuan peppercorns are not related to black peppercorns or chili peppers, nor do they "smite you with a heat wave," as the late Waverly Root wrote in his book *Food*.

The spice is rather strangely numbing, and it has a clean, spicy-woodsy fragrance that has made it popular in all regions of China for centuries. Among seasonings, only cassia and ginger have been used for as long in China. Sichuan pepper got its name because it's native to that province and probably was first cultivated there in Neolithic times.

Sichuan pepper was once a standard table condiment in China. Even wines were flavored with it, and during the Tang Period (618–907) it was the vogue to take it with tea and clotted cream. When "foreign fagara," or black pepper, was introduced from the tropics, Sichuan pepper fell out of favor with gourmets and never regained the popularity it once had, although it's still widely used.

Sichuan pepper commonly seasons roasted meats and poultry. "Seasoned salt" (see below) is a popular accompaniment to fried and roasted foods. "Seasoned oil"—made by heating Sichuan peppercorns in peanut oil until they blacken, then straining the oil and discarding the peppercorns—makes a wonderful cooking oil for stir-fried dishes, or it may be used for dressing Chinese salads.

Sichuan peppercorns are sold in Chinese markets in plastic packages, usually of 8 ounces. They keep well in a covered jar.

TO MAKE SICHUAN PEPPER: Toast Sichuan peppercorns in a dry skillet over medium heat until they begin to smoke (don't worry if a few blacken slightly), and then grind them in a mortar or spice grinder. Store excess powder in a jar.

TO MAKE SEASONED SALT: Put 2 tablespoons Sichuan peppercorns, 3 tablespoons coarse salt, and 1 teaspoon white peppercorns in a dry skillet. Toast over medium heat, shaking the pan, until the Sichuan peppercorns begin to really smoke. Transfer to a mortar or spice grinder, and grind to a coarse powder. This is traditionally served, along with lemon, with roasted fowl such as squab and with deep-fried foods.

An example of how Asian staples can elevate a dish from the ordinary, this chicken is juicy and delicious roasted or grilled. As with any roasted meat, a little dark soy sauce results in a more pleasing golden hue. The Sichuan pepper is a spicy flavor enhancer, and the sprinkling of bright green coriander is an attractive complement.

SIMPLE ROAST CHICKEN WITH SICHUAN PEPPERCORNS

Yield: 4 to 6 servings

1½ teaspoons Sichuan peppercorns	1 teaspoon freshly ground black pepper
1 chicken (4 pounds)	1½ teaspoons coarse salt
1 tablespoon dark soy sauce	¼ cup finely chopped coriander leaves

One hour before cooking, toast the Sichuan peppercorns in a small dry skillet over high heat, shaking the pan, until they begin to smoke. Transfer to a mortar or spice grinder and grind to a coarse powder. Set aside.

With a French chef's knife or kitchen shears, cut out the backbone of the chicken so it will lie flat. Rub the chicken all over with the soy sauce, and sprinkle with the two peppers and the salt. Allow to sit for 1 hour until ready to cook.

Preheat your oven to 450°F. When the oven is ready, lay the chicken skin side up on a rack in a roasting pan and roast for 20 minutes. Reduce the heat to 325°F and cook for another 30 minutes. Remove the chicken from the oven, sprinkle with the coriander, and allow to sit for 10 minutes. Serve cut, bones and all, into about 12 pieces Chinese-style, or however you like.

OTHER NAMES: Japanese pepper	SANSHO
REGION OF USE: Japan	(Zanthoxylum avicenne)

The Japanese are about the only people who don't use common pepper (*Piper nigrum*) in their cooking, and they are the only ones who sprinkle their food with *sansho*.

A close cousin of the Sichuan peppercorn—both are dried berries of a prickly ash and neither is related to black pepper—this is one of the few spices used in Japanese cooking. The fragrant leaf of the same tree, called *kinome,* is used as a garnish in Japan (see page 39).

Sansho seasons mostly fatty foods, such as grilled meat and eel, to counteract their richness—akin to Sichuan pepper mixed with salt accompanying roasted meats and deep-fried food in China. Unlike Sichuan peppercorns, however, sansho is available only ground. It comes in little shaker-top jars, sold in Japanese groceries.

OTHER NAMES: Makrut (Thai), Mak khi hout (Laotian), Ghost's lime, Lime of an evil spirit	KAFFIR LIME
REGION OF USE: Thailand, Burma, Laos, and elsewhere in Southeast Asia	(Citrus hystrix)

Only the leaves of this tree and the rind of its pear-shaped wrinkled fruit are used in Southeast Asia—for cooking, that is. Washing one's hair with a little of the juice and grated rind wards off evil spirits in Thailand. Both lime and leaves are highly aromatic—the latter, used like bay leaves, have a strong floral-lemon fragrance.

Until now, the leaves and rind of this fruit have been available only in dried form in the United States. However, the trees are being grown in Florida and California, and Thai restaurants in these states sometimes keep one in the backyard.

The dried leaves come packaged in 1-ounce plastic bags, well labeled in English, and ready to be tossed one or two at a time into soups and curries. The shredded dried rind comes in small packages, often unlabeled unfortunately, and it's best soaked in warm water before you add it, also to soups and slow-cooked dishes. (You'll find it swimming with lemon grass in Thai Hot and Sour Soup.) The rind comes powdered also, but I would avoid this. I suspect these limes and leaves will soon be on the market fresh.

DRIED ORANGE PEEL (Citrus nobilis, C. aurantium)	OTHER NAMES: Dried tangerine peel REGION OF USE: China

Even if the fruit were inedible, the orange, native to China, would have been grown just for its peel. Historically it was a seasoning on the order of ginger, garlic, fagara, and cinnamon. As a medicine, the peel was something of a panacea. There's a tradition according to a sixteenth-century *materia medica* of "servants, children, ragpickers and others" collecting it, drying it, and selling it to pharmacies. The peel of the "coolie orange," also called the Canton orange (which became the Seville orange when it hit Europe), was valued above that of the mandarin (called the tangerine after it grew in Tangiers).

Medicinally, orange peel is supposed to bring down fevers, cure acne, keep the aged in good voice, alleviate coughs, prevent convulsions, rid the body of pinworms, and act as an antidote to fish and shellfish poison. Old and dark peels—some have been aged for a century or more—are considered the most effective.

Not tossed in food as much as it used to be (though it is still important to herbal cures), orange peel is a staple in Sichuan and Fujian provinces. It's best with meat and poultry: Whole pieces added to braised duck or pork dishes along with rock sugar and dark soy sauce render them delicious and cut the richness. For stir-fried dishes, the peel may be minced or ground in a spice grinder; or it may be softened in a little Shaoxing wine, then slivered or minced and added, wine and all.

Orange peel, usually labeled "Dried Tangerine Peel," comes in small plastic packages, found on the shelf with the seasonings in Chinese groceries; but it's best to dry your own, a habit that's easy to acquire during the winter, when oranges and tangerines are in season.

TO DRY YOUR OWN ORANGE PEEL: Use oranges or tangerines with powerful flavor and fragrant peels. The peppery tangelo or Mineola, bright orange and shaped like a hand grenade, is a personal favorite, as are various tangerines. Every time you eat the fruit, put the peel, white side up, on a cutting board and cut away the white pith with a sharp knife. Toss the peel on a plate and let it dry in or out of the sunlight. Depending on the environment, it should dry in a week or so (it should still be flexible). Store in a jar.

NOTE: Orange peel does improve with age. I stay a year ahead.

OTHER NAMES: MSG, Taste essence, Aji-no-moto (Japanese), Vetsin (Vietnamese)	**MONO-SODIUM GLUTAMATE**
REGION OF USE: China, Japan, Korea, Vietnam	

One of the most controversial ingredients, MSG, sold under the brand name Accent in the United States, is ranked just above DDT by many non-Asians in terms of things they want to ingest. However, contrary to popular belief, MSG is not a wholly synthetic additive, but a salt that occurs naturally in many foods—the monosodium salt of glutamic acid, an amino acid.

Before 1908, when a Japanese scientist discovered how to extract MSG crystals from kelp, some Asians used "taste-essence," a seasoning composed of dried fermented wheat gluten (and sometimes soy protein, dried shrimp, and seaweed) that contained natural doses of MSG. Soy sauce, too, contains a trace of MSG which it comes by naturally, apparently as a result of the fermentation process.

In the early years, MSG was manufactured from wheat gluten. These days it's made from either sugar beet molasses or glucose solutions fermented with special bacteria. About 250,000 tons of the seasoning are produced annually.

The allergic reaction of some people to MSG—at least to large doses of it —dubbed "Chinese restaurant syndrome," first came to light in this country in the late 1960s. Symptoms include chest pains, headache, and numbness. Ironically, people who suffer these symptoms here may not get the same reaction in Asia.

Soups in some Chinese, Thai, and Vietnamese restaurants here seem to be the worst offenders. I'm told that cooks, in order to get the same intense flavor from their stocks as they did in Asia, may add up to a tablespoon for each couple of quarts.

For some reason, few patrons complain about side effects from dining in Japanese restaurants, even though MSG is habitually used in the cooking there. It's commonly added to table salt in Japan to enhance its seasoning ability and prevent it from caking. MSG is used with a particularly heavy hand in Japanese rice crackers and other packaged snacks, and in the pickles such as pickled daikon that are sold in bulk in Japanese markets.

MSG is available at all Asian grocery stores.

ESSENCES

REGION OF USE: Thailand
and elsewhere in
Southeast Asia

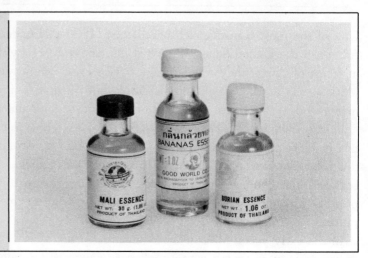

The Thais often perfume their sweets—rice pastries, coconut creams and custards, and the sweetened threads of egg yolk known as Thai Silk—with fragrances. Most popular are jasmine, called Mali Essence; pandan (screw pine) leaf extract; banana; and the essence of the notorious durian fruit, whose smell is not one of its charms. These extracts are sold in tiny bottles, ⅓ to 1 ounce, which sometimes instruct: "Used for Thai food, Cakes, Biscuit, Boiled Sweets and Ice Cream."

The Thais use a foi tong maker for this unusual and popular sweet,
in which threads of egg yolk are set in a sugar syrup and quickly removed. If
done skillfully, your serving platter should have several little pyramids of
gleaming yellow threads, almost cloyingly sweet and slightly
crunchy. Be sparing with the jasmine essence.

2 cups sugar 1 cup water 12 egg yolks 2 teaspoons lightly beaten egg white	Pinch of salt Few drops jasmine essence	**SWEET THREADS OF GOLD** (Foi Tong) Yield: 6 to 8 servings

Heat the sugar and water in a frying pan or small skillet. Let it cook until it starts to become syrupy—this may take 10 minutes.

Meanwhile, strain the yolks, the whites, and the salt through a fine-mesh strainer into a bowl. Stir in the jasmine essence.

When the syrup is almost ready, load the egg mixture into a pastry bag with a tiny opening, holding it closed with your finger. When the syrup is ready, turn the heat to low, and with a circular motion, dribble some of the egg in threads over the surface of the syrup. When set—this takes only seconds—remove with a slotted spoon. Repeat with the remaining egg mixture. With chopsticks or spoons, mound the egg threads into thin pyramids. After these sit, they should be arranged on another serving platter. When cool, they should be slightly crunchy.

NOTE: By rolling wax paper into the shape of a cone, you can eliminate the need for a pastry bag. A piece of tape should hold it; just be sure the opening is tiny.

SUGAR

Chinese brown sugar, rock sugar, and honey

"Stone honey" was what the ancient Chinese called cane sugar. For ages honey had been the only sweetener, so their first conception of sugar was of a kind of solid honey produced without the help of bees. The Chinese molded loaves, even figurines, of "stone honey," which they made by drying the juice of sugar cane in the sun.

Not native to China, although it was an early crop, sugar cane was a transplant, probably from Vietnam where it was a product known to the Chinese since at least the second century B.C. Native to somewhere in tropical Asia (it's impossible to know exactly, since it no longer grows wild), sugar cane may have originated along the coast of southeast India; in any event Indians introduced the world to sugar cane processing.

In fact the Chinese admiration for Indian sugar, a raw granular sugar which they called *sha t'ang* ("sandy sugar"), prodded them to dispatch a mission in 647 to learn how it was done. Reportedly the Chinese growers began producing a superior product. Around the tenth century the Chinese in Sichuan province produced "sugar frost," which we know as refined white sugar.

The Japanese first tasted sugar in the seventh century in Chinese confections—sweetened, salted, and fried lumps of ground grains or soybeans—which they referred to as "Chinese fruit." In 754 the Chinese introduced a crude sugar to Japan, which for centuries was only used by upper-class Japanese when they had bronchial conditions. The Portuguese and Dutch brought "barbarian sweets" to Japan in the seventeenth century, but it wasn't until around the turn of this century that sugar was widely used in Japan. Japanese sweets are mostly made with bean paste and meant to go with green tea.

Europeans first saw sugar in the twelfth century, during the Crusades (the Arabs had taken the cane to the Mediterranean from India centuries earlier), but until the early eighteenth century, when European sugar plantations in the Caribbean, Brazil, and West Africa, staffed by millions of slaves, were in full swing, sugar was a luxury item or was combined with medicines to make them palatable.

Sugar cane may be a native product, but East Asians don't come close to the 80 pounds of sugar each of us consumes yearly in the United States. The sugar-laden food at the end of a meal, which we call a dessert, was never a concept in East Asia.

Sweetened foods in Asia are traditionally snacks to be taken with tea. Whatever is put under the category of desserts in Asian restaurants here is a bow to Western convention. Responsible for enormous sugar consumption, soft drinks, now taking hold in Asia, were a recent idea imported from the West.

Besides honey and sugar cane (and beet sugar as of the eighteenth century), the Chinese have historically sweetened food with maltose and palm sugar, a staple today throughout Southeast Asia.

| OTHER NAMES: Brown sugar in pieces, Slab sugar, Brown sugar candy
REGION OF USE: China | BROWN SUGAR |

Sold in 1-pound packages or in bulk from large crocks in Chinese markets, these 6-inch wafers look like thin caramel sandwiches. You'll run across few recipes that call for this (Sweet Peanut Soup; a New Year's cake made with glutinous rice flour), but it's a fine brown sugar for any cuisine, and may be used in any recipes calling for brown sugar.

| REGION OF USE: China and elsewhere | HONEY |

Various foods, among them ginger, kumquat peels, olives, and bamboo shoots were preserved in honey in ancient China, and it was drunk diluted in water for one's complexion. It's still considered a tonic and a cure for colds. There are unusual, reasonably priced honeys for sale in Chinese markets, including "Centifloral," "Winter," and lychee. The quantities range from 12-ounce jelly glasses to jars of over 2 pounds.

MALTOSE	OTHER NAMES: Malt sugar
	REGION OF USE: China

Thick and resembling corn syrup, this has been produced by the Chinese since at least the second century B.C. The process involves converting cereal starch —wheat, barley, millet—to sugar, or "malting." Maltose is what turns to alcohol when whiskey or beer is made.

Traditionally malt sugar (or honey) is used to treat the skin of Peking duck before it's roasted. About a third as sweet as white sugar, maltose is a pleasant, flavorful sweetener, considered tonic in China. It's available in 1-pound plastic tubs, or occasionally in crocks labeled "Genuine Maltose." Try it for sweetening tea and other beverages.

ROCK SUGAR	OTHER NAMES: Yellow rock sugar, Yellow lump sugar, Rock candy
	REGION OF USE: China, Vietnam

A crystallized mixture of refined and unrefined sugar and honey, rock sugar is a necessity for the succulent braised ("red-cooked") pork and duck dishes popular around Shanghai, as it gives a sheen as well extra character to the sauce. Bird's nest soup and other sweet soups considered restorative, containing delicacies such as lotus seeds or "silver" fungus, will specify this sugar. It's an excellent beverage sweetener.

For well under $1, rock sugar is sold in Chinese and Southeast Asian markets in 1-pound boxes or plastic bags. Many of the amber crystals are big and hard. However, to measure out the proper quantities for recipes by first crushing the sugar in a cloth with a hammer, as many books suggest, is ridiculous. An estimate of the amount of sugar in a lump won't be far enough off to ruin a dish. Rock sugar may be used wherever granulated sugar is called for.

OTHER NAMES: Jaggery,
Coconut sugar, Java sugar

REGION OF USE: Southeast Asia,
including Burma, Thailand,
Indonesia, Malaysia, the
Philippines

PALM SUGAR

Probably the first man-made sugar, used well before cane sugar, palm sugar is made by boiling down the sap of various palm trees—the sugar palm, the palmyra palm, the coconut palm, and others—which are tapped like maple trees.

Palm sugar is used not just in sweets but in savory dishes as well, and not so much to sweeten them as to balance out the saltiness of soy or fish sauce, the acid of citrus juice, and the pungency of chilis.

With a maple sugar–like flavor and color that varies by brand, palm sugar is sold in Thai, Indonesian, and sometimes Vietnamese food stores. Grainy and sometimes sticky, its packaging ranges from 8-ounce plastic containers labeled "Coconut Sugar" (from coconut palm sap) to 1-pound logs of "Java Sugar." It's difficult to recommend a particular palm sugar, since although the flavor varies with the place of origin, many are delicious. Brown sugar is a barely passable substitute for palm sugar. Jaggery, sold in Indian food shops, is a better substitute.

NOTE: When "jaggery" is called for in Southeast Asian cookbooks, it means palm sugar. In India, jaggery (the name comes from the Hindu *jagri*) may be either palm sugar or raw lump sugar processed like palm sugar from sugar cane.

PALM SYRUP. A fine use of palm sugar is to melt it in a saucepan, strain it, and pour it over pancakes. In Southeast Asia, this wonderful syrup is a foil for pancakes made of rice flour and fresh coconut.

SUGAR CANE

Sugar cane was raised for eating, or at least for chewing, long before sugar was processed from it, and eating varieties are still raised. Starting in early winter, the fresh cane is sold in Chinese and Southeast Asian markets here. Once pared, the core can be gnawed on or used, as the Vietnamese do, as a thick, tasty skewer on which to grill deliciously seasoned pastes of fresh shrimp.

NUTS AND SEEDS

CHINESE ALMONDS
(Prunus armeniaca)

OTHER NAMES: Apricot seed, Apricot kernel, Bitter almond

REGION OF USE: China

Labeled either "Almonds" or "Apricot Seeds," there's confusion about the nature of these small blanched "nuts" sold by the pound in plastic packages in Chinese food stores, and in bulk in herbal shops. Closely related to the familiar "sweet" almond, and with many times the flavor—chewing on one is like taking a hit of almond extract—Chinese almonds are apricot seeds, and apricots are native to China.

Almonds, introduced to the Chinese by the Persians centuries ago, never caught on. Besides its flavor, it's hard to approach the status of the apricot seed in the Chinese pharmacopoeia. Among its powers, the extract is the base of popular cough and asthma remedies.

Because of the flavor, Chinese almonds should make a superior paste for Western desserts, and are delicious toasted. The Chinese use for them that springs to mind is the plain rectangular bars of white "almond jelly," made with agar-agar, that are wheeled around in *dim sum* parlors; it is also served in cubes with fruit cocktail.

NOTE: There is controversy about the use of apricot kernels as eating them raw in sufficient quantities can be toxic. Those in Chinese markets have been blanched but nonetheless should be put in a warm (200°) oven for 20 minutes before using.

CASHEWS
(Anacardium occidentale)

A native of Brazil, the cashew nut was planted in Malaysia by the Portuguese about 400 years ago, and the Chinese got it sometime after that. (It's safe to assume that Chicken with Cashews is not an ages-old dish.) A problem with harvesting these in Southeast Asia is that monkeys are fond of the fruit to which the nut is attached and make off with them.

The cashew nut is sold, blanched, in 1-pound plastic packages in Chinese and Southeast Asian grocery stores, and they're a relative bargain. Typically these are fried in oil until golden brown right before they're added to a dish. The oil should be heated until nearly smoking, then turned off and the cashews added so they brown evenly.

CHESTNUTS
(Castanea spp.)

OTHER NAMES: Kuri (Japanese)

REGION OF USE: Japan, China, Korea

Dried chestnuts with fresh chestnuts

Chestnuts, abundant in the fall in U.S. markets, are part of our national imagery. But Japanese and Chinese markets are just as laden with them. The Japanese, in fact, who choose among a few varieties, may incorporate chestnuts more thoroughly into their cooking than any other culture. They steam them, bake them, grill with them, and even cook them in rice. A high percentage of Japanese sweets use chestnuts.

The Chinese, mostly from Shanghai north, cook chestnuts in casseroles with duck and make a simple cabbage and chestnut dish that wouldn't be out of place on the American holiday table. A well-known banquet dessert, Peking Dust, is an ethereal mound of puréed chestnuts, walnuts, brown sugar, and cream.

The chestnut for sale at Asian markets, known as the "Chinese chestnut," is slightly smaller than the European variety. Prior to about 1940 there were forests of American chestnuts in the Eastern United States from Maine to Florida, but the trees were wiped out by a blight that came along with some chestnut saplings imported from Asia to Long Island in 1904.

Chestnuts must be peeled before using, and although the shell is no problem, the bitter inner skin takes some work. Peeling can be accomplished by slashing the tops of the chestnuts and then simmering them in water for 30 minutes.

DRIED CHESTNUTS. Peeled and dried chestnuts are delicious when reconstituted, they must be soaked for 2 to 3 hours, then simmered in water for 1 hour. They are sold in 1-pound plastic bags in Chinese markets.

GINGKO NUTS
(Gingko biloba)

OTHER NAMES: Ginnan (Japanese)

REGION OF USE: China, Japan, Korea

With fan-shaped leaves—"little duck webs" to the Chinese—the beautiful gingko tree is a relic. Thanks to millennia of Chinese cultivation, it's the lone survivor of a prehistoric family of trees. Since its introduction to the West in the eighteenth century, it has been used as an ornamental street tree in some urban areas, where it has been found to weather air pollution. The nuts from the gingko can be harvested in the fall in Manhattan—if you're fast enough.

The nut has a lengthy history as a medicine (gingko nuts are a popular Asian remedy for bladder and urinary problems) and as a food in China and Japan. In Japan, in fact, the bitterish nut is something of a staple.

Fresh gingko nuts are abundant in Chinese and Japanese markets, where they are sold in bulk. They look like little buff-colored footballs, the outer (smelly) fruit having been removed.

Besides dyeing the shells red and consuming them at weddings, the Chinese put gingko nuts in stuffings, and in anything "eight-jeweled" such as Eight-

Jeweled Duck or Eight Treasures Rice Pudding. They may be toasted, boiled, or steamed with other foods, and are an ingredient in sweet soups. The Japanese steam them in savory custards and deep-fry them on pine needle skewers.

The shell of the gingko nut may be removed with a nutcracker or by a tap of a handy utensil, taking care not to damage the soft yellow nut inside. A minute or two of simmering will loosen the brownish inside skin, which can be rubbed off while they're in the water. To cut the bitterness of the nut, it's sometimes recommended that a thin toothpick or skewer be pushed through it lengthwise to remove the central core.

Unshelled, the nuts will last a few weeks refrigerated in a sealed container (to prevent them from drying out). Gingko nuts come canned, but since it's unlikely they'll become a daily habit, use them fresh.

An exotic Southeast Asian dessert, served hot,
with fresh gingko nuts and red dates (jujubes). Freshly rendered
pork lard is best with this, and more traditional, but if this is
unavailable, use peanut oil.

WARM TARO PUDDING WITH DATES AND GINGKO NUTS

Yield: 8 servings

THE PUDDING

24 *jujubes (red dates), soaked overnight in cold water*

24 *fresh gingko nuts, shelled and peeled*

1 *pound taro root*

Water

¾ *cup sugar*

¼ *cup freshly rendered pork lard or peanut oil*

¼ *teaspoon salt*

2½ *tablespoons water chestnut powder*

THE SAUCE

2¼ *cups water*

½ *cup sugar*

2 *tablespoons freshly rendered pork lard or peanut oil*

2 *tablespoons water chestnut powder or cornstarch*

Blanch the jujubes and gingko nuts for 5 minutes in boiling water to cover. Drain, and set aside.

Peel the taro root, cut it into thick slices, and steam it for 20 to 30 minutes, until tender. Purée with ½ cup water in a food processor or with a hand mixer until smooth.

Scrape the purée into a saucepan, add 1 cup water, and bring to a boil over medium heat. Stir in ¾ cup sugar, ¼ cup lard, and the salt, and cook, stirring, 3 minutes. Add half the jujubes and gingko nuts, and continue to cook for 5 minutes or so. Meanwhile mix the water chestnut powder with ⅓ cup water, stirring until the powder is thoroughly dissolved. Mash this through a strainer into the taro. Cook, stirring, another 5 minutes. It should be as thick as a smooth porridge. Keep warm.

Make the sauce by combining 2 cups water, ½ cup sugar, and 2 tablespoons lard in a saucepan. Bring to a boil. Mix the remaining ¼ cup water with the 2 tablespoons water chestnut powder and add in the manner described above. Cook until the sauce thickens and clears, then add the rest of the jujubes and ginko nuts. Simmer for 5 minutes and turn off the heat.

To serve, transfer the taro to a platter, and pour the sauce over it.

PEANUTS (Arachis hypogaea)	OTHER NAMES: Ground nut, Monkey nut, Kachang china ("China bean," Malaysian)
	REGION OF USE: China, Southeast Asia

The route of the underground legume we call a peanut from its home in the American tropics to Asia is unclear. Native to Paraguay, Brazil, and environs, it was widely cultivated in the New World when the Europeans arrived. In the sixteenth century, either the Spanish took it across the Pacific and planted it in the Philippines, or the Portuguese took it to India or even on to Canton, or all of the above. Evidently the Chinese got it early and introduced it southward, since the peanut is often called *kachang china* ("Chinese bean") or some variation throughout Malaysia and Indonesia.

As a denizen of Asia, the peanut was no mere snack food, but was quickly appreciated as a star approaching the soybean as a source of protein and oil. Recognizing the nitrogen-enriching properties of the plant's roots, the Chinese fit it into their southern crop rotation systems, and it was all of a sudden the most important oil seed in much of South China (see page 318).

The Chinese roast peanuts and eat them salted and boiled (popular in the southern United States) for snacks, toss them in dishes (Sichuan's Chicken with Peanuts), and grind them into peanut sauce.

Because of the climate (there's not much competition from the soybean in the tropics), the peanut really took hold in Southeast Asia. Roasted and pounded in Indonesia, Malaysia, Thailand, and elsewhere, they're a base for curry-style dishes and for the dip sauces for *sate*. A peanut dressing seasons the Indonesian mixed vegetable salad *gado gado*. In Java, a fermented paste of immature peanuts is eaten boiled and fried. Crushed roasted peanuts are in fact a condiment in this region.

In China, before making a paste or sprinkling them into a dish, raw peanuts are first browned in oil. In Indonesia they're shelled and roasted, not in an oven but over a fire, in a wok filled with river sand. All is then dumped into a bamboo sieve, leaving the peanuts. But an oven will do.

Peanuts are sold shelled and skinless in 1-pound plastic packages in Chinese and Southeast Asian groceries. Before they are used, they should be fried until light gold (see peanut butter directions below), or they can be roasted in a 350°F oven. Small, tasty roasted whole peanuts from Indonesia are sold in 8-ounce packages in Chinese and Southeast Asian markets, as are larger ball-park-style peanuts from China.

PEANUT BUTTER. Southeast Asian cookbooks sometimes call for peanut butter because as a prelude to many Southeast Asian dishes, peanuts are browned and crushed in a mortar. Similarly, the best peanut butter is made from raw, skinless peanuts that have been roasted or lightly fried before they are blended in a food processor. Most commercial brands have extra vegetable oil or emulsifiers to prevent the oil from separating, and are fatty and tasteless compared to the real thing. Natural blends, nothing but peanuts and salt, are better. However, the use of salt is a little heavy-handed, and the skins, often ground with the peanuts, are slightly bitter. Health food stores with machines that allow you to grind your own are the next best thing to making it.

TO MAKE PEANUT BUTTER: Heat 2 cups of fresh peanut oil in a small heavy saucepan until hot but not smoking. Add a heaping cup of raw, skinless peanuts, stir, then immediately turn off the heat. Allow them to sit until the oil cools some, about 6 to 8 minutes, or until the peanuts are light gold. With a slotted spoon, remove the peanuts and grind to a paste in a food processor. (The oil may be used for another purpose.) If you prefer, you may roast the peanuts in a 350°F oven until light brown; in that case, add 2 tablespoons peanut oil to the food processor with the peanuts when you grind them.

This marinade for chicken is equally delicious with pork, beef, or shrimp. In fact it needn't be limited to satay; you may use it on anything you choose to grill. Use 12-inch wooden skewers, which are available at Asian markets. The skewers should be soaked in water for a couple of hours before they are used so they won't burn; or once the meat is skewered, the tips may be covered with aluminum foil.

CHICKEN SATAY WITH PEANUT SAUCE

Yield: 6 to 8 servings

1 *pound boneless, skinless chicken breasts*

MARINADE

3 *garlic cloves, finely minced*

2 *teaspoons coriander seeds, toasted and ground*

2 *teaspoons cumin seeds, toasted and ground*

2 *tablespoons brown sugar*

2 *tablespoons fish sauce*

6 *tablespoons tamarind water*

2 *tablespoons peanut oil*

DIP SAUCE

½ *cup peanut oil*

½ *cup raw peanuts*

2 *fresh green jalapeño peppers*

1 *slice fresh ginger (½ inch thick)*

4 *garlic cloves*

⅓ *cup unsweetened coconut milk (canned or fresh)*

2 *teaspoons dark soy sauce*

4 *teaspoons fish sauce*

1 *teaspoon sugar*

1 *tablespoon fresh lime juice*

Pinch of salt

½ *cup finely minced coriander leaves and stems*

Holding your knife parallel to the chicken breast, cut off wide thin slices. Cut these slices into approximately 2 × ¾-inch strips and thread them on the skewers, leaving a handle of about 4 inches. (The skewered meat should be as flat as possible.)

Mix the marinade ingredients together. Arrange the skewers in a shallow dish, handles overlapping, and pour the marinade over the meat. Allow to stand 30 to 60 minutes, turning from time to time. (You should start your fire at this point.)

Make the dip sauce: Heat the ½ cup peanut oil to nearly smoking in a saucepan. Turn off the heat and add the peanuts. The peanuts should cook to a light brown in 3 to 5 minutes (you may have to turn the heat on again, but stir the peanuts if you do). Using a slotted spoon, transfer the peanuts to the container of a food processor or blender, along with 1 tablespoon of the peanut oil (reserve the rest) and blend them to a rough paste. Add the chilis, ginger, and garlic, and continue to blend. Add the remaining ingredients except the coriander, and blend until smooth. Pour the sauce into one or two dipping bowls, stir in the coriander and reserved oil, and set out to accompany the grilled chicken.

To grill the chicken, simply cook about 1 minute on each side—do not overcook—and serve.

PINE NUTS
(Pinus spp.)

OTHER NAMES: Pine kernel, Pignolia

REGION OF USE: Korea, China

We think of pine nuts in Pesto Genovese and other Mediterranean cooking, and indeed, the esteemed "pignolia" grows on the cone of the stone pine indigenous to that area. But the Chinese and Koreans have used pine nuts for ages, and some feel the world's best come from a tree that grows in Manchuria, Korea, and northern Japan, *Pinus koraiensis*.

To the Koreans it's a staple that's used in candies, glutinous rice desserts, congee, fancy kimchi, and chopped in a kind of steak tartare. The northern Chinese use them in sweets as well as fried as a garnish for savory dishes.

For around $4 a pound, the pine nuts in Chinese groceries are a bargain no matter what kind of cooking you do. In the fall Chinese markets, at least in California, carry them freshly harvested from Utah, Nevada, and elsewhere in the West. They need to be shelled, however, and lightly fried before they're used.

An unusual dish, this could be described as the world's most luscious meat cake. It's a pork skin stuffed with hand-chopped pork and pine nuts, and it simmers for hours.

YANGCHOW PORK WITH PINE NUTS

Yield: 8 servings

3 pounds fresh bacon (pork belly), in one piece, with rind

1 cup pine nuts, browned lightly in oil or toasted

1 tablespoon minced fresh ginger

1½ tablespoons dark soy sauce

3½ teaspoons salt

1 teaspoon sugar

2 eggs

Cornstarch

6 tablespoons Shaoxing wine

Peanut oil for deep-frying

3 cups chicken stock

3 cups water

4 approximately 1-inch cubes of rock sugar

¼ cup light soy sauce

4 scallions

3 thick slices fresh ginger

1 pound spinach or hearts of Shanghai bok choy

Cut the rind from the pork, leaving at least ¼ inch of fat on the rind, and set it aside. With a heavy Chinese cleaver or French chef's knife, chop the pork coarsely by hand. (This is best done by slicing and shredding it first.) When it has approximately the consistency of ground meat, transfer it to a mixing bowl. Chop the pine nuts coarsely and add them. Add the ginger, dark soy sauce, 1½ teaspoons of the salt, sugar, 1 of the eggs, 1½ tablespoons cornstarch, and the wine. Mix thoroughly, stirring by hand in one direction.

Turn the pork rind skin side down on a cutting board, and score the fat in a diamond pattern at ¼-inch intervals. Sprinkle cornstarch over the fat and work it in. Shake off any excess. Spread the chopped pork mixture on the fat, pressing it down, and mold it into a flat cake with wet hands. Blend the other egg with 1 teaspoon cornstarch, and rub this over the ground pork.

Heat 6 cups or so of oil in a wok and when nearly smoking, slide the pork into the oil. Basting the top of the cake with a spatula, brown the pork for 5 to 7 minutes. Remove and drain.

In a clean wok or large casserole, combine the stock, water, rock sugar, light soy sauce, remaining 2 teaspoons salt, scallions, and ginger, and bring it to a boil. Slide in the meat cake, reduce the heat to medium-low, and simmer it for 2½ to 3 hours, checking it and basting the top with the sauce from time to time. (You may have to add more water if the sauce starts to thicken too soon.)

At the end of 2½ hours, transfer the cake to a large serving platter and keep warm. Strain the sauce into a clean pan, and turn the heat to high to reduce. Meanwhile, steam the spinach until it wilts and arrange it around the pork. When the sauce becomes syrupy, pour it over the pork and spinach, and serve. Needless to say, this goes well with rice. It's also excellent reheated.

NOTE: The reason you hand-chop the pork, rather than having it ground, is that the texture is infinitely more pleasing.

| OTHER NAMES: English walnut | **WALNUTS** |
| REGION OF USE: China, Korea, Japan | **(Juglans regia)** |

The Japanese credit the ancient Korean kingdom of Silla for their walnuts. The Koreans write of its introduction from China. The Chinese, who had walnut groves in the north by the year 400, supposedly got the walnut from the Persians, who are credited with first cultivating it and who also introduced it to the Greeks. No one knows how long the Tibetans have grown walnuts, but they may have introduced it to the western (Sichuan) Chinese, where today a kind of nut halvah is made from them.

The walnut came here from England, and to distinguish it from our own black walnut, it's sometimes called the "English walnut." The Old English name, *wealhhnutu,* from which we get the modern word, means, for good reason, "foreign nut."

The people of Sichuan are China's biggest nut eaters. The walnut is served crispy-fried with chicken and hot peppers. There's a duck dish in which the skin is stuffed with fried walnuts, duck meat, and seasonings, then steamed and deep-fried. Ground walnuts are used as a batter where pieces, usually of chicken, are dredged in egg white, dipped in the nuts, and then fried.

For Chinese-style whole walnuts, either golden-fried in combination with other ingredients or by themselves (sometimes first cooked in a sugar-honey syrup), the thin membrane of the walnut should be peeled off. This is done by steaming, then painstakingly pulling it away—tweezers help.

I've seen large walnut pieces in Chinese markets for $1.59 a pound, but this was in San Francisco, where not far away the bulk of this country's walnuts are harvested.

FRIED FISH IN WALNUT BATTER		
Yield: 6 servings	1½ *pounds filets of firm, white-fleshed fish such as sole*	2 *egg whites, lightly beaten*
	¼ *cup cornstarch*	1 *cup finely chopped walnuts*
	½ *teaspoon ground dried red chili pepper*	*Peanut oil for deep-frying*
	2 *teaspoons salt*	½ *cup chopped coriander leaves and stems*
	½ *teaspoon sugar*	*Lemon wedges*
	2 *tablespoons Shaoxing wine*	

Cut the filets into strips about 2 inches by ¼ inches. (They should be absolutely dry.)

Mix the cornstarch, dried red pepper, salt, sugar, and wine in a bowl. Stir the egg whites into the mixture and stir just until blended.

Dip the fish pieces, one at a time, first into the cornstarch mixture, then into the chopped nuts, making sure they're well coated. Set aside on wax paper until all are coated.

Deep-fry the fish in 350°F oil until golden, 2 minutes or so. Drain on paper towels and serve sprinkled with the coriander, with the lemon wedges on the side.

CHINESE RED DATES
(Zizyphus jujuba)

OTHER NAMES: Red date, Jujube, Indian jujube

REGION OF USE: China, Korea

According to a sixteenth-century writer in Nanking, "Among the finest of fruits are jujubes from the Yaofang Gate; they sometimes exceed two and a half inches in length and have skin as red as blood. . . . Their flesh is whiter than gleaming snow, their flavor sweeter than honey."* Too bad we can only get them dried and shriveled, in 8-ounce or 1-pound plastic bags, or sometimes in boxes in Chinese markets.

No relation to the palm date, which the Chinese named the "Persian jujube" when the Persians brought it to China in the seventh century, the jujube is a small fruit that has been cultivated in the warm, dry parts of China and India for centuries. Hundreds of varieties grow in China.

As an ingredient, dried, they're useful as a decoration for Eight-Jeweled Pudding, chopped in a sweet soup with walnuts, and braised or steamed with chicken, but they deserve note because their history is lengthy and important in China. Wines were made of jujubes; jujubes have always been offered in sacrificial rites (their red color is considered auspicious, indicating good fortune). They're one of the oldest sweetmeats, preserved in honey or salted. Some varieties have been bred just for drying.

If they're to be used in sweet dishes, jujubes should be soaked overnight in cold water. Before adding them to a braised dish, an hour or so of soaking will do, and the soaking liquid should be added. Some dishes require that they be soaked and pitted, which is tedious. (Unfortunately the best come with pits.)

NOTE: I don't know why those gummy little candies are called jujubes, although there must be a connection.

*K. C. Chang, ed., *Food in Chinese Culture* (New Haven: Yale University Press, 1977), p. 236.

A plant can be a staple of Chinese cooking for 2,000 years, which is probably the case with sesame seeds, and still be called "foreign" if it's not native. What the Chinese call "foreign hemp," sesame, is thought to be native to Africa, although some argue for Persia or even India, where it's been under heavy cultivation for millennia. The seed consists of about 50 percent oil, of a kind that keeps well in tropical heat and is fine for cooking.

Like many foodstuffs, the plant traveled from China to Japan. Unique to those countries is the wonderfully flavored amber oil made from toasted and pressed seeds (see page 319). A day-to-day ingredient in Japan and Korea, the whole seeds are toasted in a dry skillet and crushed lightly in a mortar for tossing in myriad dressings and dip sauces. The Chinese too use the whole seed toasted, but mostly as a garnish, and less frequently. They do however grind them into a paste (see next page).

BLACK SESAME SEEDS. If there's a botanical difference between black and white sesame seeds, no source I've read points it out. Black sesame seeds, and they are jet black, are used whole to dramatic effect as a garnish in both Chinese and Japanese cooking. Toasted and ground to a powder, they're mixed with sugar, yielding a kind of gray dust, to coat certain Chinese sweets—a treat only if you appreciate their taste, which is measurably earthier than the white seed.

Sesame seeds, both black and white, can be purchased in Chinese and Japanese markets in plastic packages of up to 1 pound.

SESAME SEED PASTE

OTHER NAMES: Sesame paste, Sesame butter

REGION OF USE: China

Unlike tahini, the light-colored sesame paste of the Middle East, the seeds of this Chinese condiment are toasted before they're ground, yielding a grayish brown paste not unlike smooth peanut butter. The paste is the base for sauces, among them a spicy Sichuan dressing for a summer noodle dish. It also gives substance to marinades for spareribs and barbecued pork. Like real peanut butter, it comes with solid and oil separated and must be mixed before using. In the case of sesame paste that has sat around, this can take some doing.

RECOMMENDED: Pearl River Bridge Brand "Sesame Butter," available in 8.8-ounce jars.

Lan Chi Brand "Sesame Seed Paste," from Taiwan, available in 8-ounce jars.

If done properly, these nuts look laquered and are crunchy
and not overly sweet. This recipe was intended for walnuts, but because
their skin is bitter, it means boiling and peeling them as a first step—a
tedious task. Whole pecans, native to America, work beautifully.

HONEYED PECANS WITH SESAME SEEDS

Yield: 8 to 12 servings

¼ cup white sesame seeds

¾ cup sugar

2 tablespoons honey
(lychee honey would be
nice)

½ cup water

2 cups whole pecans

Peanut oil for deep-
frying

Toast the sesame seeds in a dry skillet, shaking them just until fragrant, and set aside.

Combine the sugar, honey, and water in a saucepan, and boil until slightly syrupy. Add the nuts and cook for a minute or two, then drain in a metal colander.

In a wok or deep skillet, heat 6 cups or more of oil until hot but not smoking. Add the nuts and fry them, stirring to separate. Cook for 1 to 2 minutes, then drain in a clean colander. Immediately pour the nuts into a cool clean steel bowl, add the sesame seeds, and stir to coat. Pour the nuts onto a sheet pan and spread to cool. When cool and hardened, they will keep for several days in an airtight container.

NOTE: If the sugar syrup becomes too thick, the nuts will have a frosted rather than a glazed look; if the frying oil is too hot, they will darken and burn.

...RICE

There is no more important ingredient in this book than rice. One could say the cumulative importance of the various meats, vegetables, herbs, and sauces doesn't even add up to the importance of rice. It's not just because it's eaten two or three times a day by over half the world's population; it's that this grain, thought of as a bland accompaniment by most of us in the West, is for all practical purposes food, and one of infinite subtleties, in the minds of Japanese, Southeast Asians, and most Chinese (the northern Chinese eat wheat and wheat products). Other ingredients and the dishes made from them exist to accompany rice, not vice versa. To Asians, eating rice is synonymous with eating a meal, and they feel they haven't truly eaten unless they've had rice. The phrase "Rice is ready" calls people to dinner in China.

The cradle of rice cultivation has long been thought to be China; then as a result of archaeological discovery, the first rice cultivation was credited to northern Thailand—around 3500 B.C. In the late 1970s, the Chinese discovered rich Neolithic sites along the mouth of the Yangtze River, where rice farming took place even earlier, thus recapturing China's credit for the earliest cultivation.

Although there are thousands of varieties of rice, there are two types at either end of a spectrum from which all varieties are derived: long-grain, sometimes called Indian rice, favored by most Chinese and Southeast Asians, and the starchier short-grain "Japanese rice," eaten in Japan and by many in eastern China.

What distinguishes a type of rice, besides its length, is the amount of waxy starch molecules, called amylopectin, which cause stickiness in rice. Long-grain rice has less amylopectin than short-grain, and in fact contains a substance, amylose, that acts naturally to separate the grains. In a category of their own are the so-called glutinous rices, also referred to as "sweet" or "sticky" rice, that are nearly all amylopectin.

There is a variety of rices available for Asian cooking, and the number is increasing with the fine and unusual rices coming in from Southeast Asia.

LONG-GRAIN RICE

REGION OF USE: China, Thailand, Vietnam, and throughout Southeast Asia

Preferred by Chinese and Southeast Asians, it's long-grain rice that grows in the monsoon belt that cuts a swath across the Asian tropics. This southern "water rice," as the Chinese call it (as opposed to rice that grows on dry land), has always been considered the best, in part because of the pure whiteness that can be obtained with a minimum of milling. Although less sticky than short-grain rice, the longest and starchiest grades of long-grain rice have always been prized by the Chinese.

Chinese fussiness was compromised somewhat in the eleventh century when a famine-producing drought occurred in Fujian province. A strain of rice from Champa (now Vietnam) was introduced because of its drought resistance and its ability to grow in high altitudes; it also had a shorter growing season and in some cases could be double-cropped. Considered inferior to the familiar paddy rice, various descendants of Champa are grown today in China.

In 1694, North America became a rice grower when long-grain rice was first cultivated near Charleston, South Carolina. Carolina rice, for sale everywhere today, is perfectly acceptable for Chinese or Southeast Asian cooking. In fact most long-grain rice sold here in supermarkets and in Asian stores is domestic, raised in Louisiana, Texas, Arkansas, and California. Asian markets prefer "Extra Fancy Texas Long Grain," packaged popularly by the Comet American Marketing Company in Houston. For sale in up to 100-pound sacks, it's very good rice, reasonably priced in these markets.

Now competing with the Texas rice is a superior long-grain rice from Thailand. Called "jasmin rice," it has a refreshing fragrance when cooked. Available in markets that sell Southeast Asian foods, it comes in 10-pound bags and larger.

TO COOK LONG-GRAIN RICE: There is no strict water-to-rice ratio for cooking rice, since the larger the quantity of rice being cooked, the less water, proportionately, is required. One cup of rice may require 1½ cups of water, whereas 3 cups may require only 4 cups of water. The Chinese solve this by letting the water cover the rice by a depth of one knuckle joint (slightly over 1 inch). It should be pointed out that older rice requires more water than newer rice, and that long-grain rice requires more water than short-grain rice—something to keep in mind when using a Japanese rice cooker calibrated for short-grain rice.

First, however, rice should be washed, stirring it with the fingers until the water runs clear. Then, after the water is added, the rice is brought to a boil over medium heat. Allow it to boil vigorously for 1 minute, then turn the heat to low, cover, and cook for 18 minutes. Don't open the lid during this time. After cooking, allow the rice to sit for 7 to 10 minutes before serving. (It can sit for 30 minutes.) Uncover, fluff with a fork or paddle, and serve.

NOTE: The technique above, and there are many variations, produces what the Chinese call "steamed" rice, a term that sometimes puzzles non-Asians in Chinese restaurants who think rice cooking is more akin to boiling. It's simply a language difference.

This isn't a risotto and it's not a paella,
but there are elements of each in this Chinese dish. It's best made
in large heavy pot or casserole.

RICE POT WITH SEAFOOD AND CHICKEN

Yield: 6 to 8 servings

4 dried scallops

¼ cup water

2 cups boiling water

6 dried black mushrooms

1 whole chicken (about 3 pounds)

2 tablespoons minced fresh ginger

3 tablespoons oyster sauce

½ teaspoon salt

1 teaspoon white pepper

3 tablespoons freshly rendered chicken fat (see page 320)

1 teaspoon sesame oil

1 tablespoon Shaoxing wine

8 large shrimp

2 cups uncooked long-grain rice

4 links Chinese sweet sausage, sliced diagonally

8 littleneck clams, scrubbed

1½ cups sliced scallions, green part included

Put the dried scallops in a small bowl with ¼ cup water, and steam for 20 minutes. Meanwhile, pour 2 cups boiling water over the mushrooms and allow them to sit for 30 minutes.

While the mushrooms are soaking, bone the chicken and cut the meat, with the skin, into 1-inch cubes. Combine the ginger, oyster sauce, salt, pepper, chicken fat, sesame oil, and wine in a bowl, toss in the chicken, stir, and set aside.

Shell the shrimp, reserving the shells. Cut the shrimp in half lengthwise. Pull the scallops into shreds.

Squeeze the mushrooms out over the soaking liquid (reserve the liquid). Cut off and discard the stems, cut the caps in two, and mix the caps with the chicken. Combine the reserved mushroom liquid and the shrimp shells in a small pot. Simmer for 10 minutes; turn off the heat.

Put the rice in the bottom of a large pot, and pour the mushroom soaking liquid through a strainer over the rice. Add water until the water is about 1 knuckle joint above the rice. Bring the rice to a boil and cook over high heat about 5 minutes until the water is barely absorbed. Spread the marinated chicken and mushrooms, the scallop shreds, and the sausage slices over the rice. Turn the heat to low, cover, and cook 20 minutes. Then add the clams and shrimp, cover, and cook until the clams steam open. When the clams are done, stir in the scallions, mixing all the ingredients into the rice, and serve.

The sizzling rice comes from rice cake—a layer of brown crusted rice that comes from cooking rice 30 minutes longer than you should. This crust is then dropped in very hot oil until it puffs slightly, drained, and then immediately put on a platter and covered with a topping—in this case shrimp with tomatoes—which causes it to sizzle.
(See recipe below for making rice cake.)

SIZZLING RICE WITH SHRIMP, TOMATOES, AND WATER CHESTNUTS

Yield: 4 to 6 servings

1 *pound shrimp*

2 *teaspoons cornstarch*

Pinch + 1 teaspoon *salt*

1 *teaspoon sesame oil*

Approximately 3½ *cups peanut oil*

2 *cups peeled, seeded, and quartered ripe tomatoes*

6 *fresh water chestnuts, peeled and halved*

1½ *tablespoons minced fresh ginger*

1 *tablespoon minced garlic*

2 *small dried chili peppers, crushed in a mortar*

1 *tablespoon sugar*

⅓ *cup frozen, or parboiled very fresh, peas*

Approximately 6 pieces *rice cake (enough to cover the bottom of a platter)*

Peel the shrimp, cut them in half lengthwise, and combine with the cornstarch, a pinch of salt, and the sesame oil. Marinate in the refrigerator for 30 minutes.

Heat a skillet over high heat, and add 2 tablespoons oil. When it is smoking hot, add the tomatoes and cook, stirring, for about 5 minutes or until they make a sauce. Stir in another tablespoon of oil and set aside.

Over medium heat, heat 3 cups of oil in a wok. When it is hot, add the shrimp and cook, stirring to separate, about 20 seconds or until they just begin to curl. Drain the shrimp in a colander. Briefly fry the water chestnuts and add to the shrimp. Leave the oil in the wok over low heat.

Meanwhile, heat a clean wok or skillet and add 3 tablespoons oil. Add the ginger, garlic, and chilis, and cook, stirring, until fragrant. Add the tomato sauce, 1 teaspoon salt, and the sugar. Stir just to blend, cover, and turn off the heat.

Turn the oil up under the first wok and when it's smoking hot, add the rice cake pieces—they should puff up immediately. Turn them in the oil a couple of times, then remove and drain on paper towels. Quickly heat the tomato sauce, stir in the shrimp and peas, and cook until hot. Put the rice cake on a platter and pour the shrimp over—it should sizzle—and serve.

RICE CAKE

The best rice cake usually occurs the way it was undoubtedly discovered—when you forget to turn off the rice after 18 minutes and it continues to cook, forming a golden crust. If this happens, simply scoop out the soft rice and continue to cook the crust over low heat until it's thoroughly dried out. The pieces can then be wedged out of the pot and allowed to cool, uncovered, on a plate for a couple of hours. They can be then kept indefinitely in a plastic container.

You can make rice cake from scratch by cooking rice as you normally would, except that you let it cook for 45 minutes. Then scoop out the soft rice, leaving the crust, and follow the procedure above. The soft rice can be refrigerated and used the next day for fried rice.

FRIED RICE

Fried rice needn't be brown take-out food with soggy bean sprouts that more or less strangle whatever the main ingredient is supposed to be—the shrimp, for example, in Shrimp Fried Rice. It shouldn't be soy sauce brown.

Traditionally fried rice is a way of using leftover rice. In fact you have to start with leftover rice, preferably rice that has spent the night in the refrigerator so the granules can be separated easily by hand. Other ingredients don't have to be leftovers, although they can be. The rice should be regular long- or short-grain. (The texture of converted rice doesn't hold up well since sautéing it for fried rice would mean a third cooking; it's already partially cooked.)

To prepare fried rice: Break up the cold cooked rice into grains. Cut and assemble other ingredients, which may include meat (sliced, diced, or ground), seafood such as shrimp, vegetables cut into small pieces, seasonings including herbs, and your oil.

Heat a wok or skillet and add oil for sautéeing. When it is hot, add the main ingredients, in order according to their cooking times, and sauté until partially cooked. Add the seasonings and stir, then the rice, and continue to stir rapidly over high heat. Adjust the seasonings and continue, but don't overcook. The moist hot rice will cook the ingredients further once the heat is turned off. When the dish is piping hot, 5 to 8 minutes total time, serve and eat.

3 cups cooked rice	½ cup or more diced winter-cured pork (rind removed)	**FRIED RICE WITH WINTER-CURED PORK, CUMIN, AND PEAS**
¼ cup peanut oil		
2 teaspoons cumin seeds	½ cup peas, fresh or frozen	
1 small fresh red chili pepper, chopped (including seeds)	1½ teaspoons salt	
	1 teaspoon freshly ground black pepper	Yield: 4 servings

With your hands, break the rice into grains and set aside.

Heat a wok or skillet and add the oil. When it is hot, add the cumin seeds and stir briefly. Add the chili pepper and the diced pork and cook, stirring, until the fat of the pork is translucent, about 30 seconds. Add the peas and stir briefly, then the rice and seasonings. Stir over high heat for 3 minutes or so, until piping hot. Serve.

One of the classiest, most attractive, and tastiest
fried rice dishes—period. But first you have to make the curry paste,
which is easy if you have the ingredients.

3½ cups cooked rice, preferably that has sat refrigerated overnight	½ cup water	**YELLOW CURRY FRIED RICE WITH MUSSELS**
	2 teaspoons salt	
1 teaspoon finely minced garlic	½ teaspoon black pepper	
	¼ cup Yellow Curry Paste (see page 35)	
2 tablespoons fresh lime juice		
7 tablespoons peanut oil	1 cup minced flowering chives or regular Chinese chives cut into ½-inch lengths	Yield: 4 to 6 servings
24 mussels, scrubbed and bearded		
½ cup Shaoxing wine		

Break up the rice into individual grains.

Make a vinaigrette by shaking the garlic, lime juice, and 5 tablespoons of the peanut oil in a jar; set aside.

Put the mussels, wine, water, 1 teaspoon of the salt, and the black pepper into a pot, cover, and turn on the heat. As soon as the mussels steam open, scoop them out with a slotted spoon and transfer to a large mixing bowl. Toss them with the vinaigrette, and cover with a clean dishcloth to keep them from cooling too fast. Skim 3 tablespoons of the steaming liquid from the pot and reserve.

Heat a wok or heavy skillet and add the remaining 2 tablespoons peanut oil. Add the curry paste and stir until fragrant. Add the rice and cook, stirring, 1 minute. Add the remaining 1 teaspoon salt and the reserved broth, and stir in the chives. Drain the mussels quickly and add to the rice. Stir just until hot, and serve.

SHORT-GRAIN RICE

OTHER NAMES: Oval rice

REGION OF USE: Japan, Korea, and to some extent eastern China

Somewhat gummier than long-grain rice, this is the preferred rice of the Japanese. More than a matter of taste, these rices grow better in Japan, with its shorter growing season and longer days. Called "oval rice" by the Chinese, short-grain rice is sometimes confused with glutinous rice because of its similar shape and stickiness.

Excellent grades of short-grain rice—some claim as good or better than Japanese rice—are being grown in California, such as that packaged under the Calrose label, or the premium, Kokuho Rose. Rice in Japanese food markets here is in fact all California-grown. The Japanese prefer what they call *shinmai,* or "new rice," which reaches the market in the fall, and this too is shipped from California to Japanese grocery stores throughout the United States, and can be had in October and November.

TO COOK SHORT-GRAIN RICE: Wash and cook short-grain rice using the same method as for long-grain rice, remembering that short-grain rice requires slightly less water.

GLUTINOUS RICE

OTHER NAMES: Sweet rice, Sticky rice

REGION OF USE: China, Japan, Korea, Southeast Asia

Commonly sold as "sweet rice," sometimes called "sticky rice," opaquely white grains of glutinous rice are a staple from Korea to Indonesia. However, unlike long- or short-grain rice, this rice rarely is served plain as a foil for other foods—it's just too sticky. But its starchy richness makes it an ingredient of choice (often ground into flour) in sweet dishes, particularly the assorted little chewy cakes of tropical Asia.

Cooked and mixed with Chinese sausage, mushrooms, dried shrimps, and other ingredients, glutinous rice is also a popular Chinese poultry stuffing. Pearl Balls, seasoned ground pork rolled in glutinous rice grains, then steamed, are familiar to most of us. And *zhong,* fist-size boiled lotus or bamboo leaf packages that hang in Chinese restaurants and delicatessens, or are wheeled around on *dim sum* carts, are stuffed with glutinous rice dotted with other savories.

A Japanese staple, *mochi,* is a glutinous rice cake traditionally made by pounding hot glutinous rice with mallets in giant mortars. Machine-made and packaged in plastic, these cakes are available in Japanese groceries. They're often simply sliced, grilled, and served with soy sauce.

The Thais, in one of the simplest and tastiest uses of glutinous rice, blend it warm with coconut milk and sugar, and serve it with ripe fruit such as mango or sometimes the notoriously foul-smelling durian.

The glutinous rice available here is of two types: Chinese and Japanese groceries carry the popular stubby-grained variety common to Japan and China, and grown in California. The popular brand, and it's excellent, is Koda Farms. Southeast Asian markets have begun to carry a long-grain Thai glutinous rice, usually sold in bulk, and also of high quality.

TO COOK GLUTINOUS RICE: Unlike long- or short-grain rice, glutinous rice is steamed. First soak it in cold water for at least 8 hours or overnight, then rinse and drain. Line the top of a steamer with damp cheesecloth. Spread the rice on the cheesecloth (or spread it over a heatproof plate), and steam the rice, covered, 1 hour for the short-grained variety, 30 to 40 minutes for the longer-grained Thai type. From time to time during the steaming, sprinkle the rice with water. Taste for the consistency you want while it cooks, as you would pasta.

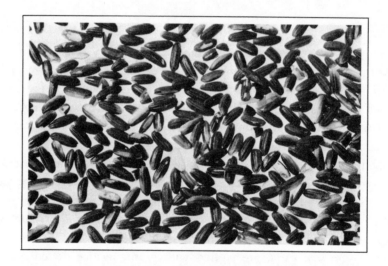

BLACK GLUTINOUS RICE. Relatively new to these shores, this intriguing rice with the bran layer still attached is indeed black (some kernels are brown) and is showing up with increasing frequency in Southeast Asian food stores. It's a staple of the Asian tropics and southern India. Usually sold in bulk, this rice is not steamed like other glutinous rice, but is cooked like regular rice, albeit longer—40 minutes or so. It may be simmered uncovered, adding a little water if necessary and tasting from time to time for doneness.

When cooked it has a nuttiness similar to wild rice. In Southeast Asia it's often served sweetened, sometimes with the addition of red azuki beans or preserved fruits such as loquat. The Chinese tout its medicinal properties, which include keeping the hair black and the blood a deep red.

Before a recent Thanksgiving
I was asked what I'd cook for the holiday. Turkey, I told
people, stuffed with a traditional Boston dressing of glutinous rice, Chinese
sausage, dried shrimp, and black mushrooms. I got some laughs about
the Boston part. But it's true—it's the traditional stuffing in the home of a
friend who grew up in Boston, albeit a Chinese home, and who was
coming for Thanksgiving. She insisted we have her mother's turkey stuffing.
This delicious version of Chinese poultry stuffing will add good taste
and texture to a holiday meal. Or it may be used to stuff a
chicken or duck for roasting any time of the year.

STICKY RICE, SAUSAGE, AND MUSHROOM STUFFING

Yield: about 8 cups

2 cups glutinous rice

1½ cups boiling water

6 to 8 links Chinese sweet sausage

12 large dried black mushrooms

½ cup dried shrimp

¾ cup chopped scallions (white part only)

¼ cup freshly rendered chicken fat (see page 320) or peanut oil

Salt and freshly ground black pepper to taste

2 tablespoons sesame oil

Soak the rice 8 hours or overnight in cold water. Spread the rice over dampened cheesecloth in the top of a steamer and steam for 1 hour, sprinkling water over it from time to time.

Meanwhile, cover the mushrooms with the boiling water, and allow to sit. Put the sausages on a plate and steam, covered, for 10 minutes.

Chop the dried shrimp or grind it in a food processor. Chop the sausages into a small dice. Squeeze the soaked mushrooms over their soaking liquid (reserve the liquid), dice the mushrooms, and set aside with the sausage and scallions.

Heat a wok or heavy skillet and add the fat or oil. Add the sausages, mushrooms, and scallions, and cook, stirring, for 1 minute or so. Stir in the rice and dried shrimp, and season liberally with salt and pepper. Stir in the mushroom soaking liquid until the rice is moistened to a desired consistency. This should take 1 cup or more.

Use the stuffing as you would any stuffing. If you want to reheat it, simply put it in a bowl and steam it. It's delicious hot, with a handful or so of fresh coriander leaves stirred in right before serving.

The Thais, in one of the simplest and tastiest uses of glutinous rice,
blend it warm with coconut milk and sugar, and serve it with ripe fruit.
Sometimes this is the notoriously foul-smelling durian; often
fresh mango is used, as here.

SWEET RICE WITH MANGOES		
Yield: 8 to 10 servings	2 *cups glutinous rice* 3½ *cups coconut milk, canned or fresh* ½ *cup sugar*	1 *teaspoon salt* 4 *ripe mangoes, pitted and sliced into strips*

Cover the rice with water and soak at least 6 hours or overnight. A couple of
hours or so before serving, spread the rice on a cheesecloth-lined section of a
steamer and steam for 45 minutes. During the steaming, sprinkle the rice twice
with ¼ cup water.

Meanwhile, over medium heat, boil the coconut milk until it's reduced by a
third. Stir in the sugar and salt, and turn off the heat.

When the rice is finished steaming and has sat for 10 minutes, blend it with
the warm sweetened coconut milk, and let stand for 10 minutes.

Arrange the rice on a platter with the mango slices on top, and serve.

BROWN RICE	
	OTHER NAMES: Genmai (Japanese) REGION OF USE: Limited consumption in Japan

If brown rice is better for you than white rice, why do billions of Asian rice
eaters, steeped in the health lore of what they eat, shun it? The answers lies
in part with the very whiteness of white rice. Removing the reddish-brown
bran layer is a refinement that took place well before the time of Confucius
(500 B.C.) and that elevated rice to the realm of the spiritual in the minds of
the Chinese. Not only was this heavy-yielding, nutritious grain an ancient,
revered staple, but it was discovered that by milling, it could be made pure
white and blemish-free, suitable for the gods, as befitted its station among
foods. Asians today don't discolor rice by dousing it with soy sauce.

Besides its pure color, milled rice had other advantages. It was easier to
cook, easier to store (it stayed fresher and more insect-free), it was easier to
digest, and there was status attached to it. (City people ate it first; rural people
couldn't afford it.) It was quite literally "refined" rice.

Also, the older hand-milling process didn't decimate the nutrients to the extent that polishing by machine did in the late nineteenth century. Over the centuries whole cuisines were built around these fluffy grains, steamy and white as snow. The heavier, nutty-flavored brown rice just didn't fit.

While some Japanese eat brown rice—it's common among Japanese on macrobiotic diets—little of it is consumed in China or Southeast Asia, and there's a dim chance it ever will be, since it would require overturning thousands of years of important tradition.

Brown rice can be purchased in Japanese markets, health food stores, and some supermarkets. It requires about twice the cooking time of white rice.

REGION OF USE: China, particularly eastern and northern	RED RICE

Not a separate kind of rice, red rice is simply uncooked rice that has been infused with a natural dye and is used as a coloring, usually for meats or for sauces used with meats. Red fermented bean curd (page 210) is colored with red rice, as are superior grades of hoisin sauce.

Sold mostly in stores that carry Shanghai foodstuffs, red rice comes in plastic packages of up to 1 pound, sometimes marked, sometimes not. Blood-red and with small broken-looking grains, it's expensive, but a little goes a long way. Typically the rice is boiled in water that's then strained. The resulting red liquid is used as the base for a sauce for braised duck or pork that includes rock sugar, salt, and sometimes star anise and cinnamon. A touch of dark soy sauce may be added to mitigate the bright red, which can take unsuspecting eaters aback. The meat simmers until cooked as the sauce reduces to a thin syrup. It's brushed with a little of the reduced sauce and served warm or at room temperature.

NOODLES
AND
WRAPPERS

Perhaps as a kind of belated thanks, in 1972 at a trade fair in Beijing, the Italians tried to interest the Chinese in a machine that, starting with flour and other basics, produced a spaghetti dish complete with tomato sauce and cheese in about five minutes. It never caught on. What had caught on in Italy about seven centuries earlier was the Asian art of pasta-making.

However, if, as the story goes, Marco Polo returned from China in 1295 with pasta, it was most likely not the first the Italians had seen of it. From Venice to the Arab lands was a short hop, and Arabs had been eating noodle-like foods since at least the tenth century. According to some sources, the spread of pasta cookery should be credited to Mongol slaves kept by wealthy Italians in the thirteenth and fourteenth centuries, because the Mongols knew the ancient Chinese noodle-making techniques.

What distinguishes Asian pasta is the large assortment of flours. Wheat flours are the rule in northern China, Korea, and Japan. Southern China uses wheat, usually with egg, as well as rice flours and others. Southeast Asians employ mostly rice flours but also make a noodle from the flour of the mung bean. Other Asian pastas are made from buckwheat, potato starch, soybean flour, bean curd, and even fresh shrimp.

NOODLES

Pasta was born, in the form we recognize—round, flat, spaghetti-like—in northern China around 100 B.C., when the Chinese began to employ techniques for large-scale flour grinding. A collection of recipes from the sixth century gives instructions for molding two lengths of flat noodles by hand, one "as thin as a scallion leaf."

For centuries, the preferred noodle of northern China has been "hand-pulled" or "hand-swung." For those of us awed by a pasta machine, seeing a Chinese chef grasp a length of dough between two hands, extend it with a toss to a length of five feet, and then continue to toss and twirl it like a jump rope while it divides into finer and finer strands as if by magic, is to witness one of the wonders of food preparation.

Chinese noodle-making left its mark on all of East Asia, as these strands of dough of various types and sizes became integral to the cuisines of Japan, Korea, and Southeast Asia.

CHINESE NOODLES

OTHER NAMES: Mein (Cantonese), Mian (Mandarin)

Noodles are rarely made at home in China, and haven't been for centuries—commercial noodle-making is an ancient craft. The noodle factory, manufacturing fresh noodles daily, is an old institution, found wherever there's a sizable Chinese community. In this country, commercial noodle-making started soon after the first Chinese immigrants came, and it's possible today to buy fresh Chinese noodles at any Asian market, including Japanese, Korean, and Southeast Asian stores. In fact most supermarkets now carry fresh Chinese noodles in their produce sections, although the quality of these nationally distributed brands seems to be consistently inferior to the local brands in Asian markets.

The Chinese eat noodles in four ways: *Stir-fried,* also known as as *lo mein* (Cantonese). The noodles are cooked, then stir-fried with various vegetables, meats, and seafood.

Pan-fried, also called Hong Kong–style *chow mein,* "shallow-fried," or "two-sides-brown noodles." These are cooked, drained, then shaped into a nest and fried on both sides until brown and crispy on the outside and soft on the inside. This stiff, golden cake is then put on a platter and smothered with a stir-fried mixture of one's choosing.

In soup. Noodles are cooked, then added to a broth which is topped with cooked meats and vegetables—sort of a meal in a bowl.

With a sauce. Most like the Western treatment of pasta, cooked noodles, hot or cold, are either tossed with a sauce or served with the sauce on the side.

Like the Italians, the Chinese make egg noodles (to which they add water) or plain flour and water noodles.

The Chinese like noodles long and uncut, since they're a symbol of longevity—noodles are traditionally served at birthdays—and eating noodles anywhere in Asia can be a noisy affair. It's polite to slurp and enjoy them.

FRESH WHEAT FLOUR NOODLES

The assortment for sale varies by locale. Cantonese-style egg noodles are most popularly sold as "regular mein," the most common, an all-purpose ⅛-inch-thick noodle to be used in any cooking method; "thin" or "extra thin" mein, which is preferred for soups but also may be pan-fried; and a fettuccine-like "wide mein," which is, in fact, a reasonable substitute for fettuccine.

Plain flour and water noodles include a thick, round Shanghai-style noodle, stir-fried or put in soups in eastern China, as well as white eggless noodles in the "regular mein" and "wide mein" sizes.

Besides flour and sometimes eggs, Chinese noodle ingredients include starch, which means cornstarch, sprinkled on the noodles as they're being cut to keep them from sticking. Salt is also added, which means it isn't necessary for the cooking water. Sometimes benzoate of soda and potassium carbonate are used to preserve Chinese noodles, although preservative-free noodles can be tracked down, for example, Richard's Noodles in San Francisco.

Fresh noodles are sold in 1-pound plastic packages; at wholesale outlets they can be purchased in 5-pound boxes at considerable savings.

TO COOK FRESH CHINESE NOODLES: Bring a large quantity of water to a boil—don't add salt or oil—and cook the noodles to taste, 4 minutes or longer. The Chinese (in fact all Asians) do not like their noodles *al dente;* they should be cooked just beyond that point. Before stir-frying, pan-frying, or using in soup, noodles may be run under cold water to stop the cooking, and tossed with a little oil to prevent their clumping up.

Sometimes called "Hong Kong–style chow mein," this is the ancestor of the dishes Americans first knew as chow mein, with the little canned fried noodles. In this case, however, you start with fresh noodles which are cooked, then pan-fried until they're crispy brown on the outside yet still soft on the inside. The topping here is beef, scallops, and mushrooms, with a shredded egg crepe garnish.

TWO-SIDES-BROWN NOODLES		
Yield: 6 to 8 servings		
	10 *small black dried mushrooms*	1 *pound bok choy, cut into 1½-inch lengths*
	8 *ounces Chinese egg noodles (regular mein)*	2 *eggs*
	Sesame oil	2¼ *cups fresh chicken stock*
	8 *ounces sea scallops*	2 *tablespoons light soy sauce*
	3 *tablespoons cornstarch*	1½ *teaspoons salt*
	8 *ounces flank steak*	½ *teaspoon sugar*
	2 *teaspoons dark soy sauce*	1 *cup peanut oil*
	½ *cup sliced bamboo shoots*	1 *tablespoon Shaoxing wine*

Put the mushrooms in a small bowl and pour boiling water over them. Allow them to soak for 30 minutes.

Meanwhile, cook the noodles in a large quantity of boiling water for 3½ to 5 minutes. Drain, rinse under cold water, and drain again. Toss with a sprinkling of sesame oil, and set aside.

Cut the scallops in half, toss with 1 teaspoon sesame oil and 1½ teaspoons cornstarch, and refrigerate. Cut the flank steak as thinly as possible across the grain. Toss it with the dark soy sauce, 1½ teaspoons cornstarch, and 1 teaspoon sesame oil, and set aside. When the mushrooms have soaked, squeeze them out over the soaking liquid, and reserve ¼ cup of the liquid. Cut off and discard the stems; cut the caps in half, and set aside with the bamboo shoots and bok choy.

Lightly beat the eggs with a few drops of sesame oil. Heat a small frying pan and lightly oil the bottom. Pour in enough of the egg to cover the bottom, pouring any excess back into the uncooked eggs. Cook just until set, and remove. Repeat until all the egg is used. Stack the egg crepes, roll them up, and slice across the roll into shreds. Set aside.

In a small saucepan, mix the chicken stock with the light soy sauce, 1½ teaspoons salt, and the sugar. Place the pan over low heat.

Meanwhile, heat a wok over medium heat. When it is hot, add the peanut oil and heat until the oil is very hot. Lower the noodles into the oil to form a nest, and let them cook until brown on one side, 8 minutes or so. Turn the noodles over and brown on the other side. (This will be much faster.) Remove to a large serving platter and keep warm.

Cook the scallops very briefly in the same oil, then remove and drain in a colander. Turn the heat off under the oil and add the beef. Stir just until the meat slices are separated and start to change color. Remove to drain with the scallops.

Pour off all but ¼ cup oil, and heat it. Add the vegetables and stir-fry 2 to 3 minutes. Add the hot seasoned stock and bring to a boil. Blend the reserved mushroom soaking liquid with 2 tablespoons cornstarch, and stir into the vegetables. Stir until the mixture thickens and clears slightly. Add the beef and scallops, and then the wine, and cook just until heated through. Pour over the noodles, garnish with the egg shreds, and serve.

For cold fresh egg noodles, this sauce is delicious; but it also may be tossed with hand-shredded cold poached chicken or chicken-stuffed wontons. Fresh coriander leaves and/or cucumber shreds are perfect garnishes.

2 cups peanut oil	1 teaspoon salt	**SICHUAN-STYLE PEANUT SAUCE FOR NOODLES**
1 heaping cup shelled raw peanuts	1½ teaspoons sugar	
½ cup freshly made tea, warm	1 tablespoon dark soy sauce	
5 garlic cloves	¼ cup fresh lemon juice	
1 tablespoon coarsely chopped fresh ginger	2 tablespoons sesame oil	
2 small fresh green chili peppers	1 tablespoon chili oil	Yield: about 3 cups

Heat the oil in a wok to nearly smoking. Add the peanuts, stir gently for 20 seconds, and turn off the heat. Allow the peanuts to sit for 10 minutes, until they are light golden. Using a slotted spoon, transfer the peanuts from the wok to the container of a food processor. Set aside ¾ cup of the peanut oil, and reserve the rest for another use.

Grind the peanuts to a coarse paste. Add a dash of the tea, and the garlic, ginger, and chilis, and continue to blend. Add the reserved ¾ cup oil, and blend briefly. Then add the rest of the tea, and the salt, sugar, soy sauce, and lemon juice, and process to a smooth consistency. Remove to a mixing bowl and stir in the sesame and chili oils. Mix thoroughly. Serve with cooked egg noodles, and garnish with coriander and cucumber shreds if you choose. The peanut sauce will keep for 2 weeks in the refrigerator.

DRIED WHEAT FLOUR NOODLES

The same Chinese noodles that can be purchased fresh are sold dried in Chinese markets in 1-pound packages, either in straight 12-inch lengths or, in the case of the thinner noodles, in nest-like swirls. These are made by local Chinatown factories, and some are imported from Hong Kong. Imported noodles sometimes include various flavorings such as fish or shrimp roe. Overlook the packaging of these imports that says "Imitation Noodle" in English; these are real noodles mislabeled by the Chinese trying to conform to FDA packaging laws.

TO COOK DRIED NOODLES: Cook them as you would fresh noodles, in a large quantity of water, albeit for a longer period of time, tasting them for doneness. With either the fresh or the dried variety, ignore the cooking directions on the package, just as any Chinese cook would. They can be wildly inaccurate.

DRIED RICE FLOUR NOODLES

Also known as "rice sticks" or "rice vermicelli," these noodles are sold in a variety of thicknesses in 1-pound clear plastic packages (each usually divided into four skeins) in Asian grocery stores. Unlike wheat flour noodles, these shouldn't be boiled before they are used. Thin ones may be soaked in warm water until softened, and then added to soups, stir-fried, or tossed with sauces; thicker ones should be covered with boiling water and allowed to stand until softened. Occasionally these are tossed, dry and uncooked, into hot deep-frying oil, which makes them immediately puff up. They are turned in the oil, removed, and drained, to be used as a bed for delicate stir-fried dishes or for use in salads. When fried, they're crisp and have an airy texture. The biggest assortment of rice noodles comes from Guandong province.

SHA HE FEN

Literally "rice noodle from Sha He," a town in Guandong province, and sometimes called "vermicelli sheets," this wide, gleaming rice noodle is sold fresh in Chinese groceries in squares that weigh about 1 pound. In *dim sum* houses, these slippery noodles are cut wrapper-size and rolled around fillings of beef, chicken, or shrimp, then steamed. The dough is slightly glutinous and virtually slithers down one's throat. Sha he fen may be cut into 8 × ½-inch noodles to be stir-fried with meat and vegetables or put into soups; sometimes they're eaten with sugar and honey as a sweet.

If not used the day they're purchased, sha he fen can be revived by allowing them to come to room temperature, then dipping them, plastic bag and all, into boiling water. Or they may be cut into the desired size and briefly parboiled.

MUNG BEAN FLOUR NOODLES

Called "cellophane noodles," "bean threads," "long rice," "vermicelli," these noodles are made from the starch of the mung bean, the same legume responsible for the familiar bean sprout. Clear, and of varying thicknesses although most are quite thin, these, like rice noodles, should be soaked in hot water rather than boiled before they are used.

A popular soup noodle, these also may be stir-fried; for example, in the famous Sichuan dish called Ants on a Tree these noodles are topped with ground pork fired with chili paste. Like rice noodles, mung bean noodles (*sai fun*) may be dropped in very hot oil, rendering them a light-as-air bed for some delicate topping. Cellophane noodles are most conveniently purchased in bundles of eight 2-ounce packages. Taiwan exports a lot of these.

This is a curious noodle dish from North China—especially unusual as dairy products are rarely used in Chinese cooking. The dish is light and attractive, and must be eaten as soon as it's cooked.

FRIED MILK

Yield: 6 servings

- 1/3 cup pine nuts
- Approximately 5 1/4 cups peanut oil
- 3 dried black mushrooms
- 2 sets chicken or duck liver (4 pieces)
- 1/3 pound shrimp
- 1/4 cup diced bamboo shoots (1/4-inch dice)
- 1/3 cup Chinese chives cut into 1/2-inch lengths
- 6 egg whites
- 3/4 cup rich milk
- 1 1/2 teaspoons salt
- 1 teaspoon sugar
- 1 tablespoon cornstarch
- 1 tablespoon sesame oil
- 1 ounce (1/2 small package) cellophane noodles

Lightly brown the pine nuts: Drop them into 1 cup hot peanut oil, and turn off the heat. When the nuts are light golden, remove them and set aside to drain.

Pour boiling water over the mushrooms and let stand 20 to 30 minutes. Cut the liver into 1/4-inch dice and the shrimp into 1/2-inch dice, and add to the bamboo shoots and Chinese chives. After the mushrooms have soaked, cut just the caps into a 1/4-inch dice and set aside with this mixture.

Beat the egg whites lightly. Blend the milk, salt, sugar, and cornstarch until the cornstarch is thoroughly dissolved, and mix well with the egg whites. Stir in the sesame oil.

Heat 4 cups or so of oil in a wok or large skillet until nearly smoking. Meanwhile, spread the noodles open so they'll cover the bottom of a platter or serving dish. When the oil is hot, pinch off a piece of noodle and add it. If it foams and swells up immediately, add the rest of the noodles. After a few seconds, when they're puffed up on one side, turn them. Remove and drain, then put them on the platter.

Heat a clean wok or skillet. When it is hot, add 3 tablespoons oil. When the oil is hot, add the liver and shrimp mixture. Stir rapidly until not quite cooked, about 20 seconds or so. Turn down the heat, restir the egg white mixture, and add it. Stir, scraping the bottom of the wok, until the egg whites have just set. (They should still be slightly runny.) Pour the sauce over the noodles, sprinkle with the pine nuts, and serve.

SOUTHEAST ASIAN NOODLES

The Chinese love affair with noodles has left an indelible mark on the countries to the south. In Thai and Vietnamese markets, a full assortment of Chinese noodles is offered because they're staples in these countries. The Thais call Chinese egg noodles *ba mee*. Also popular are the sticky sheets of fresh sha he fen, which in Thailand is called *gwaytio*. As a rule, however, more rice noodles are used than wheat noodles, and gleaming white rice noodles are for sale fresh—some flavored with dried shrimp and scallion—as well as dried. The mung bean "cellophane" noodle is also very popular. Noodles are cooked in soups, stir-fried, deep-fried, tossed in salads or with simple sauces, all in much the same way as they are in China.

See the previous section, "Chinese Noodles," for details about various noodles and their uses.

JAPANESE NOODLES

Clockwise from upper left:
cha soba, soba, udon, *and* somen

Per capita, Japan may be the most noodle-consuming country on Earth. Besides Japanese noodles, called *menrui,* Chinese varieties—especially the regular egg noodle (mein), which the Japanese call *ramen*—are enjoyed in Japan and are for sale at all Japanese food stores, made by both Chinese and Japanese manufacturers. Japanese instant noodle products in fact feature the Chinese-style noodle.

The preference for types of Japanese noodles divides geographically. From Tokyo north people favor noodles made from buckwheat flour (*soba*), and the southern Japanese prefer wheat flour noodles (*udon*).

SOBA

Enjoyed in northern Japan, these thin brownish noodles are made from wheat flour and buckwheat. Not a true cereal, buckwheat belongs to the sorrel family, and its grain yields a distinctively flavored flour. Buckwheat grows well in harsh conditions (Russia, northern Japan) and in poor soil, outsurviving in fact the weeds it competes with.

Sometimes sold fresh in vacuum-sealed plastic packages, dried *soba* is readily available in Japanese markets in packages of about 1 pound. At around $2 a pack, it's not a cheap noodle. An even more expensive beautiful green variety of buckwheat noodle (*cha soba*), made with green tea, is sold in handsome packaging.

Sometimes a course unto itself, soba is traditionally served on bamboo slats inside a square wooden box with a dipping sauce on the side, made of dashi seasoned with soy sauce, mirin, and bonito flakes. If the noodles are presented cold, the dipping sauce may be accompanied by chopped scallions, wasabi, and grated daikon to be mixed into the sauce to taste. Soba may also be served in a seasoned dashi-based broth.

Soba noodles, it should be pointed out, can substitute for udon noodles in any recipe.

UDON

A white noodle made of wheat flour, salt, and water, these come both flat and round. Dried, they're sold in packages, usually of 12 ounces or 1 pound. Udon is found fresh in most Japanese markets, often in 8-ounce packages along with a powdered "soup base" mix, as udon are typically served in broth, with chopped scallions and shichimi (seven-flavor mixture) to sprinkle on to taste.

SOMEN

A delicate thin white noodle made from wheat flour, *somen* is often served cold. Sold dried in 8-ounce packages, it also comes green, made with tea powder (*cha somen*); bright yellow, made with egg yolk (*tomago somen*); or pink, tinted with red perilla oil (*ume somen*).

Other Japanese noodles include *harusame* ("spring rain") cellophane noodles, made Japanese-style from potato starch or Chinese-style from mung beans; and *shirataki* ("white waterfall"), made from the starch of a plant called "devil's tongue." Used in Japanese "one-pot" combinations, shirataki come fresh, packed in water to which lime has been added, in 8-ounce packages. They should be parboiled first to remove the lime taste.

WRAPPERS

Legend holds that the Chinese pleated, crescent-shaped dumplings known as *jiao zi* were the prototype, via Marco Polo, for ravioli. But unlike the noodle, the origin of stuffed dough skins is unclear, except that they were popular long before the noodle. Some contend that this pasta came from central Asia, where similar foods, from the *somosa* of India, to the *pelemeni* of Russia, to the elaborate varieties in Afghanistan, have been eaten for millennia.

What is clear is that in China there is more of a tradition of making doughs to be stuffed at home, rather than buying them as you would noodles. For example, even though wrappers for *jiao zi* are available fresh in Chinese markets and some supermarkets, the dough is infinitely better if homemade. On the other hand, wontons are fine if made with a commercial flat noodle-type dough.

WONTON SKINS

REGION OF USE: Central and South China

Rapidly being adopted by American chefs for ravioli stuffed with the likes of goat cheese or thyme-scented scallop and shrimp mousse, these are available fresh at all Asian markets and in the produce section of most supermarkets. Usually 3½ inches square, sometimes round, wonton skins are made of a wheat flour and egg dough. They're sold in 1 pound packages in thicknesses varying from "extra thin" (120 to a pound) to "medium" (75 to 80 to a pound). Supermarket varieties, which should be avoided except in an emergency, come even thicker. The most practical for soft wontons or for frying are the thin variety (about 100 to the pound), sold at Chinese noodle factories or at Asian grocery stores that carry freshly made local brands.

Wonton skins freeze well before stuffing; they also freeze well after stuffing. And if you're going to boil the wontons you've frozen, you needn't thaw them first. Stuffed wontons to be fried, however, should not be frozen.

SHAO MAI. Also called *siu mai* (Cantonese), these are essentially open steamed wontons, usually filled with a pork mixture. As one of the most popular *dim sum*, they're wheeled around on carts at Cantonese tea houses. The wrappers for these, interchangeable with round wonton wrappers, are a thin wheat flour and egg pastry that's wrapped cylindrically around a filling, leaving the top exposed for garnishing. Like wonton wrappings, those bought at Asian groceries can be excellent.

The consumption of wontons, called *hun dun* in Chinese,
is recorded earlier than any other stuffed dumpling in China, where
stuffed dough products were an ancient food. The first record of wontons in
soup goes back to the Tang period (618–907), about the time wontons
were introduced to Japan. In fact the Japanese word *udon,* which is sort
of generic for "noodle," comes from the Chinese *hun dun.*
These wontons may be treated like dumplings and boiled, in which
case they're excellent as an appetizer or snack doused with Sichuan Dipping
Sauce and garnished with fresh coriander; or they may be served in an
unusual broth of seaweed (*nori*), dried shrimp, and Sichuan preserved vegetable.
Rather than tossing them in chicken broth, this eastern Chinese soup is truer
to the ancient method of serving these dumplings.

WONTONS

Yield: 70 to 80

1 *pound ground pork*

8 *ounces coarsely chopped fresh shrimp*

⅓ *cup chopped scallions*

⅓ *cup chopped coriander leaves and stems*

1 *egg*

2 *tablespoons light soy sauce*

1 *tablespoon Shaoxing wine*

1 *tablespoon cornstarch*

2 *tablespoons water*

½ *teaspoon salt*

1 *package wonton skins (1 pound)*

In a mixing bowl, stir all the ingredients (except the wonton skins) in one direction until well blended.

Put an individual wrapper in front of you and spoon 1 teaspoon of the filling into the center of the wrapper. Moisten the edges of the top half of the wrapper with your finger, and bring the bottom half of the wrapper up over the filling, folding it in half. Press the edges to seal. Pull the bottom corners of the wonton straight down, overlap them slightly, and pinch them together. The finished wonton should look like a nurse's cap. Repeat until all the wontons are made.

TO COOK THE WONTONS, bring a large quantity of water to a boil and add a portion of the wontons. They will cook in 3 to 5 minutes, and float when done. Drain them thoroughly and serve them either with Sichuan Dipping Sauce spooned over or on the side, or in the Eastern China Wonton Soup (page 300).

SICHUAN DIPPING SAUCE

Yield: 2 servings

1 tablespoon chopped fresh ginger

1 tablespoon chopped garlic

2 tablespoons light soy sauce

2 tablespoons mild vinegar

½ teaspoon sugar

½ teaspoon freshly ground white pepper

4 teaspoons sesame oil

1 teaspoon chili oil

2 tablespoons chopped scallions for garnish

Mix all the ingredients, except the scallions, together in a small bowl. When the dumplings are boiled, drained, and placed in bowls, sprinkle each bowlful with 1 tablespoon or more of this sauce, add a couple of pinches of scallions, and serve.

EASTERN CHINA WONTON SOUP

Yield: 6 servings

2 eggs

Sesame oil

15 to 20 dried shrimp, soaked and chopped

2 tablespoons chopped scallions, green part included

2 tablespoons chopped Sichuan preserved vegetable

3 sheets nori, cut into 1-inch squares

3 tablespoons freshly rendered lard

40 to 50 wontons

Light soy sauce

First make egg crepes: Beat the eggs thoroughly with a few drops of sesame oil. Lightly oil and heat a small well-seasoned skillet. Pour enough of the egg mixture into the skillet to cover the bottom; pour any excess back with the eggs. When the egg sets, peel it out of the skillet and set on a cutting board. Repeat until all the egg is used up. Stack the egg crepes, roll them up, and slice into strips.

Divide the dried shrimp, scallions, preserved vegetable, nori, and lard among 6 large individual bowls. Boil and drain the wontons, then divide them among the bowls. Bring fresh water to a boil, and pour into the bowls to just cover the wontons. Stir a few drops of light soy sauce into each bowl, garnish with the egg shreds, and serve.

These easily made, tasty little dumplings may be served
with three different sauces after they're boiled and drained. As a snack or
first course they may be set out, eight to an individual bowl, and tossed with
a tablespoon or so of the peppery Sichuan Dipping Sauce. Served like ravioli,
they should be tossed with Asian "Pesto" or with the Sichuan-Style
Peanut Sauce (see pages 18, 291).

ASIAN "RAVIOLI"

Yield: 8 to 10 servings

½ pound boneless chicken meat (fat, if any, included), cut into cubes

2 tablespoons chopped coriander leaves and stems

1 egg white

2 teaspoons cornstarch

½ teaspoon salt

½ teaspoon white pepper

1 tablespoon Shaoxing wine

1 tablespoon sesame oil

1 package thin square wonton skins (1 pound)

Put the chicken, coriander, egg white, cornstarch, salt, white pepper, wine, and sesame oil in the container of a food processor or blender, and blend to a smooth paste. Remove to a mixing bowl.

Open the package of wonton skins and keep them covered with a towel while you work. Using a spoon dipped in water, scoop a marble-size bit of filling onto the center of a wonton skin. (Use another spoon to slide the filling off the spoon so your fingers won't get oily, which would prevent the wontons from sealing where you touched them.) Brush around the edges of the skin with a little water, and cover with a second skin. Press around the filling so the two skins seal tightly.

With a pastry ring, dough cutter, or sharp knife, trim the ravioli into a round and set aside. Repeat until all the filling is used.

To cook the dumplings, bring a large quantity of water to a boil. Add the dumplings and 1 cup of cold water, and cook 3 to 5 minutes until they come to the surface. Cook another 10 seconds, until they are thoroughly done, and drain. Toss with warmed pesto or peanut sauce to taste, or put the dumplings in individual bowls and douse with the Sichuan sauce.

NOTE: These freeze well on sheet trays. When hard, they should be transferred to plastic bags. Cook frozen dumplings as directed above, without thawing. They'll just take longer to float to the surface.

One of the most popular Northern Chinese foods, these steamed, boiled, or pan-fried dumplings (the latter are known as *guo tie,* or "pot stickers") are a wheat flour and water dough stuffed with a pork mixture—traditionally pork and cabbage seasoned with a little ginger and Chinese chives. Though the wrappers for these dumpling—sometimes called "pot sticker" or *kuo tieh* or *chiao tzu* wrappers—are sold ready-made, the store-bought wrappers generally can't compare with the soft, pliable dough you can make at home. Whereas I would never make my own wonton wrappers, since the fresh commercially made wrappers can be excellent, I would never buy wrappers for northern Chinese dumplings.

| CHINESE PANCAKES | OTHER NAMES: Bao bing, Peking doilies, Mandarin pancakes, Mu shu wrappers |
| | REGION OF USE: Northern China |

These thin, 8-inch tortilla-like rounds are best known as wrappers for the crackling skin of Peking Duck, or for Mu Shu Pork. Sold fresh or frozen in Chinese markets, these are far better made at home from a recipe of your choice.

| SPRING ROLLS | REGION OF USE: Shanghai area (China) |

The original egg roll, these small golden, cylindrically shaped envelopes are a far cry from the soggy egg rolls that traditionally have been offered at Chinese-American restaurants. The wrappers for these, sometimes labeled "Egg Roll Skins" although there's no egg in the dough, are square (or sometimes round) and paper-thin. They're sold, usually frozen, in packages of 10 or 25. Spring roll wrappers with the thinness and texture of the store-bought variety are virtually impossible for the home cook to make. The skins should thaw for 3 or 4 hours before they are used. The best of these wrappers are imported, such as Oriental Mascot Brand of Hong Kong. Avoid, for any purpose, the thick "egg roll skins" for sale at American supermarkets.

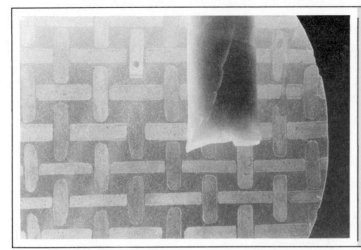

RICE PAPER

REGION OF USE:
Southeast Asia

Phyllo-thin, this Southeast Asian pastry wrapper (*bánh tráng*) is the key to what has been called Vietnam's national dish, the spring rolls known as *cha gio*. Rolled with a seafood and pork stuffing, these are fried, then served cut in sections with lettuce leaves for wrappers, fresh basil, and a fiery garlicky sauce.

Made from a dough of rice flour, water, and salt, rice paper is next to impossible to make by hand. It's one of those rare cases where a machine makes a better product.

Rice paper comes in various sizes of round and triangular pieces. The most practical for spring rolls is the 8-inch round, sold dried in 1-pound packages in stores carrying Vietnamese or other Southeast Asian goods. The yield is 45 to 50 sheets.

The sheets are brittle and must be handled with care. To soften, brush each sheet liberally on both sides with water or, better yet, beer (which yields a deeper golden color when the rice paper is fried). The sheets should then sit for a minute or two until they are soft and workable. With imagination, all sorts of fillings can be concocted—fruit fillings, for example—and the pastries can be pan-browned as well as fried (or even perhaps brushed with butter and baked).

CHA GIO

Yield: about 20

1 heaping tablespoon tree ear mushrooms

1 package cellophane noodles (2 ounces)

1 pound ground pork

½ pound coarsely chopped shrimp

1 tablespoon fish sauce

1 teaspoon salt

1 teaspoon freshly ground black pepper

2 garlic cloves, minced

½ cup chopped Chinese chives

2 tablespoons water

1 package rice paper in 8-inch rounds (1 pound)

Beer

Peanut oil for deep-frying

Large leaves from 3 heads iceberg lettuce (see Note)

1½ cups Asian basil leaves, loosely packed

2 thin cucumbers, peeled, seeded, and thinly sliced

6 to 8 red chili peppers, sliced into thin rounds

Vietnamese Dipping Sauce (see page 214)

Put the tree ears in a small bowl, cover them with boiling water, and allow to stand 15 minutes. Cover the cellophane noodles with hot water, and allow to stand 15 minutes.

Meanwhile, with a cleaver or a French chef's knife, chop the pork for a minute or two to create a finer mince. Put the pork in a mixing bowl with the shrimp, fish sauce, salt, pepper, garlic, and chopped chives. Drain the tree ears, rinse them, chop them lightly, and add to the pork. Drain the cellophane noodles and chop roughly; add 1 cup noodles to the pork. Add the water, and mix all these ingredients well with your hand or a spoon, stirring in one direction.

Taking a sheet at a time, brush each side of the rice paper liberally with beer, and set aside. After a sheet softens, which takes a minute or two, lay it in front of you. Put a heaping tablespoon of filling across the bottom third of the rice paper, stopping an inch from either edge. Fold the bottom flap over the filling, and then fold the sheet with the filling over once more, making sure that the rice paper is taut around the filling. Fold the sides in over the filling and continue to roll. Press the edges to seal. As each spring roll is finished, set it aside on a lightly oiled platter. When all are rolled, heat a large quantity of oil in a wok for deep-frying.

While the oil is heating, put the lettuce leaves on a platter or in a basket, and arrange the basil, cucumber, and chili peppers on a small platter; put both on the dining table. Set out the Vietnamese Dipping Sauce in one or two small bowls.

When the oil is hot, about 375°F, add as many spring rolls as will comfortably cover the surface of the oil. (Too many will lower the temperature of the oil.) Fry for about 5 minutes, turning from time to time, and remove to drain on paper towels. Repeat until all the spring rolls are cooked.

When all the spring rolls are done, turn up the heat slightly under the oil, and fry the spring rolls again for another minute. Remove to drain, pat lightly with paper towels, and then place on a cutting board. When they have cooled slightly, cut each into three or four sections. Arrange on a serving platter, and set out with the other ingredients.

Each eater should take a lettuce leaf, put in a couple of the spring roll sections and any or all of the garnishes, sprinkle these to taste with the sauce, roll up the lettuce, and eat.

NOTE: Any lettuce will do, so long as it is a type that won't wilt when wrapped around the hot spring rolls.

BEAN CURD SHEETS

OTHER NAMES: Bean curd skins, Yuba (Japanese)

REGION OF USE: China, Japan

Sold fresh, frozen, or dried, bean curd skins are made by heating soybean milk over hot water until it forms a skin, which is removed and dried on a bamboo mat. Fresh or frozen, they're plastic-like, malleable, and usually come in large folded rounds. Dried, they're often packaged in large, cumbersome envelopes.

Bean curd sheets are highly useful as wrappers. Buddhist vegetarians eat mock duck, fish, and other vegetarian "meats"—seasoned wheat gluten, mushrooms, and so on—enclosed by these skins. The stuffed skins are then either deep-fried or deep-fried and simmered in a seasoned sauce, both methods giving the skins a chewy real-skin quality.

Fresh or dried, they must be moistened with water before using. Buy the fresh if you can get it: Some stores in New York's Chinatown carry it; on the West Coast, it's mostly sold frozen in Chinese stores. Your best bet is stores that carry Shanghai goods. The dried, often shipped from Taiwan or Hong Kong, should be checked, as they're sometimes too broken up to be useful.

FLOURS
...AND
THICKENERS

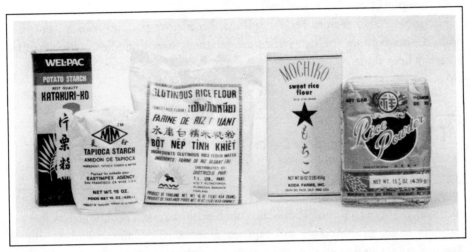

As it is elsewhere in the world, in Asia flour is used to make breads, noodles, and pastries. In China's north it's wheat flour, and in the south, it's both wheat and rice flour, as well as other starches and powders. In Japan, wheat and buckwheat flours are used in noodle-making, and rice flour is reserved for sweets. Thais and Malaysians rely heavily on rice and glutinous rice flours for noodles and the chewy little pastries of the region. Tapioca starch is also important in the Asian tropics.

The assortment of flour is also used by Asian cooks to achieve varying effects in batters and coatings for fried foods; and flours and starches from grains (such as corn) or roots (such as jicama) are common sauce thickeners.

REGION OF USE: China, Japan, Korea	WHEAT FLOUR

Not native to the Far East, wheat was introduced to China from western Asia in prehistoric times, but it wasn't until around 100 B.C. that flour-grinding techniques allowed the Chinese to produce the kinds of breads, noodles, dumplings, pancakes with onion, sesame cakes, *yu tiao* (Chinese crullers), and so on that are enjoyed today. In northern China, breads, including yeast breads, and noodles and dumplings replace rice as staple grain food. However, the southern Chinese, who do rely on rice, are also big consumers of wheat flour noodles, typically made with egg; this includes the southern Chinese wonton and egg roll wrappers.

Traditionally the Japanese use wheat flour only for noodles and deep-frying batter. The Koreans use it the same way but cook some northern Chinese-style dumplings and breads as well.

For most Asian recipes for dumplings, breads, or noodles, our all-purpose flour is fine. Among the exceptions are Japanese *somen* noodles, which require a hard wheat flour.

TAPIOCA STARCH	REGION OF USE: China, Southeast Asia

Also called "tapioca flour," this is the starch of the cassava root, which is formed into the small granules we call tapioca. For sale in Chinese and Southeast Asian markets in 1-pound packages, this starch, seldom used alone, is added in small amounts to rice flour to give Southeast Asian and Chinese pastries a translucent sheen and chewiness. It's sometimes combined with wheat starch to make the wrappers for *har gow* and *fun gor,* two *dim sum* items.

WHEAT STARCH	REGION OF USE: China

Also called "non-glutinous flour," wheat starch sounds common enough, except that buying it requires a trek to a Chinese dry-goods store. Wheat starch (*cheng fen*) is what's left when the protein is removed from wheat to make gluten, a spongy food the Chinese, especially Buddhists, value as a meat substitute. Used sometimes as a sauce thickener, wheat starch is responsible for the thin, translucent pleated wrapper that encloses the little shrimp-stuffed pastries the Cantonese call *har gow,* one of the most popular *dim sum. Fun gor,* a larger steamed *dim sum* dumpling filled with pork and mushrooms, is also wrapped in a wheat starch flour dough. Wheat starch comes in 1-pound plastic bags.

REGION OF USE: China, Southeast Asia, Japan	**RICE FLOUR**

Also called "rice powder" in Chinese groceries, rice flour is the basis of the myriad kinds of rice noodles eaten throughout Southeast Asia and southern China. It is also what binds turnip cake (*luo-bo gao*), a popular *dim sum*. Ground from long-grain rice, Chinese rice flour—used also for sweets in Malaysia and Indonesia, where it's mixed with a little tapioca starch—is sold in 1-pound plastic bags in Chinese and Southeast Asian groceries. Be sure it says just "rice flour" on the label and not "sweet rice flour," which is glutinous rice flour.

Japanese rice flour (*joshinko*) is ground from short-grain rice and is slightly more glutinous than the Chinese variety. It's used primarily for sweets.

OTHER NAMES: Sweet rice flour, Sweet rice powder REGION OF USE: China, Japan, Southeast Asia	**GLUTINOUS RICE FLOUR**

Made from glutinous rice, this flour (*shiratamako* in Japanese) is the reason for the stickiness and chewiness of the many sweet little Asian pastries such as the sesame seed rice balls of China, and the ubiquitous, sometimes garishly colored, cakes, dumplings, and coconut-covered lumps of dough eaten in Southeast Asia. The most common glutinous rice flour food is probably the plain, caramel-colored, 6- to 8-inch "sweet New Year's cake" that comes wrapped in cellophane and is stacked by the cash registers in Chinese markets during that holiday time.

Besides glutinous rice flour ground from raw rice, the Japanese make a version they call *mochiko*, ground from cooked rice, that typically is mixed with water, then boiled to make a kind of *mochi* cake (the bland white chewy Japanese staple). Mochiko, used like cornstarch, gives sauces a silken sheen.

Sweets made with rice flour and glutinous rice flour are ubiquitous in Southeast Asia. With freshly ground nutmeg in a dough made with coconut milk, and a palm sugar and macadamia nut filling, these are more interesting than most.

INDONESIAN RICE FLOUR BALLS	3 cups glutinous rice flour	3 tablespoons sugar
	1½ cups coconut milk	½ fresh coconut, grated
	1 nutmeg, freshly ground	⅓ cup macadamia nuts
Yield: about 24	¼ teaspoon salt	½ cup palm sugar

Put 2¾ cups of the flour in a mixing bowl, and stir in the coconut milk, nutmeg, salt, and sugar until the mixture forms a smooth paste. Knead the dough until it has a texture like putty or Pla-dough. If it's dry, add water or more coconut milk. Let it sit, covered, while you make the filling.

Chop the macadamia nuts coarsely in a food processor or blender, then add the palm sugar and process to a coarse paste; transfer to a bowl. Put the remaining ¼ cup flour on a little plate, and spread the grated coconut on another.

Take about 1 tablespoon of the dough and roll it into a ball. Make a deep well in it with your thumb, working it so you can fit about 1 teaspoon of filling in it. Put the nut filling in the well, pinch the dough around it to seal it, and roll again between the palms to form a ball. Repeat with the remaining dough and filling. Start a large quantity of water boiling.

When the water boils, roll the balls in the flour and drop them into the water. Stir so they don't stick to the bottom of the pan or to one another. When they float, after 5 minutes, they're done. Using a slotted spoon, remove them to paper towels to drain. While they are still warm, roll them in the coconut until well coated, and set aside to cool.

NOTE: These may be deep-fried, in which case the coconut should be finely grated, and ½ cup of it incorporated into the dough. They will fry to a golden brown in 5 minutes in 350°F oil.

	CORN-STARCH
REGION OF USE: China	

Used with a heavy hand in many Chinese restaurants, the Chinese prefer cornstarch for thickening sauces because it thickens with a clear sheen and little taste (as opposed to flour, which produces a muddier sauce and must be cooked longer than the typical stir-fried dish requires, to get rid of its raw flour taste). Cornstarch is also added to batters for Chinese deep-frying, as it gives a slightly harder crust.

To add cornstarch to a sauce, mix it with 2 to 3 parts water and re-stir right before adding. One scant tablespoon of cornstarch combined with 3 tablespoons of water should be sufficient to lightly thicken 1 cup of sauce. Any brand of cornstarch will do.

	WATER CHESTNUT POWDER
OTHER NAMES: Water chestnut starch, Water chestnut flour	
REGION OF USE: China	

Ground from dried water chestnuts, this is expensive, but it gives a clear sheen when used to thicken sauces and yields a pleasing crunchy texture when foods are coated in it and deep-fried. Water chestnut flour comes in 8-ounce boxes, the best of it from China. It is more troublesome than cornstarch to dissolve in water.

OTHER FLOURS
AND THICKENERS

Practically any starchy root will yield a "flour" more or less suitable for thickening sauces or for use in a batter. The Chinese prize the starch from *lotus root*, and *jicama* is valued in China only for the starch it yields. *Potato starch*, commonly used in East Asia, is made into cellophane noodles by the Japanese. For thickening, the Japanese favor the starch from the root of their native *kuzu*, which produces a glossy translucent sauce and thickens at low temperatures. (Known as kudzu in the U.S., this vine has spread out of control since its introduction to the American South at the turn of the century. Perhaps the people who make cornstarch should look into this.)

COOKING
FATS
AND OILS

People who are fussy about the olive oil they dribble over a salad, or who will buy only fine sweet butter, sometimes will choose a cheap vegetable oil for Asian cooking, and Asian cookbooks are partly to blame. Many of them, without discussion, call simply for "vegetable oil" as if the type didn't matter. Not just a cooking medium, oil flavors food and should be chosen carefully, and perhaps blended occasionally as Japanese chefs do for tempura.

In our fat-conscious era this may scare people, but in some cases freshly rendered pork or chicken fat is delicious. It should be remembered that Asian cuisines for the most part don't use butter or cream, fats for which we in the West aren't likely to substitute cheap vegetable oil.

Fats came first historically, and in China the first fats used were those of the pig and the dog, domesticated by the time of the late Stone Age. Obviously the pig has proved more useful in this regard—dishes such as roasted dog liver wrapped in dog fat have lost popularity over the years.

Lard, on the other hand, is still favored in many regions—such as Fujian, where pigs are bred as much for their fat as for their meat. This is also true in parts of Southeast Asia, where although vegetable oil is easier to produce, lard is preferred for its flavor.

Not as ancient as roasting, stewing, or steaming, frying is nevertheless an old cooking method. One of the earliest Chinese culinary techniques was to cook one kind of meat in the fat of a different animal, such as lamb in beef fat or fish in goat fat. Stir-frying came later; nothing resembling it is recorded much before the sixth century.

Recipes recorded in northern China in the sixth century call for either lard or the oil pressed from the seeds of perilla, a member of the basil family no longer eaten in China (see page 20). Earlier, the Chinese knew, according to a second-century text, that "you can get lard out of a soybean." Other early vegetable oils were crushed from the seeds of the mustard family—the category "rapeseed oil" includes these—and sesame seeds, which were introduced to China. Since the peanut's introduction four centuries ago, peanut oil has been a major cooking oil.

In Japan, animal fats are not used for cooking, and vegetable oils, used mostly for deep-frying, are usually blends of rapeseed, soybean, and sesame oil (the dark variety made from roasted seeds).

Besides the fresh lard used in pockets of Southeast Asia (except where there are Moslem populations), peanut oil is popular there. So is the heavy oil of the coconut, especially in the Philippines, where its known as *latik*. Coconut oil is often used at the start of a curry-type dish by boiling down coconut milk until it separates and frying spices in the oil.

VEGETABLE OIL

You can save on oil, a major expense of Asian cooking, by shopping in Asian markets and buying in quantity. Gallon or even 5-gallon tins are available. As for the kind of oil, you get what you pay for. Cheaper all-purpose oils, such as Wesson vegetable oil, Crisco oil, and others, pick up odors and break down easily when heated, which means you can't reuse them; they also have a cheap taste and odor to begin with.

The way to choose an oil is to try out different types (and brands). You may want different oils for different purposes. Whereas I prefer peanut oil for deep-frying, the best *you-tiao* (the long Chinese fried cruller, literally "oil bread") I've ever had was cooked in a flavorful corn oil.

PEANUT OIL. Peanuts, as chefs from Paris to Guangzhou know, yield one of the world's great oils, especially for frying. Peanut oil burns only at a high temperature—around 500°F. It doesn't pick up odors and tastes as readily as other oils, and thus can be strained and used again.

Aside from Planters, which is undistinguished, there are peanut oils available in Asian markets that are cold-pressed and have the fragrance of freshly roasted peanuts. Were they olive oils, they might be classified "extra virgin." Lion and Globe from Hong Kong is the most widely available. The headiest comes from China, in a red and gold 1-gallon can with absolutely no English on it except a small notation: "NET 2910 G." Panther brand, with a neutral flavor, is also good.

CORN OIL. A healthful, mostly polyunsaturated oil, corn oil is good for deep-frying and all right for stir-frying. The taste, although not that of a cheap oil, is heavy and distinct, and you have to like it. I prefer peanut oil in most instances, except for deep-fried foods where the crispy corn flavor is an enhancement.

COCONUT OIL. Heavy, saturated for the most part, this oil is tough to digest. It's good for frying, however, as it heats to about 480°F before it burns. It is used in Southeast Asia and is sold in Filipino markets here.

SOYBEAN OIL. A healthful though cheap oil, relied on by many Chinese restaurants, the taste of this can best be described as neutral to sometimes slightly fishy. Mixed with other oils, as it is in King Fong, a brand from Taiwan that's 55 percent peanut oil, it can be very good.

SAFFLOWER OIL. Touted as the most healthful oil, safflower, a decent deep-frying oil, has a tendency to pick up odors and deteriorate because of its extreme unsaturation. Like soybean oil, it can develop a fishy taste.

SESAME SEED OIL. The amber-colored sesame oil pressed from roasted seeds (see page 230) is mainly used as a flavoring; when it's heated for cooking it loses most of its flavor, and it's expensive. However, Japanese chefs blend it with other oils to fry tempura, and Koreans pan-fry with it. Cold-pressed sesame oil, for sale in health food stores, keeps well and is fine for cooking, but it's a little pricey. Perhaps worth trying is the deep golden sesame oil called *gingelly* oil, used widely in southern Indian cooking and sold in Indian food shops.

OLIVE OIL. Because of its flavor, its low burning point (280°F), and if nothing else, its expense, olive oil not appropriate for Asian cooking.

HIGHLY RECOMMENDED: Lion & Globe peanut oil from Hong Kong, available in 3-quart, 4-ounce cans.

RECOMMENDED: King Fong peanut soybean oil (from Taiwan), available in 1-gallon cans. Tung Ming peanut oil. Panther peanut oil (neutral flavor). Lion and Globe corn oil. Mazola corn oil.

NOT RECOMMENDED: Wesson vegetable oil. Crisco oil. Other inexpensive oils usually labeled "vegetable oil."

OIL FOR TEMPURA AND OTHER BATTER-FRIED FOODS: Any good oil such as peanut oil will do, but you may want to mix in 10 percent or more Chinese or Japanese sesame oil for a more authentic taste. Tempura oil from Japan, available occasionally in Japanese markets, is expensive and unnecessary.

STORING AND REUSING VEGETABLE OIL: Store oil in a tightly sealed container out of the light (or in an opaque container). Light and air turn oil rancid. Oil that is used for frying may be reused—in fact slightly used oil browns better—if it's strained and properly stored. A crock is a good choice for used oil. When it's used again, about one-third fresh oil should be added to the old. It shouldn't sit more than a few days between uses, and should be discarded after two or three times.

FAT

CHICKEN FAT

Whole chickens, especially those from Asian markets, come with fat in the cavity—a treasure that shouldn't be discarded. Around Shanghai and elsewhere, freshly rendered chicken fat is often dribbled over vegetables before they're served, or it may be used to cook the vegetables. In either case, you'll end up with a more flavorful dish using this than using a vegetable oil. Rendered chicken fat also goes well with seafood.

TO RENDER CHICKEN FAT: Take the fat from the cavity of the chicken (or ask your butcher for it), as well as any trimmed excess fat (neck skin is loaded with it) and skin pieces, and put them in a small saucepan with about 3 times the volume of water. Turn the heat to medium and let the water simmer away. When the water is almost gone, the liquid in the pan will start to make a racket. Turn the heat down slightly and pay attention. Just as the noise dies down, turn off the heat and strain off the fat into a canning jar. Allow it to cool, cover—it picks up odors like butter—and store in the refrigerator. It will keep for a week or so.

PORK FAT (LARD)

Besides making the flakiest pastry crust, if you want to take the trouble, and I feel blasphemous recommending this, freshly rendered pork fat is a delicious alternative to any vegetable oil for stir-frying shellfish or for making the sauce for a whole fish. But it must be homemade, not the chemically preserved type you find at the store, which is awful. In fact, just a tablespoon or so substituted for an equal amount of oil will make a difference. Fresh lard in combination with peanut oil is also a flavorful alternative for stir-frying the numerous strong-flavored members of the cabbage family grown in Asia.

TO RENDER PORK FAT: Buy back fat, chop it, and follow the method for rendering chicken fat. (This is best done in large quantities over a lower flame.) If you can get it, leaf lard is sometimes available in Chinese butcher shops, and this renders easily, but it is usually sold to bakeries and other commercial establishments. Lard will keep in a covered jar in the refrigerator for a week or more.

BIBLIOGRAPHY

Andoh, Elizabeth. *An American Taste of Japan*. New York: William Morrow and Company, Inc., 1985.

Brennan, Georgeanne, Isaac Cronin, and Charlotte Glenn. *The New American Vegetable Cookbook*. Berkeley, California: Aris Books, 1985.

Brennan, Jennifer. *The Complete Thai Cookbook*. New York: Richard Marek, Publishers, 1981.

Burkill, I. H. *A Dictionary of the Economic Products of the Malay Peninsula*, Vols. I & II. London: Published for the Malay Government by Crown Agents, 1935.

Burum, Linda. *Asian Pasta*. Berkeley, California: Aris Books, 1985.

Chamberlain, Basil Hall. *Japanese Things*. Rutland, Vermont, and Tokyo: Charles E. Tuttle Company, Inc., 1970.

Chang, K. C., ed. *Food in Chinese Culture*. New Haven: Yale University Press, 1977.

Claiborne, Craig, and Virginia Lee. *The Chinese Cookbook*. Philadelphia and New York: J. B. Lippincott, 1972.

Cost, Bruce. *Ginger East to West*. Berkeley, California: Aris Books, 1984.

Davidson, Alan. *Seafood of South-East Asia*. Singapore: Federal Publications, 1977.

Editors of *China Pictorial*, Beijing. *Chinese Cuisine from the Master Chefs of China*. Boston and Toronto: Little, Brown and Company, Inc., 1983.

Fairchild, David. *Garden Islands of the Great East*. New York: Charles Scribner's Sons, 1943.

Herklots, G.A.C. *Vegetables in South-East Asia*. London: George Allen and Unwin, Ltd., 1972.

Hu, Shiu-ying. *An Enumeration of Chinese Materia Medica*. Hong Kong: The Chinese University Press, 1980.

Jiangsu College of Medicine, ed. *Zhongyao Dacidian* (*Dictionary of Chinese Medicine*). Shanghai: Shanghai Kexue Jishu Press, 1977.

Khiang, Mi Mi. *Cook and Entertain the Burmese Way*. Ann Arbor, Michigan: Karoma Publishers, Inc., 1978.

Lai, T. C., ed. *Hong Kong and China Gas Chinese Cookbook*. Hong Kong: Pat Printer Associates Limited, 1982.

Laufer, Berthold. *Sino-Iranica. Chinese Contributions to the History of Civilization in Ancient Iran*, Publication 201. Chicago: Field Museum of Natural History, 1919.

Li, Hui-lin. "The Vegetables of Ancient China," *Economic Botany*, Vol. 23, 1969, pp. 253–260.

Li, Hui-lin. *Nan-fang ts'ao-mu Chuang* (*A Fourth Century Flora of Southeast Asia*). Hong Kong: The Chinese University Press, 1979.

Li, Shih-chen. *Chinese Medicinal Herbs*, trans. F. Porter Smith and G. A. Stuart. San Francisco: Georgetown Press, 1973.

Lin, Florence. *Florence Lin's Complete Book of Chinese Noodles, Dumplings, and Breads*. New York: William Morrow and Company, 1986.

McGee, Harold. *On Food and Cooking. The Science and Lore of the Kitchen.* New York: Charles Scribner's Sons, 1984.

Noh, Chin-hwa. *Traditional Korean Cooking.* Seoul: Hollym Corporation, 1985.

Ok, Cho Joong. *Home Style Korean Cooking in Pictures.* Tokyo: Japan Publications, 1981.

Schafer, Edward H. *The Golden Peaches of Samarkand.* Berkeley, California: The University of California Press, 1963.

Shim, Chung-shil. *Korean Recipes.* Seoul: Seoul International Publishing House, 1984.

Shurtleff, William, and Akiko Aoyagi. *The Book of Miso.* Berkeley, California: Ten Speed Press, 1983.

Shurtleff, William, and Akiko Aoyagi. *The Book of Tofu.* New York: Ballantine Books, 1983.

Sing, Phia. *Traditional Recipes of Laos.* London: Prospect Books, 1981.

Steinberg, Rafael. *Pacific and Southeast Asian Cooking.* New York: Time-Life Books, Inc., 1970.

Stobart, Tom. *Herbs, Spices and Flavorings.* Woodstock, New York: The Overlook Press, 1982.

Stobart, Tom. *The Cook's Encyclopedia.* New York: Harper and Row, Publishers, Inc., 1981.

Tan, Terry. *Cooking with Chinese Herbs.* Singapore: Times Books International, 1983.

Takahashi, Kuwako. *The Joy of Japanese Cooking.* Tokyo: Shufunotomo Company, Ltd., 1986.

Togo, Kuroiwa. *Rice Vinegar: An Oriental Home Remedy.* Tokyo: Kenko Igakusha Company, Ltd., 1977.

Tropp, Barbara *The Modern Art of Chinese Cooking.* New York: William Morrow and Company, 1982.

Ts'ao, Yung-ho. "Pepper Trade in East Asia," *T'oung Pao*, Vol. LXVIII, 1982, pp. 221–247.

Tsuji, Shizuo. *Japanese Cooking, A Simple Art.* Tokyo: Kodansha International, 1980.

INDEX

ABOUT THE AUTHOR

Bruce Cost has been devoted to cooking, teaching, and writing about Asian food since his introduction to fine Chinese food by a friend, Hank Cha, twenty years ago. After a stint of teaching himself the cuisine, Mr. Cost began an on-and-off seven-year apprenticeship with the late master cooking teacher Virginia Lee in Manhattan. During that time he traveled to Hong Kong and China to eat.

A popular teacher, Mr. Cost currently conducts six-week courses of Chinese and Southeast Asian cooking in San Francisco, where he lives with his daughter, Eliza. His articles on Asian food appear as a weekly column in *The San Francisco Chronicle* and regularly in *The Washington Post. The New Orleans Times-Picayune, Chicago Tribune, Dallas Morning News,* and *Portland Oregonian* have run his work, as have other newspapers via the Los Angeles Times Syndicate. He has contributed to *The New York Times Magazine, Food & Wine, Cook's,* and the late *Cuisine* magazines.

Considered by his colleagues to be one of the country's finest cooks, Mr. Cost presides over an annual Chinese New Year's banquet at Alice Waters's Chez Panisse restaurant in Berkeley, California. On a more scholarly bent, Mr. Cost is a contributor to *The Journal of Gastronomy* published by The American Institute of Wine and Food. He has lectured at the San Francisco Academy of Sciences, the University of California at Berkeley Extension, and elsewhere on Asian food and ingredients. Currently he's working in collaboration with Donald Harper of the department of Far Eastern languages at the University of Chicago on a translation of the oldest collection of Chinese recipes. Mr. Cost's first book, *Ginger East to West,* received a Tastemaker Award in 1984.